THE
CHILDREN'S HERITAGE
SOURCEBOOK

THE
CHILDREN'S HERITAGE
SOURCEBOOK

100+ BACK-TO-ROOTS ACTIVITIES FOR KIDS & TEENS

Healthy, Seasonal Cooking · Living with Animals
Gardening · Crafts & Projects

Emma Rollin Moore · Lauren Malloy · Ashley Moore

Photography by **Sara Prince**

RIZZOLI
NEW YORK

New York · Paris · London · Milan

Contents

Introduction

On every homestead of any size, whether it is a 300-acre ranch or an apartment in a big city, many hands lighten the load of the ever-abundant work. Children are usually at least as busy as any adult, and they are capable of doing more than most people would imagine. Our children help us plant, water, and harvest the vegetables, flowers, and fruit in our gardens; they feed, groom, and play with the animals and collect the eggs each morning; and they make some of the things we need in our house—candles, jam, kitchen towels, remedies, and much more—with their own hands. It feels good to support the other members of the family by helping cook meals, care for animals, and make skincare products and other items that would normally have to be purchased. All of these activities certainly could be considered work, but they are all so enjoyable they feel much more like play!

All three of our families dabble in every subject covered in this book—cooking wholesome meals from scratch, raising animals, and using creativity to make special things—although each family has a special emphasis in one area or another.

The Rollin Moore family is always cooking up something delicious, and cooking is Emma's favorite hobby. She also teaches classes in canning, fermenting, and making sourdough bread. Her children love to help prepare meals and snacks in the kitchen, and they are very happy to taste test the delicious fare. Emma's children, 13-year-old Olivia and 11-year-old Liam, know how to grow delicious veggies and fruit and how to use those ingredients to make meals the whole family can enjoy.

The Malloy family raises much of their own food and many animals, and Lauren's specialty is animal care. She even holds a degree in animal

science. Her children have daily chores, some they do even before they head to school: 11-year-old Milly feeds the three horses and two ponies, and 7-year-old June feeds the chickens, collects the eggs, and feeds the dogs. Clay, who is 2 years old, is already learning to assist his sisters and will be a big help as he gets older. To Lauren's kids, animal care is second nature, and they love getting to eat the fresh eggs from their chickens and ride their horses after all of their hard work.

The Moore family can't seem to get enough of crafting. Ashley is an early childhood teacher at the Waldorf School of Santa Barbara, and her idea of happiness is spending the afternoon with her children, making something beautiful and useful for the home or tending to the garden. All three of her children—13-year-old Isla, 11-year-old Lyra, and 7-year-old Jupiter—know how to sew, knit, and crochet; create beautiful decorations for their home; and make their own herbal remedies with plants they harvest right out of the garden.

This book is intended as a jumping-off point. It is our hope that while flipping through its pages you will be excited and motivated to try something new. Maybe you'll grow something in the garden or cook something yummy in the kitchen, or you might even get inspired to adopt a new pet or get a job working with animals. Perhaps your new interest will encourage your parents to get involved as well.

The Children's Heritage Sourcebook was written especially for kids and teens, with the assumption that younger children would be using this book together with their parents,

PICTURED FROM LEFT TO RIGHT: the Malloy family (Milly, June, Mama Lauren, Clay); the Rollin Moore family (Olivia, Liam, Mama Emma); and the Moore family (Jupiter, Mama Ashley, Isla, Lyra)

grandparents, teachers, or caregivers. Younger children will need the guidance of an adult for safety's sake. Older children will likely want to branch out on their own, and many of the projects can be beautifully accomplished by teens and tweens with very little assistance

from grown-ups. Whether you are an adult helping a child with the activities in this book or a child or teen yourself, we hope you enjoy these recipes, animal stories, and craft ideas. We wish you many creative days of cooking, raising, and making in your future!

EAT

Healthy, Seasonal Cooking

EMMA

FOOD BRINGS TOGETHER FRIENDS AND FAMILY, YOUNG AND OLD, ALL OVER THE WORLD. A good, nutritious meal offers so much more than a full belly—nourishment for our bodies, connection to our food and the farmers who grow it, perhaps even connection to family members who are no longer with us. Every time I scramble eggs, I am reminded of my grandmother, who used to make that simple dish for all of us kids when we visited. Food and memories are intertwined for us all.

Growing up on a dairy farm in the Central Valley of California, I experienced first-hand the life cycle of the plants and animals around me. We cooked what we grew and raised, and I helped my mother in the kitchen, making meals we could all enjoy together. I loved the way she bustled around, putting food on the table and gathering everyone to eat as a family. I am fond of her passion for food and the way she welcomed my four siblings and me into the kitchen to cook with her. My mother taught all five of us the importance of a home-cooked meal.

In 2008, the birth of my first child ignited my love of nutrition. Becoming a mother reminded me of the lifestyle and principles I had experienced as a child and inspired me to reclaim them. I wanted to give my kids healthy meals that were seasonal and nourishing without added preservatives, nutritious and tasty meals that would bring everyone in our family together and carry on my mother's legacy in the kitchen.

My two children, Olivia and Liam, share my love of food, holistic nutrition, and the homesteading lifestyle. You don't need acres of land to enjoy back-to-roots living. We live in a residential neighborhood and have a big backyard, where we homeschool, grow fruit and vegetables, care for our animals—a mini pony, pygmy goat, bunny, a dozen chickens, two fish, and a kitty cat—and, of course, cook nourishing meals daily. It's not the size that makes a home a homestead; it's the life you make in and around it. You can grow and prepare your own food wherever you live. With this in mind, and because our space is small, we also strive to eat locally and in season by shopping at the farmers market in our city. Even before my kids were born, I shopped at the farmers market to pick out fresh, whole food. Over the years, we've formed unique relationships with our local farmers, and I've loved swapping recipe ideas and gaining more knowledge on specific fruits, vegetables, and meats that are sourced so close to our home.

Back-to-roots living is hands-on, and everyone in the family helps with the many chores. Olivia is 13 and has a fondness for animals, especially horses and bunnies. She tends to all of our animals and exercises McQueen, a mini pony that we board for our neighbor. She takes horseback riding lessons and is a member of our local pony club. She has also taken to training Abigail, our pygmy goat, to be less skittish and more friendly. Olivia loves to help in the garden and cook sweet treats like muffins, energy bites, and cakes. She is also fond of creating delicious salads for lunch and dinner, both with me and on her own. Currently, her favorite creation includes heirloom tomatoes from our garden, cucumbers, and mint with a little lemon juice, olive oil, sea salt, and pepper.

Liam is 10 and loves raptors, so it's no surprise that in addition to other chores around our house, he tends to our hens daily, making sure they are fed and watered and all the eggs are collected punctually. Liam also enjoys cooking and can often be found lending me a helping hand by prepping ingredients for various meals and making simple snacks on his own. Currently, his favorite snack to make is a fruit, veggie, and cheese skewer that includes Gouda cheese, green olives, and whatever fruits or vegetables we have on hand.

I am so glad to share the recipes that follow with you. My heartfelt intention is to guide you into the kitchen to cook more as a family. Making whole, complete, nutrient-dense food that is good for you and tastes delicious doesn't have to be complicated. The recipes in this book are for healthy foods that are simple, satisfying, and incredibly tasty. I hope they empower you to know that anyone can bring elements of the homestead into their daily life—especially when it comes to food. Enjoy!

LACTO-FERMENTATION

Although you might not have heard of lacto-fermentation, you most likely have tried lacto-fermented foods, like pickles and sauerkraut, and have come to your own conclusions about whether you like them or not. Let's be honest, they definitely are an acquired taste due to their tang. However, I'd encourage you to give it a whirl.

What exactly is lacto-fermentation? It's a microbial process using beneficial bacteria including lactobacillus, bifidobacterium, and other lactic acid bacteria (LAB), commonly known as probiotics, which thrive in an anaerobic fermenting environment. This simple fermentation process requires nothing more than salt, fruit or vegetables, and water. No canning or fancy equipment is necessary. Lactobacillus bacteria converts sugars naturally present in fruit or vegetables into lactic acid. Since lactic acid is a natural preservative that helps fight bad bacteria, it preserves not only the flavor and texture of food, but also its nutrients. Simply put, the lacto-fermentation process works because of the lucky fact that the potentially harmful bacteria can't tolerate too much salt, while the healthy bacteria can. Beyond preservation, lacto-fermentation enhances the nutrient density of food, increases its digestibility and flavor, and improves your overall gut health.

What I love about the lacto-fermentation process is that most of the recipes take just a few minutes of active time, and all you need after that is a little bit of patience. Essentially, it's science in the kitchen. So gather your family and start fermenting!

Lacto-Fermented Seasonal Veggies with Dill and Garlic

Tangy with just the right amount of dill and garlic, these pickled veggies are the perfect gut-healthy snack or side dish. Liam loves to call these "squishy veggies" and can't get enough of them.

Enough vegetables (carrot chunks, cauliflower florets, radishes, or green beans) to fill a 1-quart mason jar

1 sprig dill

2 cloves garlic, peeled

Red pepper flakes (optional)

3 cups filtered water

2 tablespoons sea salt

Pickling spices (optional)

1. Fill a sterilized 1-quart mason jar with the vegetables, dill, garlic, and red pepper flakes (if using), making sure to leave about 1 inch of headspace at the top.
2. In a separate vessel, combine the water, sea salt, and pickling spices (if using). Stir until the salt dissolves.
3. Pour the brine over the veggies until it reaches just below the top of the jar. There should be about ½ inch of headspace.
4. Seal the jar with the lid and let the veggies sit at room temperature (out of direct sunlight) for at least 3 days and up to 2 weeks, until they are as tart as you like. It is normal for the brine to turn cloudy and bubbly. Open the jar once a day to let out the built-up air.
5. Once the texture and taste of the veggies are to your liking (they should be a combination of crunchy and sour), put the lid on tightly and store in the fridge for up to 6 months.

Lacto-Fermented Quail Eggs

Quail eggs are super cute but difficult to crack when raw due to their small size. However, by hard-boiling the quail eggs, you automatically create an easier-to-remove shell. This recipe preserves the quail eggs and makes a delicious snack or a great addition to salads and sandwiches.

1. Fill a sterilized 1-quart mason jar with the eggs, garlic, dill, and shallot, making sure to leave about 1 inch of headspace at the top.
2. In a separate vessel, combine the water, salt, bay leaf, peppercorns, mustard seeds, and red pepper flakes. Stir until the salt dissolves.
3. Pour the brine over the eggs until it reaches just below the top of the jar. There should be about ½ inch of headspace. Add the sauerkraut juice (if using).
4. Seal the jar with the lid and let the eggs sit at room temperature (out of direct sunlight) for 2 to 3 days. It is normal for the brine to turn cloudy and bubbly. Open the jar once a day to let out the built-up air.
5. Transfer the jar to the fridge; the eggs will keep for up to 2 weeks. Eat them as is, make deviled eggs, add to your favorite salad, or put on top of avocado toast.

12 hard-boiled quail eggs, peeled

2 cloves garlic, peeled and smashed

1 large sprig dill

1 small shallot, sliced

2 cups filtered water

1 tablespoon sea salt

1 bay leaf

8 whole black peppercorns

¼ teaspoon mustard seeds

Pinch of red pepper flakes

2 tablespoons sauerkraut juice (optional)

HARD-BOILED QUAIL EGGS

Hard-boiled quail eggs take 3½ to 4 minutes to cook. Bring a pot of water to a boil. Carefully add the eggs with a slotted spoon or fine-mesh strainer (this ensures the eggs don't break). Let the eggs boil for 3½ to 4 minutes. Transfer the eggs to a bowl of ice-cold water and let them sit for 5 minutes before peeling. Alternatively, you can place the cooled eggs in the fridge overnight and peel them in the morning.

Quick-Pickled Quail Eggs

If you want to preserve quail eggs quickly and like the taste of a quick pickle rather than the lacto-fermented kind, then this recipe is for you. As a family, we love to eat quick-pickled quail eggs on top of salads or rice dishes, or on their own.

12 hard-boiled quail eggs

2 cloves garlic, peeled and smashed

1 sprig dill (optional)

½ cup distilled white vinegar

½ cup filtered water

1 teaspoon sea salt

5 whole black peppercorns

½ teaspoon mustard seeds

3 or 4 allspice berries

1. Place the eggs, garlic, and dill (if using) in a clean ½-pint mason jar.
2. Bring the vinegar, water, salt, peppercorns, mustard seeds, and allspice berries to a boil in a small saucepan over medium-high heat. Stir for about 1 minute, until the salt has dissolved.
3. Pour the hot brine over the quail eggs in the jar.
4. Seal the lid on the jar and let cool to room temperature. Transfer to the fridge for at least 1 week before eating to allow the flavors to infuse. The pickled eggs will keep in the fridge for 3 to 4 months.

"Eat Your Veggies" Lacto-Fermented Ketchup

Ketchup is a preferred condiment and dipping sauce in our house. This nontraditional recipe swaps tomatoes for veggies like carrots, beets, and butternut squash. Slightly sweet and spicy, with just the right amount of tang from the fermentation process, this ketchup is a new family favorite. Use it on anything you would put traditional ketchup on. Our favorite things to dip are roasted sweet potatoes, potatoes, sausages, and eggs.

1. Place a steamer basket in the bottom of a large stockpot, then add water to just below the basket.
2. Place the carrots, beets, apples, and squash in the basket, then bring the water to a boil. Reduce the heat to medium-low, cover, and simmer for 10 to 15 minutes, until the veggies and apples are tender.
3. Put the steamed veggies, vinegar, whey, honey, onion powder, allspice, cinnamon, cloves, and salt in a blender. Blend until smooth and well combined.
4. Transfer the ketchup to a sterilized 1-pint mason jar and close with a lid. Allow the ketchup to sit at room temperature, out of direct sunlight and undisturbed, for 3 to 5 days.
5. Uncover the ketchup and give it a good stir, then cover again with the lid and transfer it to the fridge. Naturally fermented ketchup will keep for several months in the fridge.

¾ cup peeled and chopped carrots

¼ cup peeled and quartered red beets

¼ cup peeled, cored, and quartered apples

¾ cup peeled and roughly chopped butternut squash, pumpkin, or sweet potato

2 tablespoons apple cider vinegar

2 tablespoons whey or sauerkraut juice

2 tablespoons raw honey

1 teaspoon onion powder

1 teaspoon ground allspice

1 teaspoon ground cinnamon

½ teaspoon ground cloves

½ teaspoon sea salt

BARBECUE SAUCE

If you'd like to turn this into a delicious barbecue sauce, you can. Just make the ketchup as described above. After 3 to 5 days, check to see if the flavor of the ketchup is to your liking. If so, add 2 teaspoons each of cumin powder, liquid smoke, and Worcestershire sauce. Stir well and enjoy! It will keep in the fridge for up to 2 months.

Beetroot Kraut

MAKES 2 CUPS

This beetroot kraut is a great introduction to lacto-fermented foods. By using beets, red cabbage, apples (which give a touch of sweetness), dried blueberries, and a little bit of red onion, a milder kraut is created. Use it as a condiment to top sausages, burgers, or even eggs.

1 cup peeled and shredded red beets

3 cups thinly sliced red cabbage, plus 1 whole cabbage leaf

1 apple, peeled, cored, and shredded

2 tablespoons dried blueberries (optional)

⅛ cup thinly sliced red onion

1½ tablespoons sea salt, plus more if needed

½ teaspoon ground allspice

Filtered water, if needed

1. Add all the ingredients except the whole cabbage leaf and water to a large bowl and stir well to combine.

2. Transfer the mixture to a sterilized 1-pint mason jar and pack it down with the back of a wooden spoon or vegetable tamper. A liquid brine will form.

3. If there is not enough liquid to cover the kraut, mix 1 cup filtered water with 1 teaspoon sea salt in a measuring cup and stir until the salt dissolves, then add this additional brine to the jar so the kraut is completely submerged.

4. Top with the whole cabbage leaf or a fermentation weight and press down. Seal with the lid, then place in a cool, dark spot, out of direct sunlight.

5. Start checking the ferment after 3 days to make sure the kraut is still submerged. If it is not, use a sterilized spoon to press down on the top cabbage leaf to release more brine to keep it submerged. As a rule of thumb, kraut can be left to ferment for up to 2 weeks to achieve the texture and taste that you are looking for.

6. Once the kraut is to your liking, place the jar in the fridge, where it will keep for up to 2 months.

Lacto-Fermented Blueberries

Lacto-fermented fruit? Why not? These blueberries are slightly tangy, sweet, and salty all at once. They go great on top of yogurt, chia seed pudding, or oatmeal.

1. Wash the blueberries in tap water—just enough to rinse off any visible debris or dirt. You don't want them to be completely pristine; the bacteria that's found naturally on the skin of the fruit is what drives the fermentation process.
2. Mix the blueberries and salt in a small bowl.
3. Transfer the mixture to a sterilized 1-quart mason jar with a lid.
4. Fill a ziplock bag with water, seal it, and place it in the jar, covering the blueberries. (You want to minimize the blueberries' exposure to air by gently pressing the water-filled bag to fill up any extra space in the jar before it is sealed with the lid.)
5. Let the blueberries sit on the counter, out of direct sunlight, for at least 3 days. Start checking for flavor on the second day. I let mine sit out for 2 to 3 days, or, at most, 4 days. After that, they're ready to eat! The blueberries will keep in the fridge for up to 1 week.

1½ cups fresh blueberries
1 tablespoon sea salt

SOURDOUGH

When I was little, I remember taking trips to our favorite French bakery for the freshest, most delicious bread around. No surprise, my favorite was the country sourdough loaf. My mother would joke that we'd need to buy two loaves because more often than not, at least one of them would be gone by the time we arrived home. When I had a family of my own, I decided to venture into bread baking, specifically sourdough. I was interested in the beneficial effects of the fermentation process on our overall gut health and well-being, as well as the flavor that sourdough starter imparted when baking. I taught myself how to make a starter using just flour and water, then started making a simple no-knead bread.

What I have learned along the way is that the process of sourdough is pretty magical. From mixing flour and water together to letting the natural yeast in the air and flour and time do the work, there is so much fun in watching fermentation happen. Over the years, I have studied with several sourdough masters and have enjoyed creating a variety of ways to use and bake with the starter other than just bread. This chapter offers some tips on flour and water choices and describes the process of how to make your own starter. From there, you'll see three simple and delicious sourdough recipes that you can make at home. And when you are ready to up your sourdough game, our first book—*The Women's Heritage Sourcebook*—includes a no-knead sourdough recipe.

Sourdough

Flour Choices and Water

Use a good-quality flour, one that's unbleached and with no added chemicals. If you are new to baking, I recommend using bread flour. Bread flour has a higher protein content, which means it's easier to work with and can produce a better rise. All-purpose flour can be used, but because it's lower in protein, it can create a wetter dough, which is more difficult to work with. Whole-grain flours are great too, but they can be tricky since they are higher in minerals, which can speed up fermentation time and create a wetter dough. My personal preference is organic stone-ground flour, which I use whenever possible.

When baking in general, filtered and unchlorinated water helps get consistent results. Sourdough culture does not like chlorine. Using quality ingredients helps you attain the ultimate sourdough success.

SOURDOUGH STARTER

Makes 1 starter

Making a sourdough starter is a process of natural fermentation that includes a simple mixture of flour and filtered, unchlorinated water. Some sourdough starters are family heirlooms passed down through generations, which means a little piece of starter can be used in the process of making a new sourdough starter. This allows for the precious gifts of time, tradition, and fermentation to be passed along. Other starters are made from scratch and used for a short time. I created our starter about a decade ago and it's been going strong ever since. Since that time, I've added other starters to my original, including two heirloom starters gifted to me by friends and their families. Remember that a starter is living, so from the beginning we decided we needed to name it. When my daughter, Olivia, was 2 years old, she chose the name Bingo because she was taking a music class at the time and loved the song. Now, years later, Olivia and Liam have made their very own starters and named them Liath Macha and R2-D2, respectively.

¼ cup bread flour, plus more each day

2 tablespoons sourdough starter (optional)

3 tablespoons filtered water, plus more each day

1. Whisk together the flour, sourdough starter (if using), and water in a small bowl.
2. Transfer the mixture to a clean 1-quart mason jar. Put the lid on with a half turn (not tightly), and let it sit at room temperature for 12 hours.
3. After 12 hours, discard ¼ cup of the starter (or you can put it in the compost). Whisk in ½ cup flour with ½ cup water, and loosely cover again.
4. Continue discarding ¼ cup of the starter and adding ½ cup flour and ½ cup water, stirring it,

and covering the jar loosely every 12 hours for 1 week, until the starter is pillowy and bubbly.

5. As you feed your starter, make sure to thoroughly whisk the flour and water into the established starter. This will aerate it, which helps yield the best and most reliable results.

6. Make sure your jar is only half full after each feeding to accommodate the sourdough's expansion. If you've made too much starter for the capacity of your jar, discard a little (preferably into the compost).

Maintaining the Sourdough Starter

After a week, your sourdough should be sturdy enough to withstand storage. If you bake infrequently, meaning less than once a week, store your starter in the fridge. To revive it, bring it to room temperature and discard (or compost) all of the starter except for 2 to 3 tablespoons. Then feed the starter ½ cup flour and ½ cup water, stir it, cover it loosely, and let it sit at room temperature for 6 to 8 hours. Discard all of the starter again except 2 to 3 tablespoons. Then feed the starter ½ cup flour and ½ cup of water 6 to 8 hours before you plan to bake.

If you bake more frequently, meaning every day or at least a few times a week, you can store your sourdough at room temperature. This requires feeding the starter daily, by first discarding all but 2 to 3 tablespoons, adding ½ cup flour and ½ cup water, stirring it vigorously, and covering it loosely. Discard more starter to accommodate expansion, if needed, and use the discarded starter for things like sourdough biscuits, sourdough waffles, flatbread, and crepes.

If a brown liquid appears floating on top of your sourdough starter, simply pour it off. This often means the starter was fed too much water in relation to flour, or the starter has gone too long without a feeding.

The Science of Sourdough

Yeast and bacteria are present in the air, in the flour, and on your hands. You may want to use your clean hands to mix the ingredients, which will fill

them with more microbes. As the microbes begin to reproduce in the starter, the bread-friendly ones take over and crowd out any unfriendly ones.

Lactobacilli bacteria convert sugars in the flour to lactic acid and acetic acid. These acids give sourdough its distinctive sour flavor.

Acid-tolerant yeasts thrive in the starter as well. They convert sugar into carbon dioxide and ethanol. The carbon dioxide creates the bubbles that make the bread rise.

Each microbe eats different sugars, so they do not compete with one another for food.

The principal yeast in the starter is *Candida milleri*. This acid-tolerant yeast doesn't consume maltose, a sugar in flour starch. *Lactobacillus sanfranciscensis*, the bacteria found only in sourdough cultures, do eat maltose. Without it, they starve and die off. Of course, microbes do die eventually, but not before they produce their replacements. When yeasts die, they break down into compounds that the lactobacilli eat. Pretty cool, right?

Sourdough Biscuits

These biscuits are a kid's dream come true. They're just a bit different than the usual baking powder biscuits in flavor and texture, and even more delicious and flaky. You can eat them plain or with your favorite toppings. We even use them as hamburger buns.

2 cups all-purpose flour, plus more for dusting

½ cup plus 2 tablespoons cold lard, coconut oil, or unsalted butter, cut into small chunks

½ cup recently fed sourdough starter

1 tablespoon raw honey

1 teaspoon sea salt

1 teaspoon baking powder

1 teaspoon baking soda

½ cup whole milk, buttermilk, kefir, or coconut milk

1. Put the flour in a large bowl. Using a pastry cutter or knife and fork, cut in the cold lard until the mixture resembles coarse crumbs. Stir in the sourdough starter, honey, salt, baking powder, baking soda, and milk until a soft dough just comes together.

2. Flour a work surface. Roll out the dough with a floured rolling pin to a 2-inch thickness. Cut out six to eight circles with a 1½-inch round cookie cutter or glass. Place them on a parchment-lined baking sheet and put it in the fridge to chill for 8 hours.

3. Preheat the oven to 425°F. Take the biscuits out of the fridge and place them in a 10-inch cast-iron or other ovenproof skillet; they should be touching one another. Bake for 15 minutes, or until the biscuits are golden brown. Let cool for at least 30 minutes before serving.

Sourdough Cinnamon Rolls

Take breakfast to the next level! These cinnamon rolls use the sourdough biscuit recipe as a base, then cinnamon and butter and sugar are added to make them even more amazing. They are delicious and a family favorite.

1. To make the dough, put the flour in a large bowl and cut in the cold lard until the mixture resembles coarse crumbs. Stir in the sourdough starter, honey, salt, baking powder, baking soda, and milk until a soft dough just comes together.
2. To make the filling, combine the sugar, butter, maple syrup, cinnamon, and salt in a small bowl.
3. Flour the work surface. Roll out the dough with a floured rolling pin to a rectangle about 8 by 11 inches, with a 1- to 1½-inch thickness. Smear the filling over the dough and, starting from one long side, roll it into a log. Cut the log crosswise into eight 1- to 1½-inch-thick pieces. Place them cut-side down on a parchment-lined baking sheet and put it in the fridge to chill for 8 hours.
4. Preheat the oven to 350°F. Take the rolls out of the fridge and place them in a 10-inch cast-iron or other ovenproof skillet; they should be touching one another.
5. Place the skillet in the hot oven and bake for 20 to 30 minutes, or until the cinnamon rolls are golden brown. Let sit for at least 30 minutes before serving.

FOR THE DOUGH:

2 cups all-purpose flour, plus more for dusting

½ cup plus 2 tablespoons cold lard, coconut oil, or unsalted butter, cut into small chunks

½ cup recently fed sourdough starter

1 tablespoon raw honey

1 teaspoon sea salt

1 teaspoon baking powder

1 teaspoon baking soda

½ cup whole milk, buttermilk, kefir, or coconut milk

FOR THE FILLING:

1 cup coconut sugar or brown sugar

2 tablespoons unsalted butter, softened, or coconut oil

1 tablespoon maple syrup

2 tablespoons ground cinnamon

Pinch of sea salt

Sourdough Pancakes

These sourdough pancakes are crispy and full of flavor in all the right ways. I feed my starter before I go to bed so it's ready to go in the morning. Serve with a dollop of yogurt, nut butter, or maple syrup, and sprinkle with fresh fruit or dark chocolate chips—really, whatever your heart desires.

4 tablespoons ghee, unsalted butter, or coconut oil, melted

2 cups recently fed sourdough starter

2 eggs

1 teaspoon vanilla extract

½ teaspoon sea salt

1 teaspoon baking soda

Optional add-ins: zest of 1 organic lemon, 1 tablespoon maple syrup or sweetener of choice, 1 tablespoon ground flaxseed, 1 teaspoon ground cinnamon, cacao nibs, dark chocolate chips, banana slices, or blueberries

Optional toppings: butter, maple syrup, elderberry syrup, seasonal jam, powdered sugar, whipped cream, or yogurt

1. Set a 10-inch cast-iron skillet or other pan of your choice over medium heat. Add 1 tablespoon of the ghee.
2. Mix the starter, eggs, vanilla, salt, and remaining 3 tablespoons ghee in a small bowl. Stir in the baking soda (the batter will start to foam) and any of the optional add-ins (if using).
3. Drop a small dab of batter into the skillet; if it sizzles, the skillet is hot enough. Use a ¼-cup measuring cup to pour the batter into the skillet. (Work in batches to prevent the pancakes from spreading into one another. You can cook about three pancakes at a time in a 10-inch skillet.) Immediately reduce the heat a bit so the pancakes cook through without burning. When bubbles start to form on top of the pancake, flip it with a spatula and allow it to cook for an additional 30 seconds. Transfer the cooked pancakes to a platter and cover with a kitchen towel to keep warm. Repeat until all of the batter has been used.
4. Serve while still warm, topped with butter, maple syrup, elderberry syrup, or seasonal jam. Or, for an extra-special treat, sprinkle with powdered sugar or a dollop of fresh whipped cream or yogurt.

TIP: To ensure the pancakes don't stick, follow two very important rules. First, preheat the skillet before letting the batter hit the pan. A hot pan is key, plus a little ghee, butter, or oil gives the pancakes that extra crispness that makes pancakes super yummy. Second, only flip a pancake when you see little bubbles forming on top.

Gluten-Free Sourdough

The art of sourdough bread baking has been around for centuries. However, it wasn't until relatively recently that bakers began playing with the idea of gluten-free bread as a healthy and delicious alternative to traditional breads. As a rule of thumb, sourdough is prized for its health benefits because it's easier to digest. It contains the healthy gut bacteria lactobacillus, which means most of the phytic acid is broken down in the process of fermentation, preventing the spike in blood sugar that traditional bread usually causes.

The challenge is understanding how gluten-free flours work together to create a gluten-free sourdough worthy of eating. Texture and taste can be found with the right combination of gluten-free flours with the souring process. So, for those of you who follow a gluten-free diet, I have turned the three sourdough recipes in this chapter into delicious gluten-free versions.

Gluten-Free Flours

First, a word on flours. When it comes to gluten-free, it's important to know that there are many options. I have listed a variety here, and you'll notice the recipes in this chapter use a handful from this list.

ARROWROOT: This white flour from the root of a West Indian plant of the same name can be exchanged in equal quantities for cornstarch in recipes.

BEAN FLOURS: Including chickpea flour and fava bean flour, these flours are typically high in protein and have a distinct flavor. They are better suited for heartier recipes, such as bread.

BUCKWHEAT FLOUR: Even though this flour has "wheat" in its name, it is actually related to rhubarb, not wheat. Its distinct taste is best when combined with other, blander flours, like rice or millet. A little goes a long way with this flour, and it can be exchanged for equal parts oat or sorghum.

CORN FLOUR: Made from ground corn, this flour is too coarse for cakes, but is very nice for pancakes, cornbread, and tortillas. (Don't confuse it with cornmeal, also gluten-free, which is coarser and also well suited for cornbread or tortillas.) Its texture, if not its flavor, might make it a good substitute for recipes that call for semolina.

MILLET FLOUR: This nutrient-rich flour is ground from the grain of the same name. It has a subtle flavor and can be used for sweet or savory baking. In particular, it is prized for imparting a delicate crumb, so it's suitable for baked goods like muffins or quick breads like banana and zucchini. It can be exchanged for sorghum, oat, or quinoa.

NUT FLOURS: Nut flours are flours made out of nuts. They cannot be substituted in equal quantities for flour, because they are dense and too high in protein. They are used more frequently to replace just a portion of flour in a recipe. Some common nut flours used for baking are almond, walnut, and hazelnut.

POTATO FLOUR: It sounds like potato starch flour, but potato flour is very different. This is a thick, dense flour. When used for bread recipes, it can lend a soft, moist texture, but it is too dense for delicate cakes.

POTATO STARCH FLOUR: Made from ground potatoes, it looks like a fine, white powder. It is a popular flour for cakes and more delicate baked goods.

QUINOA FLOUR: The coating on the seeds of this grain, from which the flour is milled, can be bitter, so look for flour that is "debittered." This flour adds a pleasant density and nuttiness to baked goods and is well suited for scones, biscuits, and pancakes. You can substitute millet flour for quinoa flour.

RICE FLOURS: Rice flours are a key ingredient in most gluten-free baking. White rice flour is a bland-flavored flour, which works well with about any flavor, and its light texture makes it well suited for baking

cakes and delicate baked goods. Variations include brown rice flour, which is ground from unhulled rice kernels, and sweet rice flour, which is made from sticky rice and used as a thickener. Don't substitute it for white rice flour.

SORGHUM FLOUR: Made from sorghum, a relative of sugarcane, this flour is tender and adds a mild sweetness, but is rarely used alone. You can also substitute oat or millet flour.

TAPIOCA FLOUR: From the root of the cassava plant, this is a light, starchy flour that adds a superior texture and "chew" to baked goods. It is frequently used in gluten-free baking, along with other flours.

TEFF FLOUR: Made from an African cereal grass, teff is highly nutritious and high in fiber, protein, iron, amino acids, and calcium. Used with a combination of other gluten-free flours in recipes, it can add an appealing, nutty flavor and a ton of nutrition to your baked goods.

GLUTEN-FREE SOURDOUGH STARTER

Makes 1 starter

Making a gluten-free sourdough starter isn't any different than making a regular sourdough starter. All you need is flour, water, air, and time. The only difference is that gluten-free sourdough requires the use of gluten-free flour, of which there are many options. A gluten-free sourdough starter can be made in as little as 7 days. Other than the flour and water, all you need is a glass jar, preferably a clean 1-quart mason jar. Although this recipe is for creating a brown rice starter, you can also successfully make gluten-free sourdough starters with white rice, teff, sorghum, or oat flour.

½ cup organic brown rice flour, plus more each day
¼ cup filtered water, plus more each day

1. Combine the flour and water in a clean 1-quart mason jar with a lid.

2. Whisk until smooth. If it's too crumbly and dry, whisk in 1 tablespoon of water at a time to reach a thick consistency (it should not be runny). Put the lid on with a half turn (not tightly), and let it sit at room temperature.

3. After 12 hours, discard ¼ cup of the starter and add ½ cup flour and ⅓ cup water. Whisk until smooth and cover loosely with the lid. Repeat this process every 12 hours (twice a day) for the next 6 to 7 days. The starter will start to develop air pockets and become more bubbly each day.

4. If the jar gets too full of starter, simply discard some of it, but keep adding water and flour every 12 hours.

5. When your gluten-free sourdough starter is very bubbly and rises about one-third of the way up the jar, after 4 to 6 hours of feeding, you are ready to use it to make bread.

Maintaining the Sourdough Starter

Once established, your gluten-free sourdough starter just needs to be fed daily (if left on the counter) or once a week (if placed in the fridge), with the same ratio you used when creating it.

If you bake frequently (every day or a few times a week), you can store your starter at room temperature. Discard or compost ¼ cup of the starter (or use it to bake with), then feed it with ½ cup flour and ⅓ cup water once a day, stirring it and loosely covering the jar. Discard extra starter when necessary to accommodate expansion (this extra starter and any you discard when you feed your starter can be used for baking). If you bake infrequently (once a week or less), store the starter in the fridge for up to 1 week, until you are ready to use it. When you want to bake bread, take however much starter you need directly from the fridge until it runs low, then feed it to replenish your supply. The sourdough starter should have the consistency of a thick frosting when it's fed the flour and water and then mixed well.

Gluten-Free Sourdough Biscuits

Here's a gluten-free version of sourdough biscuits that is full of flavor and has a delightful texture. Serve these with a bit of butter for a savory treat, or add some honey or jam for a bit of sweetness.

1. Put the flours in a large bowl. Using a pastry cutter or knife and fork, cut in the butter until the mixture resembles coarse crumbs. Stir in the sourdough starter, psyllium husk, honey, salt, baking powder, baking soda, and milk until a soft dough just comes together.

2. Flour a work surface. Roll out the dough with a floured rolling pin to a 2-inch thickness. Cut out six to eight circles with a 1½-inch round cookie cutter or glass. Place them on a parchment-lined baking sheet and put it in the fridge to chill for 8 hours.

3. Preheat the oven to 425°F. Take the biscuits out of the fridge and place them in a 10-inch cast-iron or other ovenproof skillet; they should be touching one another. Bake for 15 minutes, or until the biscuits are golden brown. Let cool for at least 30 minutes before serving.

1 cup tapioca flour

½ cup millet flour

½ cup brown rice flour, plus more for dusting

½ cup (1 stick) plus 2 tablespoons unsalted butter, cut into small chunks, or coconut oil

½ cup recently fed gluten-free sourdough starter

3 tablespoons psyllium husk

1 tablespoon raw honey

1 teaspoon sea salt

1 teaspoon baking powder

1 teaspoon baking soda

1 cup whole milk, buttermilk, kefir, or coconut milk

Gluten-Free Sourdough Cinnamon Rolls

These cinnamon rolls are so delicious! Just like the traditional sourdough version, these use a variation on the sourdough biscuit recipe as a base, then cinnamon, sugar, and more butter and sugar are added to make them even more amazing.

FOR THE DOUGH:

1 cup tapioca flour

½ cup millet flour

½ cup brown rice flour, plus more for dusting

½ cup (1 stick) plus 2 tablespoons unsalted butter, cut into small chunks, or coconut oil

½ cup recently fed gluten-free sourdough starter

3 tablespoons psyllium husk

1 tablespoon raw honey

1 teaspoon sea salt

1 teaspoon baking powder

1 teaspoon baking soda

1 cup whole milk, buttermilk, kefir, or coconut milk

FOR THE FILLING:

1 cup coconut sugar or brown sugar

2 tablespoons unsalted butter, softened, or coconut oil

1 tablespoon maple syrup

2 tablespoons ground cinnamon

Pinch of sea salt

1. To make the dough, put the flours in a large bowl. Using a pastry cutter or knife and fork, cut in the butter until the mixture resembles coarse crumbs. Stir in the sourdough starter, psyllium husk, honey, salt, baking powder, baking soda, and milk until a soft dough just comes together.

2. To make the filling, combine the sugar, butter, maple syrup, cinnamon, and salt in a small bowl.

3. Flour the work surface. Roll out the dough with a floured rolling pin to a rectangle about 8 by 11 inches, with a 1- to 1½-inch thickness. Smear the filling over the dough, and, starting from one long edge, roll it into a log. Cut the log crosswise into eight 1- to 1½-inch-thick pieces. Place them cut-side down on a parchment-lined baking sheet and put it in the fridge to chill for 8 hours.

4. Preheat the oven to 350°F. Take the rolls out of the fridge and place them in a 10-inch cast-iron or other ovenproof skillet; they should be touching one another.

5. Place the skillet in the hot oven and bake for 20 to 30 minutes, or until the cinnamon rolls are golden brown. Let sit for at least 30 minutes before serving.

Gluten-Free Sourdough Pancakes

Just like the traditional sourdough version, these gluten-free sourdough pancakes are crispy and full of flavor in all the right ways. I feed my starter before I go to bed so it's ready to go in the morning. Serve with a dollop of yogurt, nut butter, or maple syrup, and sprinkle with fresh fruit or dark chocolate chips.

1. Set a 10-inch cast-iron skillet or other pan of your choice over medium heat. Add 1 tablespoon of the ghee.
2. Mix the starter, eggs, flour, vanilla, salt, and remaining 3 tablespoons ghee in a small bowl. Stir in the baking soda (the batter will start to foam) and any of the optional add-ins (if using).
3. Drop a small dab of batter into the skillet; if it sizzles, the skillet is hot enough. Use a ¼-cup measuring cup to pour the batter into the skillet. (Work in batches to prevent the pancakes from spreading into one another. You can cook about three pancakes at a time in a 10-inch skillet.) Immediately reduce the heat a bit so the pancakes cook through without burning. When bubbles start to form on top of the pancake, flip it with a spatula and allow it to cook for an additional 30 seconds. Transfer the cooked pancakes to a platter and cover with a kitchen towel to keep warm. Repeat until all of the batter has been used.
4. Serve while still warm, topped with butter, maple syrup, elderberry syrup, seasonal jam, powdered sugar, or a dollop of fresh whipped cream.

4 tablespoons ghee, unsalted butter, or coconut oil, melted

2 cups recently fed gluten-free sourdough starter

2 eggs

1 tablespoon cassava flour or almond flour

1 teaspoon vanilla extract

½ teaspoon sea salt

1 teaspoon baking soda

Optional add-ins: zest of 1 organic lemon, 1 tablespoon maple syrup or sweetener of choice, 1 tablespoon ground flaxseed, 1 teaspoon ground cinnamon, cacao nibs, dark chocolate chips, banana slices, or blueberries

Optional toppings: butter, maple syrup, elderberry syrup, seasonal jam, powdered sugar, or whipped cream

DAIRY AND NONDAIRY

Growing up on a dairy farm with an ample supply of milk right from the source, I developed a fondness for butter, cheese, ice cream, and the like. I remember taking a bucket to the milking parlor and filling it up with rich, creamy, frothy cow's milk. We would bring it home and drink it right away. I still remember how good that fresh milk tasted. It wasn't until I was an adult that I learned about the benefits of fermenting milk. Fermented milk products are rich in probiotics and easier to digest. On a practical note, making yogurt, cheese, and kefir at home means I can reuse containers, which reduces the amount of packaging in landfills.

In this chapter, we will take a look at both dairy and nondairy options when it comes to fermentation. With this in mind, you'll find cheese made from fresh milk and buttermilk, as well as cheese made from cashews. You'll also find yogurt made using whole cow's milk and a vegan option using canned coconut milk. Once you've created the bases, you can use these recipes to make dips, dressings, and ice cream. Yum!

Easy Farmer's Cheese

This is a perfect first cheese to make because it requires no starter culture or rennet. Instead, this simple cheese relies on the acidic nature of the lemon juice and buttermilk to cause the milk solids to separate from the whey. This recipe is one you can try to tackle on your own or with the help of a parent for a little guidance. The resulting recipe produces a mild and creamy cheese with a little bit of tang. You can enjoy it plain or with fresh herbs added in. Farmer's cheese can be a substitute for ricotta or cream cheese in recipes or it can be used as a topping or spread.

8 cups whole milk (raw or pasteurized, but not ultra-pasteurized)

1 teaspoon sea salt (optional)

1¼ cups cultured buttermilk

¼ cup lemon juice (fresh or bottled) or distilled white vinegar

Fresh herbs, such as rosemary, thyme, chives, or lavender, thinly sliced (optional)

1. Attach a milk thermometer to a medium saucepan. Put the milk and salt (if using) in the saucepan and heat on medium to 165°F, stirring occasionally to keep the milk from scorching on the bottom of the pan.
2. Remove from the heat and add the buttermilk and lemon juice, stirring gently and slowly once or twice.
3. Let the mixture sit undisturbed for 5 minutes. The acid in the buttermilk and lemon juice will begin to cause the separation of the curds from the whey.
4. Line a colander with a few layers of cheesecloth and place it over a large bowl to catch the whey.
5. Pour the curds and whey into the cheesecloth-lined colander. Let the curds strain for at least 30 minutes and up to 1 hour (the longer you strain, the firmer and drier the cheese will become).
6. Transfer the cheese to a bowl and stir in the herbs (if using). Serve immediately, or transfer to an airtight container and refrigerate for up to 1 week. If you'd like to keep the whey to use in place of water or milk in biscuits, pancakes, or other recipes, transfer it to a clean mason jar and store in the fridge for up to 2 weeks.

TIP: This recipe also works with goat's milk. If you can't find goat's milk buttermilk, you can omit the buttermilk; use the lemon juice only for a great-tasting and easy farmer's goat cheese.

Cashew Chèvre

MAKES 2 CUPS

This recipe is for kids of all ages. If you're curious about creating a flavorful cheese without the use of dairy milk, then look no further. This raw and vegan chèvre recipe uses creamy cashews as a base and is fermented over time; the fermentation process not only enhances the flavor of the cheese, but also adds a more savory and delicious quality.

2 cups raw cashews

Filtered water

3 probiotics capsules, such as Jarrow Formulas

⅛ teaspoon sea salt

2 teaspoons fresh lemon juice

2 teaspoons nutritional yeast

Dried or minced fresh herbs, such as rosemary, thyme, chives, or lavender (optional)

1. Place the cashews in a clean 1-quart mason jar. Add enough filtered water to cover the nuts by 2 inches. Soak the cashews overnight.
2. Drain the cashews and transfer to a blender. Add ¼ cup filtered water and blend on high speed, scraping down the sides from time to time, until a smooth paste forms. If you have trouble blending, add up to 2 tablespoons more water. (Add a little bit at a time; adding too much water will make the cashew cream too soft.)
3. Open the probiotics capsules and add the powdery contents; discard the casings. Blend for another 10 to 15 seconds.
4. Cut a piece of cheesecloth (about 12 inches square) and line a bowl with it. Place the mixture in the center of the square and wrap it up, shaping it into a ball. Wrap tightly and tie with string.
5. Find a dark, warm spot in your kitchen with an average temperature of 77° to 86°F. Let the cheese ferment for at least 24 hours or up to 48 hours. Taste it after 24 hours. If it has a tangy flavor, then it's ready; if it doesn't, let it ferment for another 24 hours.
6. When it's ready, open the cheesecloth ball and smell the cheese. It should have a slightly sour yet pungent aroma. If it does not, ferment in 12-hour intervals until you get this aroma.
7. Transfer the cheese to a clean bowl and mix in the salt, lemon juice, and nutritional yeast. Add herbs (if using). Mash the nut cheese with a fork until the flavorings are well incorporated. Taste and try as you go, adjusting until you achieve the desired flavor.
8. Now it's time to "age" the cheese. Take a piece of parchment paper and place the nut cheese on a long side nearest you. Roll it back and forth with your hands until you make a long log shape.
9. Close the ends of the parchment paper. Label the package with the date and place it in the fridge for as long as you can wait. Try 1 week at first, and then the next time you make it, try 2 or 3 weeks, or even up to 1 month. The longer you age the nut cheese, the richer the flavor will be and the firmer the texture will become.

10. Once you've aged the cheese, it's finally time to eat your creation.
Enjoy it as is, or roll it in herbs and serve with your favorite crackers
or raw or pickled veggies.

Milk Kefir

Milk kefir is a fermented beverage containing probiotics. It uses kefir grains to ferment the milk, which results in a tangy, drinkable beverage. You can find kefir grains at specialty stores or online. Milk kefir can be made from any animal milk—cow, goat, or sheep—as well as nondairy options such as coconut milk. If you'd like to substitute coconut milk for animal milk, follow the same procedure described below. To keep the kefir grains working properly, you will need to cycle them through animal milk every couple of batches. Make one or two batches with nondairy milk, then a batch with dairy milk, then one or two batches with nondairy milk, and so on.

1 to 2 tablespoons milk kefir grains

2 cups whole milk (cow, goat, or sheep), preferably organic, raw, or unhomogenized (never ultra-pasteurized), or coconut milk

1. Place the milk kefir grains and milk in a sterilized 1-quart mason jar.
2. Cover lightly with cheesecloth and secure with a rubber band. Leave at room temperature (70° to 75°F) for at least 12 hours.
3. After 12 hours, taste the kefir. You are looking for a slightly sour taste. If necessary, let it ferment for another 6 hours, then taste again. If you still desire more of a sour taste, check and taste every 2 hours until desired sourness is achieved.
4. Set a fine-mesh strainer over a bowl to catch the milk, then strain out the milk kefir grains. Do not rinse the grains. Either repeat the entire process in a new jar, or store the kefir grains in a mason jar in the fridge for up to 1 month.
5. Store the fermented milk kefir in the fridge in an airtight container. It will keep for up to 2 weeks.

FLAVORING MILK KEFIR AND SECOND FERMENTATION

Once the grains are separated and transferred to fresh milk, the resulting liquid is milk kefir. Since the grains have been removed, the milk kefir can be further cultured and flavored. This culturing period is the second fermentation. A good amount of time for flavoring and creating a second ferment is 2 to 6 hours. This means the kefir, with no grains in it, can sit for 2 to 6 more hours with the additional flavor and the fermentation will continue to happen. The benefits of second fermentation include additional good bacterial content, reduced lactose content, and improved flavor. Some flavor options are:

- Chai spices
- Citrus
- Vanilla extract
- Ground cinnamon
- Cocoa powder
- Pumpkin pie spice
- Fresh or frozen fruit
- Maple syrup
- Raw honey

Kefir Ice Cream

This kefir ice cream has the perfect amount of tang and just the right amount of sweet goodness. Although this recipe is for a simple vanilla ice cream, you can always add chocolate chips, nuts, or even fruit to make it even more delicious.

1. In a small saucepan, combine the eggs with the heavy cream and cook over medium heat, stirring constantly, until a somewhat thick custard forms, about 10 minutes. Remove the saucepan from the heat and allow it to cool to room temperature, about 30 minutes.
2. Mix in the milk kefir, maple syrup or sweetener, vanilla, and salt. (If sugar is your sweetener of choice, add it to the custard mixture at the end of the heating process so the heat dissolves the sugar.)
3. Transfer to an airtight container and refrigerate for at least 4 hours or overnight.
4. When ready to turn the chilled ice cream base into ice cream, pour it into an ice-cream machine, then add the optional add-ins (if using). Churn according to the manufacturer's instructions. Serve directly from the machine for soft serve, or store in an airtight freezer-safe container in the freezer for 2 to 3 months.

2 eggs, whisked

1½ cups heavy cream

1½ cups whole-milk kefir, store-bought or homemade (see page 54)

¼ cup plus 2 tablespoons maple syrup or sweetener of choice

1 tablespoon vanilla extract

Pinch of sea salt

Optional add-ins: chocolate chips, nuts, or fruit

VEGAN VERSION

To make a vegan kefir ice cream, make the kefir with coconut milk instead of dairy milk. Use coconut cream instead of heavy cream, and simply leave out the eggs.

Cilantro-Lime-Kefir Dressing and Dip

MAKES 1 CUP

This cilantro-lime-kefir dressing is perfect for salads and great for dipping too. It's also delicious mixed with mashed avocados as a topping on avocado toast.

½ cup whole-milk kefir

1 cup fresh cilantro leaves

3 cloves garlic, peeled

3 tablespoons extra-virgin olive oil

1 tablespoon fresh lime juice

½ teaspoon sea salt

½ cup whole-milk plain Greek yogurt (optional)

1. Put the kefir, cilantro, garlic, oil, lime juice, and salt in a blender. Blend on high until smooth and creamy. Chill for at least 10 minutes before using it as a dressing.
2. To make a creamy dip, transfer the dressing to a bowl and stir in the Greek yogurt.

Dairy Yogurt

Store-bought yogurt can be full of added sugars and preservatives. For this reason, we like to make our own rich and creamy yogurt. Olivia and Liam enjoy their yogurt best topped with blueberries, or any seasonal fruit, and a smidge of raw honey.

1. Attach a milk thermometer to a medium saucepan. Heat the milk in the saucepan over medium heat until it reaches 160°F.
2. Remove from the heat and let cool to 110°F. Add the starter culture to the cooled milk.
3. Pour into a sterilized 1-quart mason jar and incubate in the oven for 6 to 12 hours at 110°F. Other options are to use a yogurt maker, place in a dehydrator at 110°F, or use an insulated camping cooler with a pot of boiling water inside.
4. Place the yogurt in the fridge and chill for at least 6 hours before eating. It will thicken as it chills. Keep refrigerated and use within 2 weeks.

3¾ cups whole milk (preferably organic, raw, or unhomogenized, never ultra-pasteurized)

1 tablespoon starter culture (yogurt)

Raw, Dairy-Free Coconut Yogurt

This recipe is as simple as can be and only uses two ingredients. What's more, it does not require any extra equipment, which you might need if you had to crack open a fresh coconut. Our family likes this coconut yogurt as is, but you can always add vanilla extract, maple syrup, or raw honey for extra sweetness.

1 (14-ounce) can full-fat coconut milk

2 probiotic capsules, such as Jarrow Formulas

1. Shake the coconut milk well, then open the can and pour the coconut milk into a dry, sterilized ½-quart mason jar.
2. Open the probiotic capsules and pour the powdery contents over the coconut milk; discard the capsule casings. Stir until creamy and smooth, pushing the probiotic up against the side of the jar with your spoon to evenly disperse it.
3. Cover the jar with a tight-fitting lid.
4. Place in an oven set to 100°F. Turn the oven light on to keep the environment warm. Other options are to use a yogurt maker, place in a dehydrator at 110°F, or use an insulated camping cooler with a pot of boiling water inside.
5. Leave for 12 to 48 hours without disturbing; 24 hours is usually optimal.
6. Place the set yogurt in the fridge and chill for at least 6 hours before eating. The yogurt will thicken as it chills. Keep the yogurt refrigerated and use within 2 weeks.

TIP: It's important to select a coconut milk that is creamy and smooth (not grainy or clumpy) to ensure that the yogurt will be creamy and smooth. Our family's favorite brands are Whole Foods 365 full-fat organic coconut milk, Savoy coconut cream, and Aroy-D coconut milk. All three have produced successful results.

Coconut Yogurt Chia Pudding

MAKES 2 CUPS

Chia pudding with coconut yogurt is the perfect make-ahead breakfast or anytime snack. Try making both flavors! If you'd rather use dairy, you can easily swap out the coconut yogurt. The same goes for the almond or coconut milk. If cow's milk is your preference, it's an easy switch.

FOR THE VANILLA PUDDING:

½ cup coconut yogurt, store-bought or homemade (see page 62)

2½ tablespoons chia seeds

¼ cup almond or coconut milk

1 tablespoon vanilla extract

Pinch of sea salt

1 tablespoon maple syrup, raw honey, or other sweetener of choice (optional)

FOR THE CHOCOLATE PUDDING:

½ cup coconut yogurt, store-bought or homemade (see page 62)

2½ tablespoons chia seeds

¼ cup almond or coconut milk

1 tablespoon plus 1 teaspoon raw cacao powder

1 tablespoon vanilla extract

½ teaspoon ground cinnamon

1 tablespoon maple syrup, raw honey, or other sweetener of choice (optional)

Optional toppings: cacao nibs, almond butter, tahini, sliced banana, chopped apple, raisins, goji berries, chopped Medjool dates, bee pollen, chopped nuts, or fresh or frozen berries

1. For each flavor, put all the ingredients in a small mason jar with a lid. Mix until thoroughly combined and there are no clumps.
2. Cover with the lid and place in the fridge for at least 1 hour and up to overnight. If it's too thick for your taste, thin it a bit with a little more almond or coconut milk.
3. Once thickened, add your favorite toppings (if using) and enjoy.

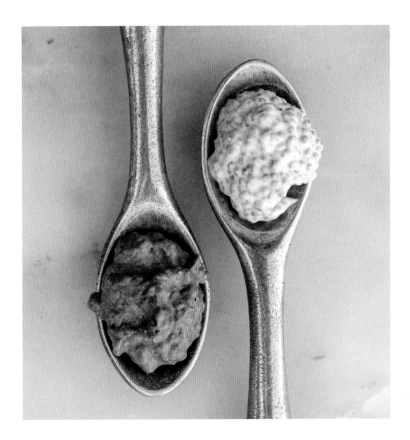

Yogurt Bowls with Seasonal Fresh Fruit

These yogurt bowls are great for breakfast or if you're looking for an afternoon pick-me-up snack. Grass-fed whole-milk yogurt is loaded with vitamin D and probiotics, and the seasonal fruit is an added benefit, full of extra fiber, vitamins, and minerals.

1. To each of four small serving bowls, add ½ cup of the yogurt and ½ cup of the fresh seasonal fruit.
2. Sprinkle on the desired toppings and drizzle with maple syrup or honey. Dust with cinnamon or cacao powder.

2 cups whole-milk yogurt, store-bought or homemade (see page 61)

2 cups seasonal fruit, such as oranges, pomegranate seeds, berries, grapes, or persimmons

Toppings, such as granola (see page 130), nuts, seeds, or bee pollen

Natural sweeteners, such as maple syrup or raw honey

Spices, such as ground cinnamon or raw cacao powder

Mint Yogurt Dip

This simple dip can be made with store-bought yogurt or made following the yogurt recipe in this book. Either way, this dip is great with seasonal veggies, fresh fruits, and crackers.

1. Combine the yogurt, garlic, mint, lemon zest and juice, salt, and pepper in a small bowl.
2. Drizzle the oil on top just before serving.

2 cups whole-milk plain yogurt, store-bought or homemade (see page 61)

1 clove garlic, minced

2 tablespoons finely chopped fresh mint leaves

1 tablespoon lemon zest

1 tablespoon fresh lemon juice

Pinch of sea salt

Pinch of freshly ground black pepper

Drizzle of extra-virgin olive oil

Cultured Butter

Did you know you can make delicious homemade butter? All you need is a mason jar with a tight-fitting lid, some heavy cream, and sea salt. This recipe includes how to culture the cream before making the butter. (For simplicity, you could also skip this step and go straight to making the butter.)

Sometimes butter gets a bad rap since it can be deemed an unhealthy fat. But it's important to note that good-quality cream from grass-fed cows can produce healthy-for-you butter that is a source of vitamins A, E, D, and K.

If making this recipe with younger kids, you might try a smaller jar so they can find success shaking the cream on their own. As a rule of thumb, whichever size mason jar you use, fill it about halfway with the heavy cream, put the lid on tightly, and start shaking.

2 cups heavy cream

2 tablespoons starter culture, such as milk kefir grains, cultured sour cream, or cultured buttermilk*

¼ teaspoon sea salt

Herbs or spices, such as chives, dill, ground cinnamon, or garlic salt (optional)

Note that unpasteurized cream will naturally ferment without any additional culture.

TO CULTURE THE CREAM:

1. Mix the cream and starter culture in a clean 1-quart mason jar. Close the lid tightly.
2. Leave the jar on the counter to culture for at least 12 hours and up to 18 hours.

TO MAKE THE BUTTER:

1. Pour the cultured cream into a clean mason jar, filling it halfway. Do not fill past the halfway mark. Screw the lid on tightly so there are no leaks.
2. Shake the jar continuously. After a few minutes, whipped cream will form. Keep shaking until you hear a thumping sound. A lump should be forming inside. Shake for an additional 30 to 60 seconds after that. You should clearly see the butterfat separating from the buttermilk. Keep shaking until all the buttermilk has separated and the butter has formed into a ball. (As a guide, around 3 minutes of shaking makes whipped cream, 6 minutes makes little cream granules, in 8 minutes the buttermilk starts to separate, and in approximately 10 minutes or more—depending on how fast you shake the jar—the butter has formed.)
3. Scoop the butter into a bowl and press it with your hands or the back of a spoon to squeeze out the buttermilk. Pour any buttermilk that comes out back into the jar. Rinse the butter with ice-cold water, then return the butter to the bowl and press it again to squeeze out more buttermilk. Pour it into the jar. Rinse the butter

with ice-cold water a second time, and press out any remaining buttermilk. Save the buttermilk to drink or use it to bake or cook with. It will keep in the fridge for up to 2 weeks.

4. Sprinkle the butter with the salt and other herbs or spices (if using). Mix everything into the butter with the spoon and put it in an airtight container for serving and storage. Salted cultured butter can stay on the counter for up to 1 week.

THE SCIENCE OF MAKING BUTTER

When fresh cream is agitated, the fat molecules get shaken out of position and clump together. This stirring or shaking causes the water molecules to be squeezed out of the solid mass. Eventually, after enough agitation, the fat molecules that clump together become butter. It's also during this process when the fat molecules get separated from the liquid in the cream that buttermilk is formed.

Shaking the cream works because cream is nothing but milk fat, a complex mixture of lipids that get stabilized by their own fat molecules. When the cream is shaken up, the fat molecules all together form a clump, leaving the water molecules, since fat and water don't mix well. This physical change is reversible. The butter can be melted and mixed with buttermilk to make cream again.

SEASONAL EATING

Eating with the seasons is one of the best ways to add variety, excitement, and nutrition to the dinner table. If you live in an area where seasons are not so defined, like here in Southern California where it is sunny most of the year, it can be hard to distinguish between the seasons. This is why we make it a point to eat seasonally as a family. Grocery stores often stock produce that is out of season or not locally harvested, but farmers markets and CSA (community-supported agriculture) programs make it easy to shop for in-season produce.

When we rely on what we can grow ourselves, or what the farmers around us are growing, we are eating food that is fresher, healthier, and more nutritious. It's also better for the planet and more sustainable, since it doesn't have to be transported far and doesn't require hothouses or pesticides. Many of the recipes in this chapter offer basic instructions that can be adapted for each season. Think of the recipes as templates. You can choose which fruit or vegetables are in season and substitute those for each creation.

Creating a Seasonal Food Menu

Seasonal meal planning is the simple act of taking some time to plan any number of your meals for the week or month ahead, incorporating what's growing now. There are a variety of reasons meal planning can be beneficial. For starters, it can save money. When you plan and cook your own meals, you are most likely saving money when compared to purchasing the same type of meal in a restaurant or buying premade items at the grocery store.

It's also healthier to create a seasonal meal plan. When you eat from what's in season, you add a wider range of nutrients to your body by mixing it up a bit and eating foods that you might not otherwise. Also, when you make an effort to choose from what's in season and plan ahead, there is often less waste, and you save time in the process because you have a plan.

My favorite part about eating with the seasons is the taste. Fresh, in-season carrots taste nothing like the ones from the store. They are sweet and bursting with flavor. When it comes to tomatoes, there really is nothing like a ripe summer tomato fresh from the garden. And the juiciest and most deliciously sweet strawberries come directly from the garden or from the farmers market.

One of the things I love about belonging to a CSA and shopping locally at the farmers market is that our CSA often shares recipes for what's in season. And when you get to know your local farmers, the perk is that they might give you extra tips on how to prepare what they are growing. You will be introduced to a variety of fruits and vegetables that you might not otherwise have tried.

As the seasons change and autumn brings cooler days and nights, we naturally crave warmth and comfort. Winter squash and root vegetables are what Mother Nature brings as nourishment for hearty meals through the fall and winter. (Winter is also a time to rely on your canned summer vegetables.) Spring emerges and brings light, bright produce, such as lettuce, greens, and peas. When we are at the height of the heat in the summer months, water-rich, juicy produce is abundant to hydrate our bodies and provide antioxidants to help protect us from the sun. There is a rhythm and purpose to foods when we eat with the seasons.

On the opposite page, you will find some basic seasonal produce and ideas of what you might create with nature's bounty.

WINTER

IN-SEASON PRODUCE: winter squash, beets, parsnips, rutabagas, sweet potatoes, cabbage, carrots, onions, Brussels sprouts

BREAKFAST IDEAS: oatmeal with apples or other preserved fruit; eggs and sauerkraut; sourdough pancakes with preserved fruit

MAIN DISHES: vegetable soup or stew with winter squash; cabbage stir-fry; parsnip and carrot fritters; grain bowls or creamy polenta with roasted winter squash, onions, beets, and carrots

SIDE DISHES: roasted winter squash; warm beet salad; parsnip and sweet potato fries; mashed parsnips and rutabagas; sautéed cabbage; preserved honey garlic–glazed carrots; sauerkraut

SPRING

IN-SEASON PRODUCE: Swiss chard, dandelion greens, kale, collard greens, spinach, lettuce, arugula, fava beans, snap peas, strawberries, broccoli, asparagus, radishes, carrots, garden-fresh herbs

BREAKFAST DISHES: scrambled eggs with spinach or other greens; fried eggs with asparagus; granola with fresh strawberries and whole milk or milk kefir

MAIN DISHES: lettuce and herb salad or dandelion greens salad topped with chicken or other protein, such as legumes or quinoa; beef and broccoli stir-fry; broccoli and spinach soup; chicken and snap pea stir-fry; grain bowls or creamy polenta with spring greens, roasted asparagus, and carrots; mashed fava bean tartine; coconut curry veggie stew; mini herb and cheese frittata; spring greens quiche

SIDE DISHES: roasted broccoli; Swiss chard with bacon and onions; kale chips; spinach and strawberry salad; sautéed fava beans; roasted asparagus; lacto-fermented radishes and carrots

SUMMER

IN-SEASON PRODUCE: tomatoes, peppers, green beans, berries, stone fruits, melons, cucumbers, eggplant, peaches, yellow squash, zucchini, new potatoes, corn

BREAKFAST DISHES: zucchini bread; yogurt with fresh seasonal fruit; eggs with fresh salsa; seasonal fruit smoothies

MAIN DISHES: pasta or pizza with tomatoes, garlic, and herbs; fajitas with peppers; roasted eggplant on pasta or pizza; stuffed peppers or zucchini; veggie kabobs; sandwiches topped with tomatoes, cucumbers, and avocado; grain bowls or creamy polenta with roasted zucchini, yellow squash, and tomatoes; zucchini and corn galette; summer veggie quiche

SIDE DISHES: cucumber and tomato salad; steamed, stir-fried, or pickled green beans; steamed or roasted potatoes; fruit salads; zucchini ribbons; lacto-fermented dill pickles

FALL

IN-SEASON PRODUCE: apples, pumpkins, kabocha squash, sweet potatoes, potatoes, butternut squash, carrots, collard greens, kale, beets

BREAKFAST DISHES: pumpkin muffins; baked apples; apple cinnamon rolls; pumpkin oatmeal

MAIN DISHES: pumpkin chili; potato soup; butternut squash soup; white bean stew with seasonal greens; roasted root vegetables with sausage over creamy polenta; sweet potato, kale, and sausage hash; sweet potato curry; grain bowls or creamy polenta with roasted butternut squash and collard greens

SIDE DISHES: roasted sweet potato and apples; sautéed collard greens; roasted carrots with carrot-top pesto; roasted beets; pickled winter squash

Creamy Ragù with Seasonal Veggies

This creamy ragù can be made with cream and cheese, or with cashew or coconut cream and nutritional yeast, if you want to try a plant-based version. Either way, it's loaded with fresh, seasonal goodness that can be adapted all year long to savor the seasons. Think winter squash in the fall and winter, or fresh peas and asparagus in the spring.

1. Bring a large pot of water to a boil with 2 tablespoons of the salt. Cook the pasta according to the package directions.
2. In the meantime, heat the oil in a heavy skillet over medium-high heat. Once the oil is hot, add the onion and cook for 2 minutes, or until it has softened. Add the garlic and stir for 30 seconds. Add the ground meat and use a wooden spoon to break it up. Cook until the meat is no longer pink, about 5 minutes. (If using lentils or beans for a plant-based version, simply add them to the pan and move on to step 3.)
3. Add the seasonal vegetables and cook for 2 minutes, until tender.
4. Pour in the heavy cream and stir to incorporate with the meat and veggie mixture. Stir in the grated cheese and cook for 7 to 8 minutes, until the sauce thickens. Add the pasta and stir to combine. Season with the remaining 1 teaspoon salt, black pepper, and fresh herbs (if using).

2 tablespoons plus 1 teaspoon sea salt

1 pound regular or gluten-free pasta, such as elbows or pappardelle

2 tablespoons extra-virgin olive oil

1 small onion, peeled and diced

4 cloves garlic, minced

1 pound ground turkey, pork, or beef, or 2 cups lentils or great northern beans

4 cups thinly sliced seasonal vegetables, such as broccoli florets, winter squash, summer squash, peas, asparagus, or mushrooms

¾ cup heavy cream, coconut cream, or cashew cream (see page 76)

½ cup grated Parmesan cheese or nutritional yeast

1 teaspoon freshly ground black pepper

Handful of fresh herbs, such as basil, mint, or dill (optional)

Cashew Cream

This cashew cream is full of flavor and adds just the right touch to thicken soups, stews, salad dressings, and pasta dishes without the dairy. It also makes a lovely cheesy dip.

1 cup raw cashews

½ cup filtered water

2 tablespoons extra-virgin olive oil

2 tablespoons fresh lemon juice

1 clove garlic, peeled

½ teaspoon sea salt

1. Place the cashews, water, oil, lemon juice, garlic, and salt in a blender. Blend until creamy and smooth.
2. Transfer to an airtight container and store in the fridge until ready to use. The cashew cream will keep for up to 2 weeks.

Seasonal Jam

This recipe uses grapes, but any seasonal fruit will do. Berries, figs, persimmons, and stone fruit are all good choices too. The ratios and measurements stay the same. What we love about making seasonal jam is that you can use the fruit when it's at its peak flavor and freshness.

1. Prepare five 1-pint mason jars by washing the jars and lids.
2. Add the grapes, sugar, and lemon juice to a medium saucepan over medium heat. Bring to a simmer, then simmer for 30 to 45 minutes, stirring occasionally to crush the fruit and dissolve the sugar.
3. Remove from the heat. Funnel the jam into the prepared jars, leaving ½ inch of headspace at the top. Wipe the jars clean and place the lids on the jars. Store in the fridge for up to 2 weeks.

4 pounds seedless grapes, preferably roughly equal quantities of red, black, and green grapes

4 cups granulated sugar

3 tablespoons fresh lemon juice

Basic Pie and Hand Pie Crust

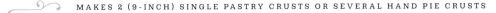

This basic pie and hand pie recipe produces a buttery, flaky crust. It is perfect for sweet or savory fillings and creations. Before your hands get messy, gather all your ingredients, plus a medium bowl, whisk, rubber spatula, 9-inch pie plate, and bench scraper or offset spatula. A ruler and a pair of kitchen shears will help too.

1¾ cups plus 1 tablespoon all-purpose flour, plus more for dusting

1 tablespoon granulated sugar

1¼ teaspoons kosher salt

1 cup (2 sticks) very cold unsalted butter, cut into ½-inch cubes

½ cup very cold filtered water

1 teaspoon apple cider vinegar

1. Whisk together the flour, sugar, and salt in a medium bowl. Toss the butter cubes in the flour, separating any stuck-together cubes with your fingers, then pinch each cube flat with your fingers to about ¼ inch thick—don't work the butter in more! Incorporate the cold water and vinegar with a rubber spatula and press and knead together until the dough comes together in a ball.

2. Dump the ball onto a heavily floured work surface, sprinkle the top with more flour, and use a floured rolling pin to roll out a rectangle about 10 by 15 inches, with the longer side closest to you, adding as much flour as you need along the way to keep the dough from sticking. (If your kitchen is very warm or if at any point the butter gets melty and sticky, gather the dough on a baking sheet and pop it into the fridge until it firms up a little, 15 minutes or so.)

TIPS FOR SUCCESS

← Your ingredients should be very, very cold. The colder the ingredients and equipment, the less risk there will be for the butter to melt or become overworked (an enemy of flaky pie crust).

← Apple cider vinegar is a secret ingredient. Add 1 teaspoon to your current favorite recipe when you add the ice water. Vinegar helps prevent the formation of gluten, which makes for a tough crust.

← Let your dough rest for at least 20 minutes. Again, it's all about gluten. After working your ingredients together and getting everything all excited, the dough needs time to relax in order for it to be on its best behavior when you're rolling it out.

← When it comes to pie dough, practice makes perfect.

← Don't stress. If you relax in the kitchen and take things step by step, knowing full well that they'll come out just fine, they will.

← Use quality ingredients. Fresh and seasonal are best. Quality really makes a difference when it comes to flavor. Search for farmers market freshness and backyard harvests to bring seasonal and local flavors to your hand pies.

3. Slide an offset spatula under the dough to loosen it from the counter, fold each 10-inch side toward the middle so the edges meet, then fold them again like a book. Fold the "book" in half, top to bottom, then slice the dough in half horizontally so you have two roughly equal-size rectangles of dough. Wrap the dough rectangles in plastic wrap and refrigerate for at least 20 minutes or up to 2 hours (or even overnight). Alternatively, the dough can be frozen for up to 3 months and thawed overnight in the fridge before baking. When ready to use, remove the dough from the fridge and bring it back to room temperature.

Gluten-Free Pie and Hand Pie Crust

This gluten-free pie dough comes together quickly and has proven to be a great alternative to an all-purpose flour crust. It holds its shape well for both sweet and savory fillings. Before your hands get messy, gather a medium bowl, whisk, rubber spatula, rolling pin, 9-inch pie plate (preferably glass; aluminum or other metal is also fine, but heavy ceramic and stoneware are not recommended), and bench scraper or offset spatula. A ruler and a pair of kitchen shears will help too.

1. To make the gluten-free flour blend, combine the rice flour, cornstarch, and tapioca flour in a medium bowl and stir to combine. Set aside 1¼ cups for this recipe and store the rest in an airtight container for future use.

2. In a medium bowl, combine the gluten-free flour blend, sugar, and salt, then add the butter. Toss the butter cubes in the flour, separating any stuck-together cubes with your fingers, then pinch each cube flat with your fingers, to about ¼ inch thick—don't work the butter in more! (If using shortening or coconut oil, it can be added without any further preparation.) Incorporate the cold water and vinegar with a rubber spatula and press and knead together until the dough comes together in a ball.

3. Dump the ball onto a heavily floured work surface, sprinkle the top with more flour, and use a floured rolling pin to roll out a rectangle about 10 by 15 inches, with the longer side closest to you, adding as much flour as you need along the way to keep the dough from sticking. (If your kitchen is very warm and the butter gets melty and sticky, gather the dough on a baking sheet and pop it into the fridge until it firms up a little, 15 minutes or so.) Form the dough into a disk. Since the dough is so crumbly and does not hold together at this point, I find it easier (and far less messy) to pour the mixture into a large food-storage bag and use the bag to help form it into a disk. Close up the bag and store the dough in the fridge for at least 1 hour and up to 3 days before using.

FOR THE GLUTEN-FREE FLOUR BLEND:

3 cups rice flour (brown or white)

2½ cups cornstarch

1½ cups tapioca flour

FOR THE DOUGH:

1¼ cups gluten-free flour blend, plus more for dusting

1 tablespoon granulated sugar

¾ teaspoon kosher or fine sea salt

½ cup (1 stick) very cold unsalted butter, cut into ½-inch cubes, or ½ cup solid all-vegetable nondairy shortening or coconut oil

2 to 4 tablespoons very cold filtered water

1 teaspoon apple cider vinegar

Pizza Margherita Hand Pies

These hand pies make a fun appetizer, snack, or meal. They are savory and stuffed with all the ingredients you might enjoy on a pizza. You could also add prosciutto or ground beef. Other flavor combination ideas include caramelized onions and feta or ham, sautéed mushrooms, or roasted potatoes or veggies with cheese.

1 pie crust dough
(see page 78)

Brown rice flour or pizza flour, for dusting

6 tablespoons homemade tomato sauce (see page 85)

6 slices fresh mozzarella

4 sun-dried tomatoes, thinly sliced (optional)

6 fresh basil leaves

1 egg, beaten

1. Take the dough out of the fridge and bring it to room temperature, 20 to 25 minutes. Flour a work surface. Roll out the dough with a floured rolling pin to a circle of ⅛-inch thickness. Use a 6-inch round cookie cutter to cut out 12 circles.

2. Spoon 1 tablespoon of the tomato sauce on six of the circles, leaving a ½-inch border all around. Top with 1 slice of mozzarella cheese, several slices of sun-dried tomato (if using), and a fresh basil leaf, pressing down slightly. Top each circle with another circle of dough and seal the edges with a fork.

3. Transfer to a parchment-lined baking sheet and prick the centers of each hand pie to make air holes. Brush the tops and edges with the egg wash.

4. Refrigerate the pies for 20 minutes. While the pies are chilling, preheat the oven to 375°F.

5. Once the pies have chilled, remove them from the fridge and bake for 25 to 30 minutes, or until golden brown.

6. Place the pies on a cooling rack until cool enough to handle, then serve. They can also be served cold (or reheated in the oven before serving).

Homemade Tomato Sauce

This is a basic sauce that is full of flavor. Using fresh tomatoes from the garden or farmers market makes a big difference. In a pinch, you can substitute canned diced tomatoes for the fresh ones.

1. If using fresh tomatoes, the tomato skins need to be removed. Bring a large pot of water to a boil. Have a bowl of ice-cold water nearby. Remove the tomato stems, and score the bottom (non-stem end) of each tomato with a small X. Working in stages, place the tomatoes (about four to six at a time) in the boiling water for 30 to 60 seconds, or until you see the skins split. Use a slotted spoon to remove the tomatoes and place them immediately in the bowl of ice-cold water. When cool enough to handle, slip the skins off. Halve, quarter, and dice the tomatoes.

2. Heat a large Dutch oven or cast-iron skillet over medium-high heat. Add the oil, vinegar, diced tomatoes, bell pepper, salt, onion powder, basil, oregano, black pepper, and red pepper flakes (if using). Use the back of a spoon or fork to mash the tomatoes and help them break down a bit.

3. Bring to a low boil, constantly stirring, until the mixture has reduced by half, 45 minutes to 1 hour.

4. For a smooth consistency, let the sauce cool for 1 hour, then place in a blender and puree to the desired consistency. Skip this step if you want your sauce to be chunky. Let the sauce cool, then store in the fridge in an airtight container for up to 1 week, or freeze for up to 3 months.

2 pounds tomatoes (plum or beefsteak) or 1 (28-ounce) can peeled and diced tomatoes

1 tablespoon extra-virgin olive oil

1 teaspoon balsamic vinegar

2 tablespoons finely chopped seeded red bell pepper

1 teaspoon sea salt

¼ teaspoon onion powder

¼ teaspoon dried basil

¼ teaspoon dried oregano

¼ teaspoon cracked black pepper

Pinch of red pepper flakes (optional)

Seasonal Jam Hand Pies

This recipe uses jam (though you could also use fruit butters) to make a scrumptious homemade toaster pastry. Dusted with cane sugar, these seasonal jam hand pies are delicious.

1 pie crust dough
(see page 78)

Brown rice flour or pizza flour, for dusting

6 tablespoons seasonal jam

1 egg, beaten

Cane sugar, for sprinkling

1. Take the dough out of the fridge and bring it to room temperature, 20 to 25 minutes.

2. Flour a work surface. Roll out the dough with a floured rolling pin to a round with a ⅛-inch thickness. Use a 6-inch round cookie cutter to cut out 12 circles.

3. Spoon 1 tablespoon of the jam onto six of the circles. Top each circle with another circle of dough and seal the edges with a fork.

4. Transfer to a parchment-lined baking sheet and prick the center of each hand pie to make air holes. Brush the tops and edges with the egg wash and then sprinkle with the cane sugar.

5. Refrigerate the pies for 20 minutes. While the pies are chilling, preheat the oven to 375°F.

6. Once the pies have chilled, remove them from the fridge and bake for about 20 minutes, or until the edges have slightly browned.

7. Transfer to a wire rack to cool completely.

Brown Sugar Apple Pie

This classic apple pie recipe is a real treat, with a flaky, buttery crust and a tender, lightly spiced apple filling. Use a combination of your favorite apples for the best flavor, and bake until the top is golden and the filling is bubbly.

1. In a large bowl, mix together the lemon juice, brown sugar, cinnamon, allspice, nutmeg, salt, and 2 teaspoons of the bourbon (if using). As you peel, core, and thickly slice your apples, toss them into the bowl with the sugar-and-spice mix. (The lemon juice in this mixture will keep the sliced apples from browning.)

2. Toss the apples with the sugar-and-spice mixture. Let sit at room temperature for 1 hour to allow the fruit to release any juices.

3. Using a fine-mesh strainer over a small bowl, strain out ½ cup of the apple mixture's juices. The rest of the juice can be discarded.

4. Put the juice and butter in a small saucepan. Cook over medium-high heat until it becomes thick and syruplike, about 10 minutes.

5. Combine the resulting syrup, cornstarch, and remaining 2 teaspoons bourbon (if using) with the apples and mix together.

6. Place one oven rack in the lowest position and put a large rimmed baking sheet on it (to catch any drips from the pie). Position a second rack the next rung up (still in the lower third of the oven) and preheat the oven to 375°F.

7. Remove two disks of dough from the fridge and let them sit at room temperature for 5 to 10 minutes. Place the first disk on a lightly floured work surface. Using a floured rolling pin, roll out the pie dough into a 12-inch-diameter circle that's about ⅛ inch thick. As you roll out the dough, check to make sure it isn't sticking. If it starts to stick, gently lift it up and sprinkle a little more flour on the work surface or on the dough to keep it from sticking. Gently place the rolled-out dough on a 9-inch pie plate. Press down to line the pie dish with the dough.

8. Mound the apples in the dough-lined pie plate.

9. Roll out the second disk of dough, again to a 12-inch-diameter circle about ⅛ inch thick. Gently place it over the apples. Trim the excess dough with kitchen shears, leaving a ¾-inch overhang from the edges of the pie plate.

1 tablespoon fresh lemon juice or apple cider vinegar

½ cup dark brown sugar

½ teaspoon ground cinnamon

¼ teaspoon ground allspice

¼ teaspoon ground nutmeg

Pinch of sea salt

4 teaspoons bourbon (optional)

3 pounds apples, such as Granny Smith, Jonagold, Golden Delicious, Fuji, or Braeburn

2 tablespoons unsalted butter

3 tablespoons cornstarch

2 pie crust doughs (see page 78)

1 egg, beaten

2 tablespoons granulated sugar or raw sugar, for sprinkling

Vanilla ice cream, for serving

10. Fold the dough under itself so that the edge of the fold comes right to the edge of the pan. Press the top and bottom dough rounds together as you flute the edges using your thumb and forefinger, or press with a fork.

11. Brush the egg wash over the top and edges of the pie. Use a sharp knife to cut slits in the top of the pie crust for steam vents. Sprinkle it with the sugar.

12. Place the pie on the oven rack centered over the baking sheet. Bake the pie until the crust begins to lightly brown, about 20 minutes, then reduce the heat to 350°F. Bake until the crust is golden and juices are bubbling, anywhere from 45 minutes to 1 hour more, depending on the type of apples used. (About halfway through baking, check to make sure the crust isn't browning too quickly. When it's nicely browned, tent the pie with a large piece of aluminum foil to keep the crust from browning further.)

13. Transfer the apple pie to a rack and cool for at least 2 to 4 hours before serving. Serve slightly warm or at room temperature, with a scoop of vanilla ice cream on the side.

LATTICE-TOP CRUST

If you want to make a lattice-top crust, roll out a disk of pie dough into a 12-inch circle. Using a wheel cutter or knife, cut an even number of vertical strips out of the dough, at least six to eight. You can use a ruler or measuring tape to make perfectly even strips, eyeball it, or make a bunch of different-size strips. It's totally up to you. Then follow these steps:

1. Lay one strip horizontally across the center of the filling.
2. Lay another strip vertically across the middle so it's perpendicular to the first strip.
3. Lay two strips perpendicular to that strip, on either side.
4. Peel back one side of the bottommost strip, lay a strip down perpendicular to that one, and cover it.
5. Repeat on the other side. Continue this weaving process until you've used all the strips of dough and the surface of the pie is covered.
6. Trim the edges to line up with the overhang of the bottom crust.
7. Press the top and bottom dough together as you flute the edges using your thumb and forefinger, or press with a fork.
8. Brush the egg wash over the lattice and the fluted edges of the pie, and sprinkle with sugar.
9. Bake as directed above.

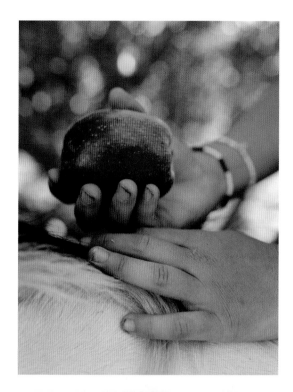

Seasonal Farmers Market Macro Bowls

Serves 4

A macro bowl is a balanced, nutritious, delicious, and fairly easy way to make a meal. "Macro" is short for macronutrients—protein, fat, and carbohydrates—which our bodies need for energy as well as to maintain structure and function. The ingredients in a macro bowl are the perfect combo of all three nutrients. We typically enjoy macro bowls for dinner, but you can eat one for any meal.

To make a healthy and nourishing macro bowl, you will simply start off with a base of leafy greens. Top with a variety of nutrient-dense veggies, proteins, carbs, and healthy fats. Then bring it all together by drizzling or sprinkling with some delicious add-ons. Get creative and have fun. The options are endless!

Step 1: Base

Start off with a base of seasonal leafy greens. Some options include spinach, kale, arugula, mixed baby greens, romaine, red-leaf lettuce, Swiss chard, sprouts, or microgreens.

Step 2: Toppings

You can sprinkle your choice of these ingredients on top, or arrange them in little piles by type—whatever makes you happy!

SEASONAL VEGGIES: They can be raw, roasted, or grilled. Some options include carrots, cucumbers, cabbage, zucchini, beets, mushrooms, peppers, radishes, broccoli, cauliflower, snap peas, green beans, asparagus, or Brussels sprouts.

PROTEIN: Some options include nuts, seeds, beans, lentils, quinoa, tempeh, tofu, eggs, fish, or meat (for example, chicken, turkey, or beef). If choosing animal protein, focus on quality sources. Perhaps you have a local farmers market, butcher, or CSA program in your area that sources quality meat.

WHOLE-FOOD CARBOHYDRATES: Some options include roasted sweet potatoes, quinoa or rice, corn, squash, beans, or peas.

HEALTHY FATS: Some options include avocado, nuts, seeds, olives, olive oil, tahini, or salmon.

Step 3: Add-ons

Add-ons are the yummy things that you drizzle or sprinkle over the top to bring your macro bowl all together. Some options include homemade or quality store-bought dressings or sauces; fermented veggies like sauerkraut or kimchi; and nuts, seeds, hempseeds, salsa, hummus, fruit, cheese, guacamole, pesto, nutritional yeast, fresh lemon juice, herbs, or your favorite spices or seasonings.

1 to 2 cups seasonal veggies

1 to 2 cups protein

1 to 2 cups whole-food carbohydrates

2 to 3 cups leafy greens

1 cup healthy fats

Sprinkle of add-ons

1. Cook the seasonal veggies, protein, and carbohydrates as desired.
2. Fill four bowls with ½ cup or more of the leafy greens, then add ¼ to ½ cup each of the veggies, protein, and carbohydrates. Top with the healthy fats and a sprinkling of add-ons.

Seasonal Quick-Pickled Veggies

As much as I love lacto-fermenting a variety of vegetables, quick pickling is a fast and flavorful option if you don't want to wait for your veggies to ferment.

15 cloves garlic, peeled

6 Kirby cucumbers, quartered lengthwise

6 young spring carrots, peeled and halved lengthwise

1 handful large scallion pieces or green beans

Other seasonal veggies, such as radishes, cauliflower, winter squash, or summer squash

Several sprigs fresh dill

½ teaspoon celery seed

½ teaspoon coriander seed

½ teaspoon mustard seed

8 whole black peppercorns

1 bay leaf

Pinch of red pepper flakes (optional)

1½ cups filtered water

1½ cups distilled white vinegar

1 tablespoon sea salt

1. Fill a clean 1-quart mason jar with the garlic, cucumbers, carrots, scallions, other seasonal veggies, dill, celery seed, coriander seed, mustard seed, black peppercorns, bay leaf, and red pepper flakes (if using), making sure to leave about 1 inch of headspace at the top.

2. In a medium saucepan, bring the water, vinegar, and salt to a simmer over medium-high heat, stirring until the salt dissolves. Remove from the heat.

3. Pour the hot brine over the vegetables to cover completely. Let the jar cool to room temperature, then cover and refrigerate. The pickles will taste good in just a few hours or even better after a couple of days. They'll keep in the fridge for about 3 months.

Kid-Pleaser Seasonal Salad

Kids like salads too! We love to put together a seasonal salad bar, where we start with a base of lettuce, then we each get to choose what else goes on our prized greens. You can get really creative with this recipe. We even divide up the slicing and dicing so that everyone in the family gets involved.

1. Place the lettuce in a large bowl.
2. Add your preferred other greens, herbs, veggies, fruit, dried fruit, cheese, nuts and seeds, proteins, and grains and toss until combined.
3. Add the salad dressing and toss to coat. Season with the salt and pepper, and toss to incorporate.

4 cups torn butter, gem, or romaine lettuce leaves

Other greens, such as spinach, kale, or arugula

Herbs, such as cilantro, mint, chives, basil, or dill

Seasonal veggies, such as carrots, fennel, cucumbers, sweet peppers, corn, or peas

Seasonal fruits, such as berries, avocados, tomatoes, pomegranate seeds, persimmons, apples, citrus, or pears

Dried fruit, such as cranberries, raisins, or Medjool dates

Cheese crumbles, such as feta, or other cheeses, such as shaved pecorino or Manchego

Nuts and seeds, such as pepitas, sunflower seeds, sprouts, pecans, almonds, or walnuts

Proteins, such as hard-boiled eggs, chickpeas, roasted chicken, or smoked or grilled salmon

Grains, such as brown rice, quinoa, or millet

⅛ cup salad dressing (see page 98), or more if needed

Sea salt

Freshly ground black pepper

Basic Salad Dressing with Lemon Zest

There are health benefits to making your own salad dressing. When we make our own, we are able to control how many additives, if any, we wish to use. Plus, the oil we choose makes a big difference. For this reason, try using olive or avocado oil. Both are less likely to spoil and are prized for their health benefits. Add brightness to your salad by including lemon or orange zest in your basic dressing.

⅓ cup fresh lemon, tangerine, or orange juice or apple cider vinegar

1 heaping teaspoon Dijon mustard or mayonnaise (or both)

2 teaspoons lemon zest

2 teaspoons finely chopped fresh herbs, such as thyme or parsley leaves

1 teaspoon sea salt

½ teaspoon freshly ground black pepper

1 clove garlic, minced

½ cup extra-virgin olive oil

1. In a container with a lid, such as a mason jar, combine the lemon juice, mustard or mayonnaise, lemon zest, chopped herbs, salt, pepper, and garlic. Add the oil last. Tightly cover with the lid, and shake until blended.

2. Set aside for 45 minutes to allow the flavors to combine. Shake again before using. The dressing will keep in the fridge for up to 2 weeks.

THE SCIENCE OF SALAD DRESSING

Did you know there is some science behind salad dressing and what helps it all come together? Oil and water usually don't mix. But many salad dressings are a combination of oil and vinegar that come together to form a sauce. What helps them stay mixed? The answer lies in the molecules that make up vinegar and oil. The water molecules in the vinegar are polar, meaning each one has a positive and a negative charge. Opposite charges attract, so the positive ends of the water molecules stick to the negative ends of other water molecules, forming tight bonds. Oil molecules are nonpolar. They don't have a positive or negative charge, which means they can't stick to the water molecules. To combine oil and vinegar, you need an emulsifier. Emulsifiers are special molecules that bridge the gap because they have the ability to attract and "hold hands" with both polar and nonpolar molecules simultaneously. In the food world, mustard and mayonnaise are emulsifiers, so if you add them to the oil and vinegar, it will help the dressing stay smooth and combined for a much longer time, even after you stop shaking the jar.

Farmers Market Soup for All Seasons

SERVES 4

This is a simple vegetable soup recipe that is easy to make and adapt for each season. This soup is especially good if you place some cooked pasta at the bottom of the bowl, then ladle over some soup, top with grated pecorino, and serve with crusty sourdough bread.

2 tablespoons extra-virgin olive oil, plus more for drizzling

1 medium onion or large leek, diced

2 medium carrots, diced (2 cups)

2 stalks celery, diced (2 cups)

1 bulb fennel, diced (1 cup; optional)

4 cloves garlic, minced

1½ teaspoons herbes de Provence or 1 tablespoon chopped fresh herbs, such as thyme or parsley leaves

2 cups diced zucchini, summer squash, or winter squash, such as butternut or kabocha

2 cups chopped green beans or whole peas

6 cups bone broth, veggie stock, or meat stock of choice

1 bay leaf

1 teaspoon sea salt, plus more if needed

Kernels from 1 ear corn or ½ cup frozen corn

¼ cup thinly sliced fresh basil leaves

1. In a large pot or Dutch oven, heat the oil over medium heat. Add the onion or leek and sauté until deeply golden and fragrant, 5 minutes.
2. Add the carrots, celery, fennel (if using), garlic, and herbes de Provence. Cook, stirring often, for 7 minutes.

PICKING SEASONAL VEGGIES

The most important thing to consider when making soup for your family and friends is how to create a flavorful broth. Once you have a flavorful base, you are good to go! Start with aromatics like onion, garlic, carrots, celery, or fennel.

When picking seasonal vegetables, see if your parent or guardian can take you to the farmers market or a local vegetable stand, and pick out what veggies sound good to you. If you're not sure where to start, try some options from the following list (if you're not sure what is in season, check out our seasonal food guide on page 72 for help).

- Onions, leeks, or shallots
- Garlic
- Celery
- Fennel
- Carrots
- Root veggies, such as parsnips, rutabagas, or turnips
- Potatoes
- Bell peppers
- Green beans
- Summer squash, such as zucchini and yellow squash
- Winter squash, such as butternut, kabocha, or pumpkin
- Mushrooms
- Corn
- Peas
- Tomatoes
- Red or green cabbage
- Greens, such as kale, chard, spinach, or collards

3. Add the zucchini, green beans, broth, bay leaf, and salt. Bring to a simmer. Cover and simmer until the carrots are just tender, 10 to 12 minutes. Add the corn. Cook uncovered for an additional 3 to 4 minutes, then stir in the fresh basil.

4. Taste the soup. Add ½ teaspoon or more of the lemon juice (a little at a time) until the flavor is to your liking. Season with the pepper and taste the soup again. If it's bland, add more salt as needed.

5. Serve with cashew cream or pesto, grated pecorino or Parmesan, a drizzle of good olive oil, and crusty bread.

TIP: Other possible soup additions include diced tomato, diced bell peppers, diced potatoes, shredded cabbage, sliced kale, cooked beans (like chickpeas or white beans), or a cooked grain. If going the tomato route, feel free to add 1 tablespoon tomato paste, which can give the soup even more richness. If you are a meat lover, you can add leftover cooked chicken or little meatballs to the simmering broth.

½ teaspoon fresh lemon juice or apple cider vinegar, plus more if needed

Freshly ground black pepper

Drizzle of cashew cream (see page 76) or pesto

Grated pecorino or Parmesan cheese

Crusty bread, for serving

Farmers Market Feast

A fun way to eat seasonally as a family is to create a menu and then let the kids do the shopping for the feast at the farmers market. Try creating a budget for spending. The more everyone is involved in choosing the produce, the more we all become invested in eating seasonally. We'll also be more inclined to eat fresh fruits and vegetables than we might otherwise. Below is a sample summer menu (recipes for each item appear in the following pages). Use it as a jumping-off point. You can always create your own menu too!

You can choose a few of the recipes from the sample menu to make with your family and friends, or you can make everything that is listed. Whatever you decide, I suggest including the entire family, especially your children, in picking the recipes to use, writing the shopping list, shopping and picking out ingredients, and more. This is also a great time to delegate who is responsible for making each item. For example, in the kitchen my son tends to prefer chopping and combining ingredients for each dish (he makes a great sous chef), but my daughter loves making drinks and desserts all on her own. So you might ask each member of your family who would like to be responsible for each dish. You might pair older kids with younger kids, or, if the children are really little, you can decide which dishes you'd like to make with their help and which you'd like to cook on your own.

The night before your feast, I suggest soaking the beans (if cooking them from scratch), as well as making the sauce for the street corn, the cookies, and the whipped cream. Then, the rest of the recipes can be prepped about 1½ hours before serving. You might want to start with making the beans and the homemade tortilla dough. From there, chop the veggies to roast, make the guacamole and the tomato salad, and cook the ground beef. Then, when everything else is ready, make it a family affair to press and cook the tortillas so they are hot off the griddle to enjoy with the entire meal.

SAMPLE SUMMER MENU

Grass-Fed Ground Beef Tacos with Green Cabbage, Lime, and Cilantro Slaw
(see page 105)

Refried Pinto Beans
(see page 106)

Quick-Pickled Red Onions
(see page 107)

Pico de Gallo Heirloom Tomato Salad
(see page 108)

Roasted Street Corn and Zucchini
(see page 111)

Guacamole with Carrot and Radish Chips
(see page 112)

Creamy Strawberry Agua Fresca
(see page 115)

Almond Shortbread Cookies with Whipped Cream and Seasonal Berries
(see page 116)

Grass-Fed Ground Beef Tacos with Green Cabbage, Lime, and Cilantro Slaw

This combination of grass-fed beef and green cabbage, lime, and cilantro slaw on homemade tortillas is flavorful and a sure crowd-pleaser. If you're looking to omit the ground beef, you can substitute refried beans (see page 106) for a plant-based vegetarian taco.

TO MAKE THE TORTILLAS:

1. Mix the salt into the masa in a large bowl. Slowly pour the hot water into the masa to create a doughlike consistency. The dough should be firm and springy when touched, not dry or sticky. If it is too sticky, add a teaspoon of masa at a time until it is the correct consistency; if it is too dry, add a teaspoon of water at a time.
2. Let the dough rest for about 1 hour, covered with a damp kitchen towel.
3. Heat a cast-iron skillet or griddle over medium heat. Divide the dough into 2-inch balls. Using a rolling pin, press the dough between two pieces of wax paper, or flatten using a tortilla press, aiming to make 6-inch circles.
4. Place a tortilla in the hot cast-iron skillet and cook until the top starts to look cooked, about 1 minute. Flip and heat the other side for 1 minute. Repeat with the rest of the tortillas.
5. To keep the tortillas warm while preparing the rest of the components, preheat the oven to 250°F. Wrap the tortillas in foil, then put them in the oven. When you are ready to serve, remove them from the oven, but leave them wrapped in the foil so they don't dry out.

TO MAKE THE SLAW:

1. Combine the cabbage, lime juice, and cilantro in a medium bowl.
2. Toss well and season with the salt and pepper.

TO MAKE THE FILLING:

1. Heat the oil in a large skillet over medium-high heat. Add the ground beef, breaking it up with a spoon. Cook, stirring once or twice, until browned and cooked through, 3 to 5 minutes.
2. Add the salt, cumin, onion powder, and paprika and cook, stirring gently, until the beef is coated, about 1 minute more.
3. To assemble the tacos, fill the tortilla with meat (or refried beans, if you prefer), then top with the cabbage slaw.

FOR THE TORTILLAS:

½ teaspoon sea salt

2 cups masa harina (corn flour)

2 cups hot water

FOR THE SLAW:

½ green cabbage, shredded

Juice of 2 limes

1 cup chopped fresh cilantro leaves

Sea salt

Freshly ground black pepper

FOR THE FILLING:

1 tablespoon avocado oil

1 pound grass-fed ground beef

1 teaspoon sea salt

1 teaspoon ground cumin

1 teaspoon onion powder

Pinch or more of paprika

Refried Pinto Beans

Although you can easily buy prepared refried beans, making them from scratch is worth the effort. The end result is a rich and creamy addition to tacos, burritos, or just a side of rice.

1 tablespoon extra-virgin olive oil, plus more if needed

½ cup finely chopped yellow onion

2 cloves garlic, pressed or minced

¼ teaspoon fine sea salt

¼ teaspoon ground cumin

3 cups cooked pinto beans or 2 (15-ounce) cans pinto beans, drained and rinsed

½ cup filtered water

1. Warm the oil in a medium saucepan over medium heat. Add the onions. Cook, stirring occasionally, until softened, 5 to 8 minutes.

2. Add the garlic, salt, and cumin. Stir well, then add the pinto beans and water. Stir again, cover, and cook for 5 minutes.

3. Reduce the heat to low and uncover. Use the back of a spoon to mash up some of the beans until you reach your desired consistency. Continue to cook the beans, uncovered and stirring often, for 2 more minutes, or until tender.

4. Remove from the heat. If the beans seem dry, add a very small splash of oil and stir to combine. Cover until ready to serve.

Quick-Pickled Red Onions

You might think red onions are too spicy or too bitter for kids to enjoy, but think again. This is Liam's favorite condiment (other than ketchup). Containing only red onions, vinegar, water, and sea salt, it's amazing how this quick-pickle method smooths the flavor of the onions and transforms them into the perfect tart and tangy topping for tacos, salads, sandwiches, and even pizza.

1. Put the onion in a clean 1-pint mason jar.
2. Bring the vinegar, water, and salt to a boil in a small saucepan over medium-high heat and stir for about 1 minute, until the salt has dissolved.
3. Pour the hot brine over the onion in the jar, making sure the liquid completely covers the onion. You may need to top it off with a bit more vinegar to make sure the onion is totally submerged.
4. Let the jar cool to lukewarm, then seal with the lid and refrigerate. The quick-pickled onion will be ready after just a few hours, but will stay good in the fridge for up to 4 weeks.

1 red onion, thinly sliced
½ cup apple cider vinegar
½ cup filtered water
1½ teaspoons sea salt

Pico de Gallo
Heirloom Tomato Salad

SERVES 4

This simple salad highlights summer heirloom tomatoes at their finest. The saltiness of the cotija cheese adds extra flavor to the tomatoes, and the freshly squeezed lime juice makes this dish come alive. The cilantro adds an herbaceous quality to the dish, but it can be omitted if you're craving something simpler.

2 large heirloom tomatoes, thinly sliced

¼ cup crumbled fresh cotija cheese

¼ cup fresh cilantro leaves (optional)

Sea salt

Freshly ground black pepper

Juice of 1 lime

Drizzle of extra-virgin olive oil

1. Place the tomato slices on a serving platter. Sprinkle with the cheese and cilantro (if using), and season with the salt and pepper.
2. Squeeze the lime juice over everything and then drizzle with the oil.

Roasted Street Corn and Zucchini

This street corn recipe comes together quickly and can be roasted in the oven. The best part is the sauce, which can always be made ahead of time or prepared on its own to top salads or rice dishes.

1. Preheat the oven to 400°F. Place the corn on a foil-lined baking sheet. Roast for 30 to 40 minutes, turning every 10 minutes or so, until lightly charred all over but not burned. About 20 minutes into cooking the corn, place the zucchini on another foil-lined baking sheet. Roast for about 20 minutes.
2. Meanwhile, in a small bowl, mix together the mayonnaise, sour cream, feta, cilantro, garlic, and lime juice.
3. Once the corn and zucchini are roasted, remove from the oven and brush generously with the sauce. Top with the extra cheese and cilantro and serve immediately with lime wedges.

4 ears corn, shucked

3 zucchini, cut into ¼-inch-thick slices

¼ cup mayonnaise

¼ cup sour cream

¼ cup crumbled feta or cotija cheese, plus more for garnish

½ cup chopped fresh cilantro leaves, plus more for garnish

2 cloves garlic, minced

Juice of ½ lime, plus wedges for serving

Guacamole with Carrot and Radish Chips

MAKES 1½ CUPS

Nothing beats fresh guacamole as an addition to a summer farmers market feast. You can serve it with carrot and radish chips or the traditional tortilla chips.

2 ripe avocados, pitted and peeled

2 to 4 tablespoons minced red onion

2 tablespoons finely chopped fresh cilantro (leaves and tender stems)

1 tablespoon fresh lime juice

¼ teaspoon sea salt, plus more if needed

Pinch of freshly ground black pepper, plus more if needed

Red radish and carrot slices or tortilla chips, for serving

1. Mash the avocados in a medium bowl. Add the onion, cilantro, lime juice, salt, and pepper and stir to combine. Taste and season with more salt and pepper, if needed.

2. Serve with the radish and carrot slices or tortilla chips.

Creamy Strawberry Agua Fresca

MAKES 8 CUPS

This refreshing drink combines fresh strawberries, milk, yogurt, and raw honey for a sweet treat. You can use coconut, almond, or cow's milk. We love this version with coconut milk. It's the perfect drink to accompany tacos with all the fixings.

1. Put the strawberries and 1 cup of the water in a blender. Blend thoroughly.
2. Using a fine-mesh strainer set over a pitcher, strain the strawberry mixture to remove the seeds.
3. Add the coconut milk, yogurt, honey, and remaining 2 cups water to the pitcher with the strawberry liquid. Stir to thoroughly combine, then serve over ice, garnished with the reserved strawberries.

2½ pounds strawberries, hulled (reserve ½ pound for garnish)

3 cups filtered water

2 cups coconut milk

1 cup plain coconut yogurt or yogurt of choice

¼ cup raw honey

Almond Shortbread Cookies with Whipped Cream and Seasonal Berries

MAKES 12 COOKIES OR ASSEMBLED CUPS

These almond shortbread cookies come together quickly and are such a delicious dessert. They're yummy on their own, but in this recipe we dress them up with whipped cream and seasonal berries.

1½ cups almond flour

3 tablespoons maple syrup

3 tablespoons coconut oil

1 teaspoon almond extract

¼ teaspoon sea salt

1 cup cold heavy cream or 1 (14-ounce) can coconut cream, chilled in the fridge overnight

2 tablespoons powdered sugar, raw honey, or maple syrup

½ teaspoon vanilla extract

2 cups fresh seasonal berries

1. Preheat the oven to 350°F.
2. Place the almond flour, maple syrup, coconut oil, almond extract, and salt in a medium bowl and mix to thoroughly combine.
3. Form the dough into 1-inch balls and place on a parchment-lined baking sheet. Use a fork to slightly flatten each cookie, just enough to leave a mark.
4. Bake for 8 to 10 minutes, until lightly golden.
5. Remove from the oven and let cool. The cookies can be stored in an airtight container in the fridge for up to 1 week.
6. To make the whipped cream, pour the cream, powdered sugar, and vanilla into a medium bowl. Whisk with a handheld mixer on high speed until medium to stiff peaks form, about 1 minute.
7. To assemble the cups, divide the whipped cream among 12 small mason jars or cups. Divide the fresh berries among the jars and top each with a shortbread cookie.

HEALTHY SNACKS

Creating healthy do-it-yourself snacks is fun for kids of all ages. The best snacks are not loaded with refined sugars or preservatives. Instead, they include fresh, seasonal ingredients that are good for your brain and body. The recipes in this chapter have it all because they are healthy and they taste incredible. Plus, they are meant to be made by parents and children together. In fact, I find when I include my children in making their own snacks, they are more likely to eat them. This chapter has a variety of snack ideas for your lunchbox or as an after-school or anytime treat. Enjoy!

Gluten-Free Seeded Herb Crackers

These crackers are flaky, crispy, salty, and savory. They come together really quickly, and most important, our entire family approves of them. The nuts and seeds are an added bonus and provide our bodies with healthy fats, as well as vitamins and minerals.

1 cup almond flour

½ cup cassava flour, plus more if needed

2 tablespoons finely chopped fresh herbs, such as rosemary, thyme, or chives

1 tablespoon ground flaxseed

1 tablespoon sesame seeds

1 tablespoon pumpkin seeds

½ teaspoon sea salt, plus more for sprinkling

Pinch of freshly ground black pepper

¼ cup extra-virgin olive oil or ghee, plus more for brushing

¼ cup filtered water, plus more if needed

½ teaspoon everything bagel seasoning, garlic salt, or finishing salt (optional)

1. Preheat the oven to 375°F.
2. In a bowl, whisk together the almond flour, cassava flour, chopped herbs, flaxseed, sesame seeds, pumpkin seeds, salt, and pepper. Set aside.
3. Whisk the oil and water in a small bowl, then stir into the flour mixture.
4. The dough should be smooth and not too sticky or dry. As the dough forms, if it is too sticky, add 1 teaspoon more cassava flour at a time and mix so that the dough comes together. If it is too dry, add 1 teaspoon more water at a time until the dough has enough moisture to hold together.
5. Separate the dough into two balls. Place one ball between two sheets of parchment paper and roll it out with a floured rolling pin to a rectangle about 8 by 11 inches, with a ¾-inch thickness.
6. Remove the top layer of parchment and cut the dough into eight pieces with a pizza cutter or sharp knife. Use a fork to prick each piece of dough a few times. Brush with more oil and sprinkle with everything bagel seasoning or salt (if using).
7. Transfer to a baking sheet on the bottom piece of parchment paper. Repeat with the second ball of dough.
8. Bake for 10 to 15 minutes, until the crackers are golden. Let them cool completely before serving.
9. Enjoy as is or with your favorite dip. Store in an airtight container at room temperature for up to 1 week.

Raw Zucchini Roll-Ups

Super simple and oh so cute, these raw vegan zucchini roll-ups are the perfect snack. You need very thin strips of zucchini for this dish, and a mandoline is the best tool. If you are a kid or teen making this recipe, please ask an adult for help with the mandoline, as it is extremely sharp.

1 large zucchini

8 to 10 asparagus tips

1 cup cashew chèvre (see page 52) or farmer's cheese (see page 50)

Small bunch fresh chives, finely chopped

Small bunch fresh mint leaves, finely chopped

Small bunch fresh dill leaves, finely chopped

Sea salt

Freshly ground black pepper

Zest and juice of 1 organic lemon

1. Using a mandoline, veggie peeler, or sharp knife, slice the zucchini lengthwise into very thin strips.
2. Cut the asparagus tips into 2- to 3-inch-long pieces. Halve any thicker ones lengthwise.
3. Put a dollop of cheese at the end of a zucchini slice. Top with the asparagus, chives, mint, and dill. Season with the salt and pepper.
4. Roll up tightly and place on a serving plate. (If you're having trouble getting them to stand, place them seam-side down on the plate.) Repeat with the remaining zucchini slices.
5. Drizzle with a little bit of zest and lemon juice.

Fermented Honey Garlic

Some call it honey-infused garlic or garlic-infused honey because this recipe works much like a combination of infusion and fermentation. Honey-fermented garlic is used by herbalists to combat colds and flus in the winter, and it's used by cooks as a condiment to add a honey-garlic flavor to any dish. It goes great with stir-fried quail eggs (see page 126), but it can also be used for so many other things. Drizzle it over pizza, serve it alongside roasted veggies, use it in a glaze for grilled pork or fish, or add it to stir-fries.

1. Add enough garlic cloves to a clean 1-pint mason jar to fill it about two-thirds full. Add enough honey to completely cover the garlic cloves, then put the lid on.
2. Let the mixture sit in the jar on the counter for 1 month before consuming. There is no need to refrigerate after opening. It will keep on the counter for up to 3 months.

About 4 heads garlic, cloves separated and peeled

About 1 cup raw honey

Dolmas

This recipe is definitely a labor-intensive one, but the energy you put into making these dolmas from scratch is worth it in terms of flavor. If you want to skip the step of preserving the grape leaves, you can look for preserved grape leaves at specialty stores.

FOR THE PRESERVED GRAPE LEAVES:

2 tablespoons sea salt, plus more for the water

25 grape leaves

¼ cup fresh lemon juice

Splash of apple cider vinegar

4 cups filtered water

FOR THE DOLMAS:

4 tablespoons extra-virgin olive oil

½ red onion, finely chopped

1 cup sprouted short-grain brown rice

1¼ cups vegetable broth

¼ cup finely chopped fresh dill

⅛ cup minced fresh mint leaves

¼ cup pine nuts, toasted

2 tablespoons dried currants

1 tablespoon lemon zest

3 tablespoons fresh lemon juice

Sea salt

Freshly ground black pepper

TO PRESERVE THE GRAPE LEAVES:

1. Bring salted water to a boil in a medium saucepan over high heat. Set up a bowl with water and ice. Working in batches, boil the grape leaves for 1 minute, then transfer to the bowl of ice water. Dry the leaves with paper towels and set aside.

2. Stir together the lemon juice, vinegar, water, and salt in a medium saucepan over high heat. Bring to a boil.

3. Stuff the grape leaves into a clean 1-quart mason jar and pour the hot liquid over them.

4. Let cool, then seal the jar and store in the fridge for at least 48 hours before using. The leaves will keep in the fridge for up to 2 weeks.

TO MAKE THE DOLMAS:

1. Pour 2 tablespoons of the oil into a medium saucepan and heat on medium.

2. Add the onion and sauté until soft, about 5 minutes.

3. Add the rice and stir to combine. Sauté for another minute.

4. Pour in 1 cup of the broth, cover, and lower the heat. Simmer the rice for about 15 minutes, until the liquid has been absorbed and the rice is half cooked.

5. Add the dill, mint, pine nuts, currants, lemon zest, and 1 tablespoon of the lemon juice to the rice. Stir until all the ingredients are well combined. Season with the salt and pepper. Let the mixture cool to room temperature.

6. Place a preserved grape leaf shiny (smooth) side down, vein (bumpy) side up, on a hard, flat surface.

7. Place 2 tablespoons (more or less, depending on the size of the grape leaf) of the rice filling at the base of the leaf, near where the stem was. Fold the stem end up over the filling. Fold the edges of the leaf inward.

8. Continue rolling the leaf until it forms a neat rolled package. (Do not roll too tightly; the rice will expand a little during cooking, and if you

roll it too tightly, the leaf will unravel as it cooks.) Squeeze the roll gently to seal. Repeat the process until all the filling has been used.

9. Place the rolls at the bottom of a 12-inch skillet with a lid. Don't be afraid to pack them snugly; this will help keep them intact as they cook. Make a single layer on the bottom of the skillet. When you run out of room, make a second layer on top.

10. Pour the remaining 2 tablespoons oil, ¼ cup broth, and 2 tablespoons lemon juice over the stuffed grape leaves. Bring to a simmer over medium heat.

11. Reduce the heat to low, so the liquid is slowly simmering, and place an inverted heat-safe plate on top of the stuffed grape leaves to weigh them down and keep them secure as they cook.

12. Cover the skillet. Let the grape leaves cook for 30 to 40 minutes, until fork-tender.

Stir-Fried Quail Eggs

This snack is a favorite! Since the quail eggs are small and absorb the sweet and savory flavors of the soy sauce, sesame oil, and fermented honey garlic with ease, they explode with flavor when you eat them. They also make a great appetizer for sushi night and are so good on top of a stir-fry or salad.

1 tablespoon toasted sesame oil

2 tablespoons soy sauce

12 soft-boiled or hard-boiled quail eggs, peeled

1 tablespoon fermented honey garlic (see page 123)

Sesame seeds

Handful of thinly sliced fresh scallions

1. Heat the oil in a small skillet on high.
2. Add the soy sauce and quail eggs and cook, stirring constantly, until the soy sauce has reduced to a glaze, about 3 minutes.
3. Stir in the fermented honey garlic and cook for 1 more minute, until it has caramelized. Remove from the heat and sprinkle with the sesame seeds and chives. Serve immediately.

Green Pea "Hummus"

This pea "hummus" makes a tasty snack dip or even sandwich or wrap spread. Instead of chickpeas, the sweet and flavorful green pea takes center stage in this recipe. You can replace the frozen peas with fresh peas, if you have them. The tahini is optional, but it makes the dip creamy.

1. Place the peas, oil, lemon zest and juice, tahini (if using), garlic, and salt in a food processor and process until pureed.
2. Transfer the mixture to a bowl, drizzle with the additional oil, sprinkle with the additional salt, and serve with fresh-cut veggies, sourdough bread, or crackers.

1 pound frozen baby sweet peas, thawed

¼ cup extra-virgin olive oil, plus more for drizzling

Zest and juice of 1 organic lemon

2 tablespoons raw tahini (optional)

1 clove garlic, grated

¼ teaspoon sea salt, plus more for sprinkling

Fresh-cut veggies, sourdough bread, or crackers, for serving

Rosemary Roasted Nuts

This nut mixture is a combination of a variety of nuts, all tossed together with a little bit of olive oil, sea salt, and fresh rosemary, then baked. The result is a savory and salty nut mix that is bursting with flavor. It is perfect for a snack at home, or you can pack it for a special treat on a midday hike.

1. Preheat the oven to 375°F.
2. Mix the almonds, cashews, and walnuts in a medium bowl and toss with the oil, salt, and rosemary.
3. Transfer to a baking sheet and roast in the oven for 10 minutes, until golden brown.
4. Store in an airtight container on the counter for up to 1 week.

1 cup almonds

1 cup cashews

1 cup walnuts

1 tablespoon extra-virgin olive oil or melted ghee

1 teaspoon sea salt

1 tablespoon finely chopped fresh rosemary leaves

Nut-and-Seed Granola

This nut-and-seed granola is gluten-free and sweetened with a bit of coconut sugar and maple syrup. The result is a nutty, seedy, maple-flavored granola that is perfect on its own or a fantastic addition to yogurt, pudding, or even milk.

¼ cup coconut oil or ghee

3 tablespoons coconut sugar

2 tablespoons maple syrup

1 teaspoon vanilla extract

¼ teaspoon sea salt

2 cups slivered blanched almonds

1 cup unsweetened shaved coconut

1 cup sprouted nuts and seeds, such as a combination of pumpkin, sunflower, sesame, and chia seeds

1. Preheat the oven to 325°F.
2. Combine the coconut oil, coconut sugar, maple syrup, vanilla, and salt in a small saucepan. Heat on medium-low until the sugar dissolves and the ingredients are thoroughly incorporated. Remove from the heat.
3. In a large bowl, combine the almonds, shaved coconut, and sprouted nuts and seeds. Add the coconut oil mixture to the bowl with the nuts and seeds. Toss thoroughly to coat.
4. Transfer the mixture to a parchment-lined baking sheet. Bake for 20 to 30 minutes, until golden brown.
5. Let cool for 1 to 2 hours, or until hardened. Break it apart and transfer to an airtight container. It will keep on the counter for up to 2 weeks.

Rhubarb-Strawberry Applesauce

When you think of rhubarb, you probably think of pie (that recipe is in our first book, *The Women's Heritage Sourcebook*). If you have a lot of rhubarb on hand, though, you'll need more options, and this rhubarb-strawberry applesauce is pretty amazing. You can eat this delightful sauce on its own or layer it with yogurt or chia seed pudding to create a parfait. Olivia and Liam love the sauce topped with a drizzle of raw honey and an extra sprinkle of cinnamon.

1. Place the rhubarb, apples, and water in a small saucepan over medium-high heat and bring to a boil. Then cover, reduce the heat to low, and simmer for 10 minutes, until the rhubarb and apples are tender.
2. Add the strawberries and simmer for an additional 5 minutes, until softened.
3. Cool the mixture to room temperature, then place it in a blender along with the cinnamon and salt. Blend until thoroughly combined and pureed.
4. It's ready to eat right from the blender, or you can transfer it to a clean 1-pint mason jar and keep it in the fridge for up to 2 weeks.

2 stalks rhubarb, diced

1 apple, peeled, cored, and diced

¼ cup filtered water

8 strawberries, stemmed and diced

½ teaspoon ground cinnamon

Pinch of sea salt

Banana Trees (Banana Sushi)

These little bites are a staple at our house, perfect for breakfast or snacking. The best part is that you can get as creative as you like in preparing and serving them.

1 banana

Almond butter or nut or seed butter of choice

Optional toppings: chia seeds; cinnamon; coconut shavings; goji berries; bee pollen; raw cacao powder; cacao nibs; dark chocolate chips; dried berries, such as blueberries, cranberries, or cherries; or freeze-dried berries, such as raspberries, strawberries, or blueberries

1. Peel the banana and slice it into rounds about ¼ inch thick. Place the banana slices on a small plate.
2. Add a dollop of nut butter on top of each slice and add your toppings of choice (if using).

Seasonal Fruit Skewers

MAKES 6

Seasonal fruit skewers are a super easy and fun way to showcase what's in season. This recipe uses fresh berries, but you can also use other seasonal fruit, such as citrus, stone fruit, apples, pears, or persimmons. You could do the same thing with seasonal veggies, if you prefer.

1. Using a skewer, thread the blueberries, strawberries, and blackberries in a pattern.
2. Arrange the skewers on a cutting board or platter and serve.

24 blueberries

12 strawberries

12 blackberries

Seasonal Fruit Gummies

This recipe uses tangerine juice, but any seasonal fruit, juiced or pureed, will do. If you're looking for a fun twist, you can add organic coconut milk to the mix. If you choose to go this route, substitute 1 cup coconut milk for 1 cup of the fruit juice. One of our favorite combinations is 1 cup coconut milk and 2 cups passion fruit juice. The gummies are so good!

3 cups fresh tangerine juice, or any fresh seasonal fruit juice or puree

¼ to ½ cup raw honey, depending on the sweetness of the fruit

Pinch of sea salt

½ cup powdered gelatin, such as Vital Proteins

Unsalted butter, for greasing

1. Taste the fruit juice to check sweetness. Add the fruit juice, honey, and salt to a small saucepan and whisk to combine. Heat the mixture on low heat until it just barely warms. (You don't want it to get too hot.) Slowly whisk in the gelatin.

2. Pour the mixture into a greased 8-inch square glass baking dish. Place in the fridge for 2 hours or until firm. Cut into bite-size pieces.

3. Store in an airtight container in the fridge for up to 2 weeks. The gummies will soften some (but still hold together) if left out at room temperature.

VITAMIN C

Did you know that tangerines and most other citrus fruits are packed with loads of vitamin C? With the addition of gelatin, this seasonal treat is not only a yummy snack but also great for your hair and skin.

Seasonal Fruit Leather

Seasonal fruit leather is a fun snack that combines a delicious fruity taste with the added bonus of portability. It's simple—and all you need are fresh fruit, a blender, and your oven.

1. Preheat the oven to 200°F, or the lowest temperature your oven will go, making sure it's 200°F or below.
2. Add the fruit, coconut sugar (if using), lemon juice, cinnamon (if using), and salt to a blender. Blend until you have a smooth puree. Pour the puree onto a parchment-lined baking sheet and smooth using a knife or spatula.
3. Bake for 6 to 8 hours, or until the leather is no longer loose and wet. Remove from the oven and allow to cool completely before using a pizza cutter or knife to cut the fruit leather into strips for fruit roll-ups or into rectangles for pieces of fruit leather. If you would like to roll it, cut a strip of parchment the same size as the fruit leather to roll up with it so it does not stick to itself.

3 cups chopped (and peeled, if necessary) fresh ripe seasonal fruit

3 tablespoons coconut sugar or raw honey (optional)

1 tablespoon fresh lemon juice

1 teaspoon ground cinnamon (optional)

⅛ teaspoon sea salt

FLAVOR COMBINATIONS

Nearly any fruit can be made into fruit leather, which means you can use this recipe in any season. You just need to be able to make the fruit into a puree. You can even make vegetable leather or mix and match for delicious flavor combinations. Here are some suggestions to help you get started:

- Berries, such as strawberries, blueberries, raspberries, or blackberries
- Stone fruits, such as apricots, plums, or peaches
- Tropical fruits, such as mangoes, bananas, pineapples, or papayas
- Citrus, such as oranges, lemons, or grapefruit
- Other fruits, such as apples, pears, watermelons, kiwis, grapes, or passion fruit
- Vegetables, such as pumpkin, rhubarb, zucchini, spinach, or kale (yes, kale!)
- Herbs, such as basil, mint, or rosemary
- Spices, such as cinnamon, nutmeg, cardamom, allspice, clove, ginger, or chai spice

Chocolate Zucchini Muffins

This muffin recipe proves that chocolate and zucchini really do go well together. These muffins are moist, fluffy, and full of flavor. It's also worth noting that they are gluten-free and sweetened with maple syrup and a ripe banana, making them a perfect plant-based treat.

Coconut oil, unsalted butter, or ghee, for greasing

1½ cups shredded zucchini

¾ cup almond butter

⅓ cup raw cacao powder

⅓ cup maple syrup

1 teaspoon baking soda

1 teaspoon vanilla extract

1 egg

1 ripe banana, mashed

¼ teaspoon sea salt

½ cup dark chocolate chips or mini chocolate chips

1. Preheat the oven to 350°F. Grease or line a muffin tin.
2. Place the shredded zucchini in a strainer and press down on it with a spoon to release as much liquid as possible. Set aside.
3. In a large bowl, combine the almond butter, cacao powder, maple syrup, baking soda, vanilla, egg, banana, and salt and mix until smooth.
4. Stir in the zucchini and chocolate chips.
5. Spoon the batter into the muffin tin. Bake for 20 to 22 minutes, until the tops of the muffins are not soft.

Easy Mixing Bowl Superfood Energy Bites

MAKES 12 BITES

These superfood energy bites are simple and make a tasty snack to eat as is, crumble on yogurt, or sprinkle on top of a smoothie or oatmeal for some extra flavor. Loaded with good-for-you nuts and seeds that are full of healthy fats, antioxidants, and immune-boosting qualities, you'll want to keep these around for a daily dose of goodness.

1. Place the oats, hempseeds, nut butter, honey, salt, chocolate chips, sesame seeds, goji berries, bee pollen, and vanilla in a large bowl and stir thoroughly to combine.
2. Roll the mixture into 12 (1½-inch) balls. For added yumminess, roll the balls in cacao powder, ground cinnamon, sesame seeds, or maca powder to coat.
3. Store the balls in an airtight container in the fridge for up to 2 weeks.

TIP: If you want to try a date-sweetened version, omit the honey. Pulse 1 cup pitted Medjool dates in a food processor and add them to the mixture instead.

1½ cups gluten-free oats or almond flour

2 tablespoons hempseeds, chia seeds, flaxseed, or unsweetened shredded coconut

½ cup nut or seed butter

¼ cup raw honey

¼ teaspoon sea salt

½ cup dark chocolate chips, cacao nibs, raisins, or pitted Medjool dates

1 tablespoon or more sesame seeds

1 tablespoon or more goji berries

1 tablespoon or more bee pollen

1 teaspoon vanilla or almond extract

Raw cacao powder, ground cinnamon, sesame seeds, or maca powder, for rolling (optional)

Honey-Cacao Bars

This recipe uses tahini instead of nut butter to create a raw cacao bar that is nut-free. Since this recipe includes raw cacao powder and honey, you are getting extra doses of antioxidants and polyphenols. They are great for your brain and immune health too. All good stuff!

¼ cup raw tahini

3½ tablespoons raw cacao powder

2 tablespoons raw honey

1 tablespoon coconut butter

½ teaspoon vanilla extract or flavoring of choice, such as orange oil

Pinch of sea salt

Optional add-ins: sesame seeds or other seeds, such as flaxseed, sunflower, or pumpkin; goji berries or other dried fruit, such as raisins or currants; bee pollen; cacao nibs; adaptogens; spices; or edible flowers, such as lavender buds or rose petals

1. Place the tahini, cacao powder, honey, coconut butter, vanilla, and salt in a medium bowl and mix until thoroughly combined.

2. Divide the mixture into four blobs and place them on parchment paper. Sprinkle with your preferred add-ins (if using).

3. Shape and fold the blobs into small rectangles to look like candy bars.

4. Store the finished bars in an airtight container in the fridge for up to 2 weeks. (They soften when you take them out.) They will keep for several weeks in an airtight container or freezer bag in the freezer. When ready to eat, let thaw for 1 hour.

SWEET GIFTS

These bars are not only yummy, but also make sweet gifts. Why not make a bunch and give them out around Valentine's Day? They make nice party favors too. Just make sure to keep them refrigerated until you pass them out.

Raw Sea Salt Caramel Chocolate Truffles

MAKES 15 TRUFFLES

These truffles are truly delicious. The tahini, sea salt, and date combination creates a creamy, caramel-like taste. Although you can save these for special occasions like holidays or birthdays, you can also keep a jar in the fridge to add a little sweetness to a regular day.

1. Place the dates in a food processor. Pulse a few times to break up the dates. Add the tahini, cacao powder, vanilla, and salt. Process until smooth, stopping as needed to scrape down the sides of the bowl with a rubber spatula. The mixture will be a little sticky, but it should be thick and smooth. If there are any lumps, scrape down the sides of the bowl and process again.
2. Transfer the mixture to a bowl or plate. Cover with a kitchen towel and refrigerate until firm enough to roll.
3. Form the firmed-up mixture into truffles that are roughly the size of a large marble. Roll the truffles in the maca and cacao powders to coat. If you need more for rolling, add equal parts maca powder and cacao powder to a bowl. Roll the truffles in any add-ins (if using).
4. Store the finished truffles in an airtight container for up to 2 weeks in the fridge. They will also keep for several weeks in an airtight container or freezer bag in the freezer. When ready to eat, let thaw for 1 hour.

1 cup packed pitted Medjool dates (about 15 large)

¼ cup raw tahini

3 tablespoons raw cacao powder or unsweetened cocoa powder, plus 1 tablespoon for rolling

1 teaspoon vanilla extract

¼ teaspoon coarse sea salt, plus more for sprinkling

1 tablespoon maca powder, for rolling

Optional add-ins: sesame seeds or other seeds, such as flaxseed, sunflower, or pumpkin; goji berries or other dried fruit, such as raisins or currants; bee pollen; adaptogens; spices; or edible flowers, such as lavender buds and rose petals

Coconut Milk Caramel

This coconut milk caramel is delicious on its own, served with apple slices, or drizzled over yogurt, granola, or fruit—you get the idea!

1 (14-ounce) can full-fat unsweetened Thai coconut milk

¾ cup coconut sugar

¼ teaspoon sea salt

1 apple, cored and sliced, for serving

1. Stir the coconut milk and sugar together in a medium saucepan and bring to a boil over medium heat. Stirring constantly, establish a steady, strong simmer and cook for about 15 minutes, until the mixture has thickened.

2. Add the salt and cook for another 5 to 7 minutes, until the salt is completely incorporated.

3. Let the caramel cool completely; it will thicken further as it cools.

4. Transfer the cooled caramel to a clean mason jar. It will keep for up to 2 weeks in the fridge.

5. Put the apple slices on a plate and serve drizzled with the caramel.

DRINKS AND TONICS

Kids of all ages, especially me, love specialty drinks and tonics. My childhood was filled with fun drinks. My mother wasn't a fan of giving us soda, but she would make other drinks for us to indulge in. I remember she would make tea (both iced and hot) and snacks (cucumber and cream cheese sandwiches were our favorite) so that my sister and I could host little backyard tea parties with our friends complete with a cozy blanket, fancy teacups, and stuffed animals. And when it was county fair season (I showed dairy cattle at our local fair each year from grade school through high school), and we had to wake up extra early to take care of our animals and muck out the stalls, my mother would send us off with the most magical hot cocoa.

Those memories carried me into my adult years and motherhood. Over the years, I have noticed that our table is not complete without a fun drink to enliven the mood and table setting.

This chapter includes a collection of some of our family favorites. From chicken bone broth to smoothies to homemade sodas and vinegar tonics, there are so many healthful drinks that provide extra hydration and flavor all at once.

Chicken Bone Broth

The benefits of bone broth are plentiful. This nutritious beverage is said to have anti-inflammatory properties, is healthy for your gut, and may help protect your joints. It also happens to be super tasty and is our family's go-to beverage during the winter months. For this recipe, I like to use a chicken carcass left over from roasting a chicken and pieces from the chicken as well. If you don't want to roast a whole chicken, you can use about 3 pounds of chicken backs, wings, and necks.

1 leftover chicken carcass and pieces of a whole roasted chicken or 3 pounds chicken backs, wings, and necks

1 garlic head, halved crosswise

1 yellow onion, quartered

1 bunch parsley or herb of choice (optional)

2 bay leaves

2 tablespoons whole black peppercorns

1 tablespoon extra-virgin olive oil

1 tablespoon apple cider vinegar

1 tablespoon sea salt (optional)

12 cups filtered water

1. In a large stockpot, add the chicken carcass, garlic, onion, parsley, bay leaves, peppercorns, oil, vinegar, and salt. Pour in enough filtered water to cover the bones (about 12 cups).
2. Cover the pot and bring the broth to a boil over medium-high heat, then reduce the heat to low and simmer, with the lid slightly ajar, for 12 hours. During the first few hours of simmering, a frothy or foamy layer will form. Just skim it off with a shallow spoon and discard.
3. Remove from the heat and let cool. Strain out the bones and vegetables using a fine-mesh strainer set over a bowl. Discard the bones.
4. When cooled to room temperature, transfer to a clean 1-gallon mason jar and store in the fridge for up to 5 days, or freeze in a freezer-safe container for later use.

Basic Shrub (Drinking Vinegar)

MAKES 3 CUPS

Simply put, a shrub is a drink that includes vinegar, fruit, and sugar—a drinkable vinegar. Once the drinking vinegar is created, you can add bubbly water to create your own natural soda. There are so many different ways to make shrubs. Some recipes call for heating all the ingredients before straining and drinking; others require no cooking at all. I prefer the latter. This method is called the cold method. I also love to use Bragg apple cider vinegar due to its raw, unfiltered quality. With their combination of raw vinegars and certain fruits or herbs, drinks and sodas made with shrubs can be teeming with probiotics and digestive enzymes. The beauty of shrubs is that you can use a basic template to make them year-round using seasonal ingredients.

1. In a clean 1-quart mason jar or other container with a tight-fitting lid, combine the fruit and sugar. Use the back of a wooden spoon or a muddler to smash the fruit a bit.
2. Cover tightly with the lid and let it sit on the counter for 24 hours.
3. Using a fine-mesh strainer over a bowl, strain out the fruit and discard it. Add the vinegar. Stir well, taste, and add more sugar or vinegar, if necessary, so the taste is to your liking. Pour the shrub into a clean 1-quart mason jar, cover tightly, and refrigerate for 1 week so the flavors come together.
4. To make a bubbly, probiotic-rich soda, add 1½ parts shrub to 2 parts sparkling water (more or less sparkling water can be added given your taste preference).

2 cups diced fruit, cleaned, peeled, and seeded, if necessary

2 cups granulated sugar, plus more if needed

2 cups apple cider vinegar, plus more if needed

Sparkling water, for serving

TIP: Shrub sodas are a fun drink to serve for special occasions, such as birthday parties, dinner parties, holidays, or other celebrations. Olivia's and Liam's favorite shrub flavor is fresh strawberries. Experiment with the seasons and see which flavors become your favorites.

Ginger Bug

What is a ginger bug, you might wonder? Simply put, it's a mixture of fermented yeast and sugar water. By creating a ginger bug, you capture the beneficial microorganisms from wild yeasts and bacteria in the same way a sourdough starter does. When mixed with a flavored sweet tea, fruit juice, or other base, the wild microorganisms in the ginger bug begin to consume the sugar in the base liquid, and as they do, they reproduce and emit carbon dioxide. The result is a fizzy, effervescent, naturally fermented soda that is rich in beneficial bacteria—critical to gut health and immune system function.

Make sure to use fresh organic ginger because it has the best chance of having a strong colony of yeast and bacteria. There is some debate about whether or not to include the skin. I leave the skin on; the good bacteria and yeast on it will help you have a successful ginger bug. It is also important to use granulated sugar to start the culture; honey, stevia, and other sweeteners will not work. And make sure to use filtered water so it does not contain chlorine, which can affect the culturing process.

1 fresh organic ginger root, unpeeled, plus more each day

2 to 3 tablespoons granulated sugar, plus more each day

2 cups filtered water

1. Cut a piece of ginger root about 1½ inches long and dice it to make 2 to 3 tablespoons.
2. Place the ginger in a clean 1-quart mason jar and add the sugar and water. Stir with a spoon. Cover it loosely with the lid and store on the counter at room temperature.
3. Each day, for the next 5 days, stir the mixture, add 1 teaspoon diced ginger and 1 teaspoon sugar, and stir again. (It may take up to 8 days of adding sugar and ginger to create an active culture. The culture is active when there are bubbles forming around the top of the mixture, it "fizzes" when stirred, and it takes on a sweet and mildly

KEEPING YOUR GINGER BUG ALIVE

To keep the bug alive, you need to feed it regularly. Add 1 teaspoon diced ginger and 1 teaspoon sugar per day if kept at room temperature. You can also rest it in the fridge, feeding it 1 tablespoon diced ginger and 1 tablespoon sugar once a week. To reactivate it, remove it from the fridge, let it warm to room temperature, and begin feeding it again. When you borrow liquid from your bug, you'll need to replace it. Dissolve 2 tablespoons granulated sugar in ¼ cup filtered water for every ¼ cup of ginger bug you remove.

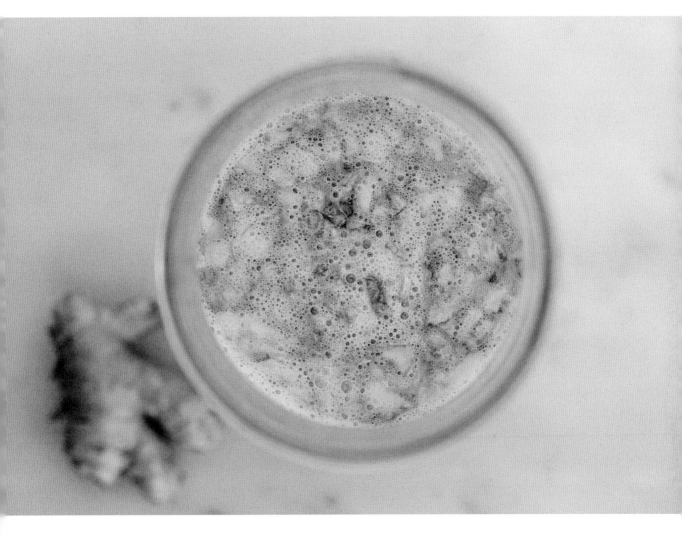

yeasty smell. It will also become somewhat cloudy. If the mixture hasn't taken on these characteristics by day 7 or 8, discard it and start again. If mold appears on the top, scrape it off if it can be removed. If it cannot be removed, or if this happens more than once, discard the mixture and start again.)

4. Once the ginger bug has cultured, mix it well, and transfer it to a flip-top bottle. Close the top and allow it to ferment on the counter at room temperature, away from direct sunlight, for 1 to 3 days. Transfer to the fridge and allow it to chill before opening. It can now be used to create fermented sodas and drinks at the ratio of ¼ cup ginger bug to 1 quart sweetened herbal mixtures (for ginger ale or root beer) or diluted fruit juice (for fruit-flavored sodas).

Ginger Soda

Once you've made a ginger bug, you can use it to make fermented sodas. You'll need flavorings—whether that's fresh herbs, fruit juice, or a concoction of herbs, flowers, roots, and bark. While a ginger bug itself benefits from a loosely lidded environment, homemade fermented sodas benefit from a tightly capped container that prevents the escape of the carbon dioxide produced during fermentation. This gas, a natural by-product of fermentation, ensures that the resulting homemade soda is fizzy, bubbly, and pleasantly effervescent when opened.

1 to 2 inches fresh organic ginger root, unpeeled and finely chopped

4 cups filtered water

¼ cup granulated sugar

¼ cup ginger bug (see page 156)

¼ cup fresh lemon juice

1. Place the ginger, 1½ cups of the water, and sugar in a medium saucepan and bring to a boil over medium-high heat.
2. Reduce the heat to medium-low and simmer until the sugar dissolves.
3. Remove from the heat and add the remaining 2½ cups water. Let cool to room temperature.
4. Once the ginger mixture has cooled, strain it through a fine-mesh strainer into a large bowl.

THE SCIENCE OF WILD SODA

This is a perfect kitchen recipe to introduce the science of microbiology by demonstrating how a carbonated drink such as ginger soda can be made using yeast, a single-celled organism.

For starters, what do you think makes soda fizzy? It's the dissolved carbon dioxide in the liquid. Of course, you can just add carbonation to drinks. That is how the soda sold at grocery stores is made. However, another way of carbonating drinks is to use a microorganism called yeast. Yeast are tiny, single-celled, living plants. When placed in a warm, moist place and given sugar as a food source, the yeast become active and multiply. Just as they do in humans, these metabolic processes produce waste. The metabolic waste made by yeast is carbon dioxide, a gas that can make drinks fizzy.

If a drink that's being carbonated is placed in a sealed container, the space between the liquid and the lid fills up with carbon dioxide. As the concentration of carbon dioxide increases, the gas starts to get pushed into the solution and the bubbles stay in the water. This makes the drink fizzy. If the lid were loose, the gas would escape and you would get "flat" soda. As long as the yeasts have enough sugar to eat, they keep making carbon dioxide. When the yeasts run out of sugar, they start another metabolic process called fermentation, then carbonation occurs.

5. Before adding the ginger bug, stir it and pour it through a fine-mesh strainer as well. Then add the ginger bug and the lemon juice to the ginger mixture and stir.

6. Pour the ginger soda mixture into a clean 1-quart mason jar and close with a tight-fitting lid.

7. Let the jar sit on the counter for 1 to 3 days, then transfer to the fridge. It will keep for up to 1 week.

Fermented Orange Juice

This fermented orange juice is an easy way to get good-for-you probiotics (good bacteria) in your belly. It's also loaded with vitamin C. This means that you are not only boosting your gut health with a healthy dose of cultured goodness, but also doing your immune system and skin a favor too.

1. Put 3 cups of the orange juice in each of two clean 1-quart mason jars.
2. Add ½ cup of the filtered water, a pinch of salt, and 2 tablespoons of the whey to each jar. Stir thoroughly.
3. Tightly close each jar and let them sit at room temperature for 24 to 48 hours, away from direct sunlight, until they're bubbly.
4. If the lid starts bulging or you see bubbles forming at the top of the liquid, you may need to burp the jars once a day (which sounds silly, but it simply means you need to unscrew the lid, which lets out any air that might be accumulating) to prevent too much pressure from building up. If air is accumulating, that is good! It means the good bacteria in the mixture are eating up the sugars in the orange juice, and the outcome is a bubbly drink without added carbonation.
5. Drink immediately, or store the jars in the fridge for up to 1 week.

6 cups fresh orange juice (from about 24 navel oranges)

1 cup filtered water

Sea salt

4 tablespoons whey, veggie starter culture, water kefir, or sauerkraut juice

TIP: You can use the leftover whey from making the farmer's cheese (see page 50) to make this bubbly drink. Or you can even use the leftover fermented juice culture from the beetroot kraut (see page 24), which adds a pretty pinkish-red color to the beverage.

Basic Nut, Seed, or Oat Milk

You can make your own nut, seed, or oat milk! It's easy, and when you make your own, you are ditching the packaging and using reusable containers, which is better for the earth. You can control how much water you add for nutritional purposes too. Plus, like anything, when you make it fresh from your kitchen, it tastes better, has fewer additives and ingredients, and is customizable, made just the way you like it.

1 cup raw almonds, cashews, hempseeds, or pumpkin seeds

Filtered water

Pinch of sea salt

Optional add-ins:
½ teaspoon vanilla extract, 1 or 2 pitted Medjool dates, 1 tablespoon raw honey, ½ teaspoon ground cardamom, ½ teaspoon ground cinnamon, 1 tablespoon raw cacao powder, 1 teaspoon maca powder, ½ teaspoon activated charcoal, ½ teaspoon chlorella, or ½ teaspoon spirulina

1. Add the nuts or seeds to a clean 1-quart mason jar or bowl. Add enough filtered water to cover the nuts or seeds by 2 inches, and soak on the counter at room temperature for 7 hours. (There's no need to soak hempseeds.) Pour off the water and rinse the nuts or seeds well.

2. Add the soaked nuts or seeds, 2 cups filtered water, salt, and any add-ins (if using) to a blender and blend for 1 to 2 minutes on high speed, until thoroughly combined.

3. Line a fine-mesh strainer or colander with an opened nut milk bag or two layers of cheesecloth and set over a bowl or container. Pour the nut mixture through the strainer. Once the milk has run through, squeeze the bag and cheesecloth gently to wring out the rest of the milk. You should have about 2 cups.

4. Transfer the milk to a clean 1-quart mason jar. It will keep in the fridge for 4 to 6 days. Compost or discard the solids.

Green Sea Dragon Smoothie

SERVES 1

This smoothie contains spirulina, a type of blue-green algae with strong antioxidant effects. Spirulina is believed to be one of the oldest life-forms on earth. Super cool!

1. To a blender, add the banana, almond milk, almond butter, spinach (if using), spirulina, dates, salt, and ice cubes. Blend until icy, creamy, and smooth, scraping down the sides as needed.
2. If the smoothie is too thick, thin with more almond milk; if it is too thin, thicken with more ice. Taste and adjust the flavor as needed, adding more banana for sweetness or spirulina for green color.
3. Serve immediately, topped with blueberries, granola, or nuts and seeds (if using). It is best enjoyed fresh.

1 banana, plus more if needed

1 cup almond milk or coconut milk, plus more if needed

¼ cup almond butter or raw almonds

1 cup spinach or other greens (optional)

1 teaspoon spirulina

3 or 4 Medjool dates, pitted

Pinch of sea salt

½ cup ice cubes, plus more if needed

Optional toppings: fresh blueberries, granola, or nuts and seeds

Dairy-Free Hot Cocoa Mix

This recipe came together because we love camping and wanted a better cocoa mix than what was available at our local grocery store. If you'd like, you can add collagen, maca powder, and cinnamon to your mix for extra flavor and nutrients. When ready to make hot cocoa, add about 2 tablespoons of the mix to 1 cup of hot water. Stir well, then top with marshmallows or a sprinkle of cinnamon.

½ cup raw cacao powder

¾ cup coconut milk powder

¾ cup coconut sugar

3 tablespoons grass-fed beef collagen, such as Vital Proteins (optional)

1 tablespoon maca powder (optional)

1 heaping teaspoon ground cinnamon (optional)

1. Sift all the ingredients together through a fine-mesh strainer into a large bowl.

2. Stir until the cacao mixture is thoroughly combined.

3. Store the mixture in an airtight container at room temperature for up to 2 months.

FORAGED FOODS

Over the years, our family has enjoyed connecting more to the wilderness, which has created a deeper appreciation for the wild plants and weeds in our area. One way to get closer to nature is by foraging for and cooking wild ingredients. For a deeper understanding of plant knowledge and a plant identification guide, please see our first book, *The Women's Heritage Sourcebook*, and have fun identifying, harvesting, and experimenting with the edible wild plants and weeds that grow near you.

It is important to note that not all plants are edible. Some are very toxic, and some can cause serious harm if they are even lightly touched. Before making anything from this chapter of the book, please be sure you can properly identify each of these plants. You will need at least two plant identification books and a grown-up to go with you. If even one part of the plant is different from what is described and pictured in your identification books—if the leaves are the same but the flowers are different, for example—it's most likely a completely different plant. Once you get to know the plants around you, you'll have an easy time identifying them and will have more confidence to use them in your cooking.

Elderberry Chia Seed Strawberry Jam

MAKES ABOUT 5 CUPS

Elderberries and elderflowers are not only used in many recipes, but also beloved by herbalists, who use them in their medicines. This wild foraged jam comes together quite easily and is the perfect alternative to conventional jam, since it is sweetened with raw honey instead of sugar.

2 cups filtered water

½ cup dried or ¾ cup fresh elderberries, stems removed

¾ to 1 cup raw honey

1 pound fresh or thawed frozen strawberries, sliced into quarters

Pinch of sea salt

6 tablespoons chia seeds

1. Add the water and elderberries to a medium saucepan and bring to a boil over medium-high heat.
2. Reduce the heat to low and simmer, uncovered, until the liquid is reduced by half, 45 minutes to 1 hour.
3. Using a fine-mesh strainer over a bowl, strain out the elderberries and discard. Measure the elderberry liquid that is left, add the same amount of honey to it, and stir. (It should be anywhere from ¾ cup to 1 cup liquid.)
4. Return the elderberry-honey mixture to the saucepan and add the strawberries and salt. Set over medium heat. Once the mixture starts to bubble, reduce the heat to medium-low.
5. Stir the strawberries as they soften. Once the berries have softened and are falling apart, add the chia seeds and stir them in. Reduce the heat to low and cook for an additional 15 minutes, until the jam has thickened. Remove the pan from the heat.
6. If you like your jam a bit chunky, simply pour the mixture into two clean 1-pint mason jars and cover tightly with the lids. Let cool, then store in the fridge until ready to enjoy. If you prefer jam with a smoother texture, allow the mixture to cool to room temperature, then put it in a blender and pulse a handful of times until you reach your preferred texture. Pour it into two clean 1-pint mason jars and cover tightly with the lids, then store in the fridge until ready to enjoy. The jam will keep in the fridge for up to 2 weeks.

TIP: While the jam is still hot, it may seem more fluid than you think is correct. The chia seeds need a bit of time to work their magic, so make sure to let it cool and then put it in the fridge for a few hours to achieve a jamlike texture. Try this jam on sourdough biscuits (see page 32) and pancakes (see page 36).

Elderberry-Honey Tonic

Honey-fermented elderberries can be used as an immune booster or simply as a condiment to add sweetness to any dish. You can drizzle the tonic on pancakes or add it to bubbly water for a fizzy drink.

1. Add enough elderberries to a clean 1-quart mason jar to fill it about two-thirds full. Add enough honey to completely cover the elderberries, then put on the lid.

2. Let the elderberry-honey mixture sit at room temperature for 1 month, then stir the mixture, strain out and discard the berries, and transfer the liquid to a clean mason jar. The tonic will keep for up to 3 months. There is no need to refrigerate.

Fresh elderberries, washed and stemmed

Raw honey

Honey-Elderflower Cordial

This recipe makes a delicious, seasonal elderflower cordial sweetened with raw honey. Although it's an impressive drink, don't be intimidated. It is a very easy recipe to make. You simply mix, stir, and let it steep for a few days before storing. The cordial is delicious diluted with still or fizzy water or used as a flavoring in ice cream, fruit fool (pureed fruit mixed with whipped cream), and other recipes.

1 cup elderflower blossoms, washed

2 organic lemons

3¼ cups filtered water

16 ounces raw honey or 1 pound granulated sugar

1. Remove the blossoms from the elderflower heads, discarding as much stem as possible, and place them in a large bowl. Zest the lemons with a fine grater over the bowl, then slice the lemons and add them to the bowl.

2. Heat the water in a saucepan or kettle until just simmering, but not boiling. Pour the hot water over the elderflower mixture. Set aside to cool to between 96° and 104°F, checking the temperature with a kitchen thermometer. Add the honey and use a wooden spoon to stir until it dissolves completely.

3. Place a finely woven cloth or tea towel over the bowl and set in a cool, dark place to steep for 2 to 3 days, checking the flavor after the second day. If you'd like it to be stronger, leave it until the third day.

4. Once the cordial has finished steeping, strain it through a fine-mesh strainer into a glass measuring cup, then pour it into a sterilized 1-quart mason jar or flip-top bottle. Keep in the fridge for up to 1 month, or freeze in a freezer-safe container for longer storage.

Stinging Nettle, Lemon, and Poppy Seed Doughnuts

It takes a little preparation to blanch stinging nettles, but after that this recipe comes together so beautifully. Be sure to wear kitchen gloves when chopping the stinging nettle leaves. If you don't have a doughnut pan for baking, you can always use a muffin pan instead.

FOR THE DOUGHNUTS:

Unsalted butter, for greasing

All-purpose flour, for dusting

1 cup stinging nettle leaves

2 tablespoons fresh lemon juice

6 tablespoons unsalted butter, at room temperature

½ cup organic cane sugar

1 egg

2 tablespoons poppy seeds

1 cup all-purpose flour or gluten-free flour blend

1 teaspoon baking powder

½ teaspoon sea salt

FOR THE GLAZE:

1 tablespoon stinging nettle leaves

¼ cup filtered water

½ cup powdered sugar

2 teaspoons fresh lemon juice, plus more if needed

Pinch of sea salt

Optional toppings: lemon zest, edible flowers, sprinkles, freshly picked berries, or nettle leaves

TO MAKE THE DOUGHNUTS:

1. Preheat the oven to 350°F. Grease and flour a doughnut or muffin pan.
2. Wearing gloves, remove the nettle leaves from the stems, wash, and let dry.
3. Bring a large pot of water to a boil over high heat and set up a bowl of ice water.
4. Once the water begins to boil, add 1 cup of the nettle leaves and blanch for 1 to 2 minutes to remove the sting.
5. Use tongs or a slotted spoon to remove the nettle leaves from the boiling water and place them in the bowl of ice water. Once cool, drain the nettle leaves and press down on them with a spoon to remove as much liquid as possible.
6. Use tongs or a slotted spoon to transfer the nettle leaves to a blender with the lemon juice. Blend until well combined.
7. In a large bowl, cream together the butter and sugar until light and fluffy. Beat in the egg, then beat in the pureed nettles and poppy seeds.
8. Slowly add the flour, baking powder, and salt to the mixture, using a rubber spatula to stir until thoroughly mixed.
9. Spoon the mixture into the prepared pan, pushing the batter to the edges of each indentation and making it level.
10. Bake for 10 to 12 minutes, then insert a toothpick into the center of one of the doughnuts to see if it comes out clean; if not, bake a little longer, about 2 minutes.
11. Cool in the pan for 10 minutes, then turn onto a wire rack to cool completely before glazing.

TO MAKE THE GLAZE:

1. To make the stinging nettle juice, wash the nettle leaves first. Puree the nettle leaves and water in a blender until well combined, then strain through a fine-mesh strainer over a bowl. Discard or compost the pulp.

2. Whisk together the stinging nettle juice, powdered sugar, lemon
   juice, and salt in a medium bowl. If the glaze is too thick, add
   additional lemon juice until it reaches the desired consistency.

3. Dip the doughnuts in the glaze, return them to the wire rack, and
   immediately top with lemon zest, edible flowers, sprinkles, or freshly
   picked berries. If you want to decorate them with nettle leaves, be
   sure to gently blanch the leaves first.

4. Allow the glaze to set at room temperature for about 30 minutes
   before stacking or serving the doughnuts.

Stinging Nettle Pesto

Stinging nettle might seem a little intimidating, but with a little blanching (submerging the greens in boiling water), you can remove their sting and turn these wild greens into something quite fantastic. You can drink the nutrient-rich cooking water just like tea, and once the pesto is made, you can spread it on fresh veggies or wraps or top flatbreads, eggs, soup, or even a macro bowl with it. If you aren't able to forage some wild nettle greens, try using kale or spinach instead.

4 cups stinging nettle leaves

2 or 3 cloves garlic, peeled

3 tablespoons pine nuts, walnuts, almonds, pecans, or hempseeds

½ cup extra-virgin olive oil

¼ cup grated Parmesan cheese or nutritional yeast

¼ teaspoon sea salt, plus more if needed

Freshly ground black pepper

1. Wearing gloves, remove the leaves from the stems (reserve the stems for making tea, if you'd like), wash, and let dry.
2. Bring a large pot of water to a boil over high heat and set up a bowl of ice water.
3. Once the water begins to boil, add the nettle leaves and blanch for 1 to 2 minutes to remove the sting.
4. Use tongs or a slotted spoon to remove the nettle leaves from the boiling water and place them in the bowl of ice water. (Use the leftover nettle cooking water as a tea or for steaming veggies, making rice, or boiling pasta.)
5. Once cool, drain the nettle leaves and press down on them with a spoon to remove as much liquid as possible.
6. Place the nettle leaves and garlic in a food processor and process until well combined.
7. Add the pine nuts, oil, cheese, salt, and pepper to taste. Process until the pesto is thoroughly combined. Taste and add more salt and pepper, if necessary.
8. Store in a mason jar in the fridge for up to 3 weeks, or freeze in the jar or another freezer-safe container for up to 6 months.

Dandelion Fritters

SERVES 2 TO 4

These wild springtime blossoms are such a fun creation and make a tasty snack. They are also packed with good-for-you nutrients like iron, vitamin A, and vitamin C. When foraging for dandelions, there are two important things to remember. First, always pick in a clean area, away from pesticides, power lines, and pet urine. Second, be 100 percent sure that you have properly identified your flowers. Always double-check with an adult. Also note that the dandelions must be used immediately after picking or the flower heads will close up.

½ cup all-purpose flour or gluten-free flour blend

½ cup corn flour

1 cup milk of choice

1 egg

1 teaspoon baking powder

½ teaspoon sea salt

¼ cup avocado oil or coconut oil, for frying

1 cup freshly picked dandelion flower heads, washed

1. Whisk together the flours, milk, egg, baking powder, and salt in a medium bowl.
2. Warm the oil in a small cast-iron skillet over medium heat. Dip the dandelion flower heads in the batter and fry in the hot oil, flower side down.
3. When they are golden brown, flip them and fry the other side until golden brown.
4. Drain on a towel and serve immediately, while they are hot and crispy.

Pickled Dandelion Flowers

This recipe uses dandelion flower heads as a pickle, but you could substitute the flowers of chives or the petals of small flowering roses as well. You can even try using yucca and calendula flowers.

1. Gently wash and dry the dandelion flower heads and place them in a clean ½-pint mason jar.
2. In a small saucepan, bring the vinegar, water, sugar (if using), and salt to a boil over high heat, then reduce to medium-low and maintain a simmer. Let simmer for 1 minute, or until the sugar and salt dissolve.
3. Pour the brine over the dandelions to fully cover. Seal the lid while hot and invert the jar for 1 minute (this means you turn the jar upside down, which helps heat the air inside the jar and makes it more likely to get a better seal as it cools).
4. Allow the jar to cool, then put it in the fridge. Store in the fridge for at least 24 hours or up to 3 days before opening. Once opened, the pickled dandelions will keep in the fridge for 6 to 12 months.

20 to 30 freshly picked dandelion flower heads

¼ cup rice vinegar or distilled white vinegar

⅛ cup filtered water

1 tablespoon granulated sugar or drizzle of raw honey (optional)

⅛ teaspoon sea salt

Prickly Pear Ice Pops

MAKES 6 ICE POPS

Prickly pear, the fruit that grows on the opuntia cactus, can be used to create a delicious, plant-based ice pop made from fresh fruit. The fruit of the prickly pear yields a bright pink juice that pairs nicely with strawberries and lime.

6 prickly pears, cleaned

⅓ cup fresh lime juice

⅓ cup strawberries, fresh or thawed frozen

¼ cup agave nectar or raw honey

Generous pinch of sea salt

1. Wearing thick gardening gloves, slice off both ends of the prickly pear and discard. Using the tip of a knife, make one long, vertical cut down the body of the prickly pear. Slip your finger into the cut and grab hold of the skin. Peel back the thick, fleshy skin completely and discard it. Transfer the edible portion of the fruit to a blender.
2. Add the lime juice, strawberries, agave nectar, and salt to the blender and blend until thoroughly pureed.
3. Pour the mixture into ice pop molds and freeze for at least 3 hours before eating.

Vegan Lemonade Berry Curd

Rhus integrifolia, also known as lemonade berry, is a shrub native to California. Folks make lemonade berry lemonade by steeping its ripe berries in water. The result is a tart, lemony beverage. It's so hard to wait for the berries to ripen though. While we wait, we make other things with the flower buds of the same shrub, like this yummy vegan lemonade berry curd. You can eat the curd on its own, pair it with fruit, or try it with almond shortbread cookies (see page 116).

1 (14-ounce) can coconut cream

Zest of 1 organic lemon

3 tablespoons cane sugar, coconut sugar, or maple syrup

¼ cup lemonade berry flower buds

½ cup fresh lemon juice

2 tablespoons arrowroot powder or cornstarch

1. Place the coconut cream, lemon zest, cane sugar, and lemonade berry flower buds in a saucepan. Whisk to combine.
2. Place the lemon juice and arrowroot powder in a small bowl and whisk to combine.
3. Add the lemon juice and arrowroot powder mixture to the saucepan. Stir well.
4. Cook over medium heat, being careful not to let it boil. Once the mixture starts bubbling and thickening, reduce the heat to medium-low and continue cooking until the mixture is thick and jiggly, about 5 minutes.
5. Remove from the heat and strain through fine-mesh strainer over a bowl; discard the solids. Let the curd rest for 10 to 15 minutes, then whisk one more time before transferring it to a clean ½-pint mason jar. Store in the fridge for up to 2 weeks.

Outdoor Cooking

KATIE COTA

Katie Cota loves to cook! She has a way with food, and is able to make eating outside by a campfire in the woods taste like a gourmet-cooked meal. Katie began cooking when she was a young girl. She loves to cook outdoors not only because she loves being outside, but also because she thinks food cooked over an open fire is more delicious—and we, her tasters, agree! After a long day of outdoor activities like horseback riding or hiking, knowing that Katie is grilling or cooking makes everyone extra hungry with anticipation.

Katie's kids—Cassie, Jack, and Clara—started cooking outside as early as they could walk. They helped by carrying cooking items, stirring food, and planning menus. As they got older, they did more and more. The kids are currently 13, 12, and 10, so they are now able to do pretty much all aspects of the cooking. They help with coming up with recipes, prepping the food to go, packing coolers and dry boxes, finding a camping location, prepping and building the fire, cooking, and cleaning up the mess. Katie's family car camps, backpacks, and horse packs as often as possible. Cooking and being outdoors is something her kids have grown up with and will hopefully continue throughout their lives. They have the basic skills now, and there is always more to learn.

Katie enjoys cooking over an open fire and cooking over coals. Each has its own purpose, and certain recipes seem to taste better using one or the other. For example, she loves meat and veggies grilled, but if you are making a stew or chili, she thinks a Dutch oven is better for more of a long, slow cooking time.

There are so many good places to cook outdoors: your own backyard, the beach, camping spots, cattle brandings, or grilling in the backcountry. Katie loves cooking for people! She loves trying to make something that is special that people will enjoy, and she loves the effort that goes into the meal. For her, it's more about the people than the specific location. That being said, she says outside is always better, and the Sierra Nevada mountains seem to add that extra little something. And, of course, after a long day outside, pretty much anything tastes good!

Cooking with Coals

To get coals ready to be cooked on, you can do one of two things. You can either use wood to build a fire and wait for the wood to become like coals, or you can use store-bought charcoal. You will need to light your charcoal or fire and wait for the wood or coals to burn down in order to cook in the Dutch oven. Coals are ready when the fire has subsided and the coals are covered in a gray ash. As the coals burn down, they continue to turn to ash; this means the coals are ready to be spread out and cooked on. This can take anywhere from 10 to 20 minutes. Dutch ovens can be placed directly on the charcoal, and will also need to have charcoal placed on the lid to cook evenly. Cook times vary, so check your Dutch oven throughout cooking, but if you have an appropriate amount of coals, cook times should be similar to the time in an oven.

Safety

Only have a fire with an adult present. Make sure your fire is in a designated safe place, and always have a fire extinguisher or water nearby. Use a shovel or tongs to place the charcoal over the Dutch oven lid, and always use heatproof gloves when handling the cast iron. You will need an adult to help you get the coals ready, and you will need to take appropriate safety precautions around the fire.

Cooking with Cast Iron

Cast iron is great to cook with, whether you're using a skillet or a Dutch oven, because you can use less oil. The more you cook with it, the more it is "seasoned," and it fortifies what you cook with iron. A cast-iron Dutch oven is required when cooking with coals so that you can put coals on the lid in order to create warmth, almost like an oven. This ensures the contents cook evenly.

Food Preparation

Katie likes doing most of her prep at home, which saves her time and energy when on an adventure. Being prepared gives her more time to play and

explore the outdoors with friends and family. So, for the recipes included here, she added what parts are good to prepare beforehand at home and what she likes to do at the campsite. Of course, the choice is up to you. Always check with an adult before prepping food or cooking.

SQUASH BOWLS WITH SAUSAGE

Serves 4

Extra-virgin olive oil

1 red onion, diced

4 cloves garlic, peeled and diced

1 pound sausage or any ground meat

Sea salt

Freshly ground black pepper

Seasonings of choice

Bunch of spinach, chopped

1 cup chanterelle mushrooms, chopped

Butternut squash, acorn squash, or sugar pumpkins

AT HOME:

1. Heat 1 tablespoon of olive oil in a large skillet over medium heat. Add the onion and garlic, sauté for 5 minutes, then add the sausage and cook until the meat is browned. Season with salt and pepper to taste and any other seasonings of your choice.
2. Add the spinach and chanterelle and sauté for 5 more minutes. Let cool, then store the mixture in an airtight container with a lid in the fridge for up to 3 days before going to the campsite.

AT THE CAMPSITE:

1. To create a bowl using a butternut squash, acorn squash, or sugar pumpkin, halve the squash and scoop out the seeds.
2. Oil, salt, and roast the squash to your liking.
3. Fill the squash bowl to the top with the sausage filling.
4. Wrap the squash and filling in aluminum foil.
5. Put the squash directly in the coals.
6. Check the squash in 10 to 15 minutes; it should be tender when pierced with a fork. Eat when warm.

DUTCH OVEN APPLE CRISP

Serves 8

2 cups oats

2 cups crispy rice cereal

½ cup (1 stick) unsalted butter, softened

2 tablespoons plus ¼ cup dark brown sugar

2 teaspoons ground cinnamon

½ teaspoon sea salt

¼ teaspoon ground nutmeg

1 tablespoon all-purpose flour or
   gluten-free flour blend

8 Granny Smith apples

Juice of 1 lemon

1 teaspoon vanilla extract

AT HOME:

1. To prep the topping, mix the oats, crispy rice
   cereal, 4 tablespoons (½ stick) of the butter,
   2 tablespoons of the brown sugar, 1 teaspoon
   of the ground cinnamon, and ¼ teaspoon
   of the salt in a bowl. Transfer to an airtight
   container. It will keep on the counter for up
   to 3 days.
2. To prep the filling, mix the remaining ¼ cup
   brown sugar, 1 teaspoon ground cinnamon,
   ¼ teaspoon salt, nutmeg, and flour. Store in a
   second container with a lid.

AT THE CAMPSITE:

1. Peel, core, and dice the apples. Cut the
   remaining 4 tablespoons (½ stick) butter
   into bite-size pieces.
2. Mix the apples, lemon juice, vanilla, and
   butter with the prepared filling in the
   Dutch oven.
3. Top with the prepared topping and cover
   with the lid.
4. Put the Dutch oven directly on the
   ready coals and add more coals on the top
   of the lid.
5. Check in 20 minutes. If the filling is bubbling
   up and the topping is crispy, it is ready.

DUTCH OVEN RIBS AND SWEET BEANS

Serves 4

FOR THE BEANS:

1 bell pepper

¼ cup barbecue sauce

¼ cup dark brown sugar

¼ cup molasses

¼ cup ketchup

2 tablespoons honey mustard

1 tablespoon Worcestershire sauce

1 pound bacon, cooked

Homemade cooked navy beans (2 cups dried
    navy beans plus 1 teaspoon sea salt) or
    2 (28-ounce) cans baked beans

FOR THE RIBS:

1 tablespoon olive oil

1 to 2 yellow onions

2 racks of pork ribs

Honey mustard

Dry rub*

Barbecue sauce

Orange juice

*If you'd like to make your own dry rub, mix
together 1 tablespoon brown sugar, 2 tablespoons
paprika, 1 teaspoon garlic powder, 1 teaspoon
onion powder, 1 teaspoon ground cumin, 1 teaspoon
sea salt, and 1 teaspoon freshly ground black pepper.*

AT HOME:

1. Dice the bell pepper and add it to a bowl.
2. Mix in the barbecue sauce, brown sugar, molasses,
   ketchup, honey mustard, and Worcestershire
   sauce.
3. Mix in the cooked bacon. Store in an airtight
   container in the fridge for up to 3 days before
   going to the campsite.
4. If cooking beans from scratch, put them in a bowl,
   cover with about 2 inches of cold water, and soak
   overnight. Drain the beans and put them in a large
   pot with a tight-fitting lid. Add 1 teaspoon salt and
   enough cool water to cover the beans by 2 inches,

DUTCH OVEN PIZZA

Serves 4

Olive oil

Pizza dough (store-bought or made ahead of time)

Your favorite sauce (Katie's family likes pesto)

Your favorite toppings (Katie's family likes mozzarella,
    sausage, artichoke hearts, garlic, and olives)

1. Oil the bottom of your Dutch oven.
2. Stretch the pizza dough to fit the bottom of the
   Dutch oven.
3. Top with your favorite pizza sauce and toppings.
4. Cover the Dutch oven with its lid and place it on
   the coals, then cover the lid with more coals.
5. The cook time depends on your dough and the
   heat of the fire, but you should check after
   15 to 20 minutes. The dough should be slightly
   browned, the toppings should be cooked, and the
   cheese should be melted.

then cover with the lid. Bring to a boil over high heat, then lower the heat to maintain a simmer and cook gently, stirring occasionally, until the beans are just tender (but not mushy), 30 to 40 minutes. Drain and rinse the beans under cold water to stop the cooking process. Transfer to an airtight container and store in the fridge for up to 3 days before going to the campsite.

AT THE CAMPSITE:

1. Oil the inside of the Dutch oven.
2. Slice 1 or 2 onions into rings.
3. Line the bottom and sides of the Dutch oven with the onions.
4. Prep the ribs by cutting off any extra membranes. Pat dry.
5. Brush on enough honey mustard to coat the ribs.
6. Pat on the dry rub.
7. Brush the barbecue sauce on top to your liking.
8. Place the ribs in the Dutch oven in a circle, using the onions to prevent the ribs from touching the bottom or sides.
9. Put the bacon mixture and beans in the center of the ribs and cover the ribs with orange juice.
10. Put the Dutch oven directly on the coals, cover with its lid, and add more coals to the lid. Cook for 2 to 3 hours, or until the ribs are beginning to fall off the bone.

RAISE

Living with Animals

LAUREN

SINCE THE DAWN OF HUMAN EXISTENCE, OUR LIVES HAVE BEEN INTERTWINED WITH the animals with which we share this earth. Some large animals, such as the cave bear and the saber-toothed tiger, saw early man as prey and hunted us. Many animals, such as large snakes and crocodiles, frightened us terribly and we chose to avoid them. Others, such as deer and buffalo, we learned to track, trap, and hunt for their meat, fur, and bones. It is thought that early humans first domesticated dogs for protection, and eventually were able to domesticate other, more docile animals, like goats and other milk producers. After that, it was the beasts of burden, such as yaks and oxen, and eventually we "tamed" horses. We humans evolved around and with animals, so it is no wonder that we are so fascinated by them.

There is so much to learn when it comes to animals, whether they are wild or domestic. Science has made huge strides in understanding the natural histories, behaviors, emotions, and needs of different animals, but there is still so far to go. Throughout this section, I will introduce you to some animal science basics and share insight into several domestic animals, including the horse, pig, dog, cat, and more. We will examine the natural history of each animal and try to understand its past in order to understand its behaviors, its ways of communicating, and how to meet its basic needs.

It is easy to see a cute, cuddly animal and want to take it home. However, you need to take the time to understand that animal and what it needs before committing to taking care of it. When considering owning an animal, you must be ready to take responsibility for that animal's health and well-being, both now and in the future. We will explore this process deeper and in more detail for each featured species in the following pages. Please make sure to learn the important key terms associated with each animal. And remember, your parent or guardian must be on board when it comes to getting an animal, or even if you are looking to get some hands-on experience with an animal.

There are many reasons why owning a pet can be beneficial. Learning to care for an animal can help improve confidence while teaching you responsibility. Having relationships with animals can help reduce feelings of stress and loneliness and increase feelings of love and acceptance. Did you know children who own pets tend to play outside more and that having a pet when you are young could actually help reduce allergies?

But there are also reasons why owning a pet could be a problem for you. Cost, time commitment, energy, training, and safety are just a few things to consider. It is very important when thinking about getting an animal of your own to consider the pros and cons of being a responsible pet owner. When you become the owner of a pet, it should be for that animal's entire life span. Knowing as much as you can about the animal's natural history, behavior, and basic needs is a great way to start.

I was lucky enough to grow up with animals in my backyard, and I learned how to care for them through daily experiences with my family. I then studied animal science in college and even got to study cheetahs and black rhinos in Africa and Przewalski's horses in China. After college, I worked at an animal rescue center in California, and now I am raising my family surrounded by—guess what—lots of animals. Currently we have three horses, a pony, a mini mule, two pigs, 10 chickens, two dogs, and a cat. (The quail and bunny chapters in this section were shared by Ashley and Emma, respectively.) Can you guess who helps me feed, muck, and take care of all these animals? If you guessed my kids, you were right, so let me introduce you to Milly, June, and Clay.

Milly is 10 years old. She has loved animals ever since she was a baby and has a particularly special bond with horses. She is very independent and works hard at her chores. She feeds all three horses, the pony and mini mule, dogs, and cat before and after school every day. Milly has been taking riding lessons since she was 4 years old. She is now a very competent and confident rider and is even learning how to rope cattle from horseback. Milly likes to ride all our horses, but her favorite is Peaches. She also enjoys training our border collie and spends a lot of time working on obedience and commands with him.

June is 7 years old. She also loves animals, especially pigs. June's chores are to feed the chickens, collect the eggs, and feed the piglets. Sometimes she has to be reminded, but once she is doing her chores, she does a very thorough job. She sometimes feeds the horses by herself. June has also been taking horseback riding lessons for a few years and is getting more and more comfortable. She rides Peaches too. She loves learning about animals and is very good at socializing our piglets.

Clay is 2 years old. He likes to ride the pony, Trigger, and he is very serious about putting hay in the feeders. We have to watch him carefully, as he will quickly crawl under the fence or gate and try to go in with the horses, which could be dangerous. He's not old enough to have his own chores yet, but he will soon.

You will see Milly, June, Clay, and some of our friends throughout this section. I hope it inspires you to learn even more about the animals that spark an interest for you.

ANIMAL BASICS

When working with animals, there are certain basics we humans should learn in order to better understand their behavior and adapt ours. Learning about an animal's natural history and how it evolved can help us understand why that animal behaves the way it does. Learning and understanding an animal's needs—and considering if we can meet those needs—is an important part of caring for an animal. Looking at the different ways animals communicate with one another (and with us) is important in understanding and adjusting our interactions with animals. And if you learn some of the key terms in this chapter, you can use them and sound like a pro.

ANIMAL SCIENCE: The study of domesticated animals, such as livestock

ANIMAL HUSBANDRY: The science of caring for, raising, and breeding domesticated animals

ANIMAL BEHAVIOR: The way an animal acts and how it interacts with its environment

BODY LANGUAGE: How the body, or parts of the body, are used to express an emotion or intention

NATURAL HISTORY: The scientific study of plants and animals through observation rather than through experimentation

EVOLUTION: The way that animals and plants can change and adapt to their environment over time

DOMESTICATION: The process of taming an animal to live around humans

LIVESTOCK: A domesticated group of animals, usually kept for profit, such as beef cattle, dairy cows, horses, sheep, pigs, and poultry

WILD ANIMAL: An animal that lives in the wild and is not tamed by humans; it finds its own food and water

GENETICS: Inherited characteristics in DNA

GENUS: An animal's common biological classification

SPECIES: A group of living organisms with similar genes that can reproduce and have fertile offspring

SPECIES EPITHET: The name that follows the genus and distinguishes it from other animals of the same genus

POPULATION: An organism or species living together

TRAIT: A distinguishing characteristic that an animal commonly displays

CHARACTERISTIC: A specific behavior, personality, or appearance that is common to a person, place, or thing that can help identify it

SOCIAL HIERARCHY: Ranking within a group; some hold dominance over others

Natural History

The natural history of an animal is the history of that particular animal through time and evolution. The evolution of a particular animal has been studied very carefully, and by discovering an animal's history, we can then develop a deeper understanding of its behavior, instincts, and needs. Simply put, understanding an animal's past can help you understand how and why that animal acts and responds the way it does today. When learning about any animal, remember that it is important to start with its natural history.

Communication and Behavior

Animals cannot tell us in words how they are feeling, but they certainly communicate with us in other, nonverbal ways. Learning about different species and how they communicate is an extremely important part of your journey in understanding the animals you are interested in learning more about and looking to communicate with. Each species has its own unique way of communicating. It can be through body language, sight, sound, touch, or even through the use of scent chemicals (think of skunks). Animals use these different ways of communicating to show affection, danger, fear, anger, dominance, joy, and so much more.

ACTIVITY

Write down your favorite animal. Next, write how that animal communicates with its own species. Now, explore how that animal might communicate with you.

In order for us, as humans, to understand animals better, we must first understand their unique natural histories, and then study how they communicate with one another. By doing that, we will more adeptly know what they are feeling and be able to adapt our own behavioral response to them more appropriately.

Needs

Animal husbandry is the science of caring for, raising, and breeding domesticated animals. When we take care of an animal, we are responsible for all its needs. This includes its physical health—food, water, grooming, shelter, safety, and vet care—and its mental health— mental stimulation, attention, and exercise. We want our animals to live the healthiest, happiest lives possible, so before considering getting an animal, it is very important that you learn exactly what its needs are and will continue to be as it grows older. This way you will be totally prepared to be a responsible, caring owner and friend to that animal. It is very important to realize that when you make a commitment to caring for an animal, it is a long-term one that should last for that animal's entire life span.

Domestic vs. Wild

Domestication is the process of taming wild animals to live comfortably alongside humans. Early humans domesticated animals for food, for

<hr>

ACTIVITY

Think about what animals mean to you. What animals are you most curious about? How could you learn more about the animals you are interested in?

<hr>

protection, and to help with work. We needed them for carrying our burdens, for plowing our fields, and eventually even for transportation. Humans domesticated animals by meeting their needs and even learned to manage the breeding of these animals. Humans have domesticated approximately 40 species, and in many ways we have advanced and evolved alongside—and with the help of—these domesticated species.

Dogs may well have been the earliest domesticated animals. They provided not only warmth and comfort in cold drafty caves, but also the earliest known alarm system. Their persistent barking and growling warned those around them of imminent danger. They aided early hunters in the tracking and retrieval of game, which they needed to survive, and since dogs are natural scavengers, they kept caves free of food debris. How handy and helpful dogs were to early humans.

Most domesticated animals were raised primarily for food—animals like goats, cows, and chickens. Others helped make work easier, like water buffalo, horses, and oxen. All animals that were domesticated demonstrated certain behaviors and traits. For example, many lived in herds where they respected social hierarchies, weren't picky eaters, were docile and easy to contain, and could be bred in captivity. Perhaps most important, though, they had the right temperament to be around and handled by humans.

So why aren't lions, rhinos, and hundreds of other animals domesticated? Animals that stayed wild tended to be predators that were more aggressive toward humans, or were just too large and strong to contain. A great example of humans having trouble domesticating an animal is the zebra, and yes, humans have tried. The zebra seems similar to a horse, but it is not. Zebras are known for being very mean and aggressive, making them virtually untrainable by humans. Their unsuitability for domestication stems from their highly attuned flight instinct and their fierce reaction when cornered. They simply lack respect for domination, which makes them extremely difficult to train. They are also able to jump much higher than horses, so fencing would need to be much more extensive to contain them. Consider, too, that their backs are narrower and shorter, making a zebra very difficult for a human to ride. In the end, it wasn't worth the time or effort for humans, so zebras remained wild.

Jobs with Animals

Have you ever dreamed of working with animals when you grow up? If so, there are lots of awesome and rewarding jobs out there to consider. You could choose to work with either domesticated or wild animals. Many of these interesting jobs you may never have imagined or even heard about. Below are a few domestic and wild animal-based careers to think about, and these are just a few of the many great jobs out there for animal lovers. In this section, you will meet a mule and horse packer, cattle rancher, and wildlife rescuer, so keep on reading!

Animal Breeder

Animal breeders are folks who breed animals in order to improve their genetic lines. This can range from breeding small animals, such as dogs and cats, to breeding large animals, such as horses and mules. For example, selective breeding can help increase milk production or the amount of wool a sheep produces. Also, there are very specially trained animal breeders who are working diligently to help endangered species breed in captivity in order to save them from becoming extinct.

Animal Groomer

An animal groomer provides cosmetic services for pets like washing, cutting coats, trimming nails, and brushing teeth. Animal groomers also work with wild animals in zoos and wildlife preserves, keeping all varieties of animals physically healthy. I have watched an elephant at the Santa Barbara Zoo getting a pedicure, using a very large nail file. This was not an easy task, and no bright red nail polish was applied.

Animal Rescuer

Animal rescue work, both with domestic and wild animals, is another career that has risen out of the need to protect and care for injured and abandoned animals. Unfortunately, there are some pet owners who, for whatever reason, abandon or mistreat their animals. Many people feel that irresponsible overbreeding, particularly of cats and dogs, accounts for many of these neglected animals. There are also wild animals who are harmed by living too close to humans and suffer from environmentally caused issues, such as oil spills, injuries caused by cars and boats, and even unintended poisonings. Someone who works for an animal rescue center or organization usually works at a shelter specifically designed to fit the needs of those particular animals. Your job would be to help with the daily tasks of the shelter: cleaning, feeding, walking, and nurturing the animals, and also preparing them to go to new homes or be released back into the wild. I worked at the California Wildlife Center and helped rehabilitate many raptors and other native wildlife before releasing them back into the wild. What a liberating feeling it was to release one of those regal birds and watch as it powerfully disappeared out of sight!

Animal Trainer

How about becoming an animal trainer by learning how to teach animals to exhibit certain behaviors when given specific cues? This could range from training animals to simply be obedient and follow verbal commands or hand gestures—such as agility trainers who teach dogs to compete over and around obstacles—to training animals who learn to assist people with disabilities so they can live more independently. You could also learn to train dogs to assist law enforcement or to rescue people who may be trapped in fallen buildings or under the snow after an avalanche. Have you ever thought about the animals you see in the movies or on your favorite TV show? Most of those animals, large or small, wild or domesticated, had to be trained to be handled and to entertain by performing specific tasks.

Conservation Biologist

A conservation biologist studies the earth's biodiversity and how to manage and protect it. That means they want to help protect and restore our planet's different species, their habitats, and their ecosystems. A conservation biologist might work in the field doing research to gather information on a particular species or habitat, or they might work for a private or public agency to help manage biological communities.

Kennel Manager

A kennel manager is someone who runs a dog kennel and helps manage its daily operations. Kennels usually board people's animals and many also offer training and obedience classes for dogs that are having obedience issues.

Pet Sitter

A pet sitter is someone who watches pets when their owners are unable or unavailable. This could mean anything from dog walking to housing people's pets. Some pet sitters even run dog daycare centers.

Wildlife Biologist

A wildlife biologist studies the life and behavior of wild animals and how an animal interacts with its habitat or the place it lives. Understanding an animal and how it lives in and uses the environment around it helps us learn what it needs and therefore what needs to be protected. This job often takes people to remote places to study animals in their natural habitats.

Wildlife Veterinarian

A wildlife veterinarian is someone who cares for injured wild or captive animals. They can work with all different kinds of wildlife, from mammals and birds to amphibians and reptiles. Can you imagine knowing how to care for all those different kinds of animals? A wildlife vet can work in a clinic, but many work out in the field, traveling to help their wild patients.

Zoologist

A zoologist is a scientist who studies the behavior, classification, and distribution of animals. Though a zoologist is similar to a wildlife biologist, a zoologist studies an animal's behavior and certain characteristics to understand them better.

ACTIVITY

Make a list of animal jobs you can think of. Write about what job you could see yourself doing in the future, and make sure to draw a picture of yourself doing it.

A zoologist may work in a lab or out in the field. Jane Goodall is one of the world's most famous zoologists. She has studied chimpanzee behavior for more than 60 years, helping us understand these animals and therefore understand much more about how to protect them.

Common Names vs. Scientific Names

Humans have developed systems to organize and classify things, and this has been a useful tool in animal science. Taxonomy is the science and process of naming and classifying all things. Animals have two names: a common, everyday name by which we, the general public, know them, and a scientific name. Every recognized and documented species on earth is given a two-part scientific name. It sounds complicated, but when you learn the system you can more easily understand animals' histories.

For the scientific name, each species has a generic (more common) name followed by a species name. The first part is known as the genus and the second part is known as the species. The genus is always capitalized, and the species is always lowercased. For example, the four-legged animal we like to ride has the scientific name *Equus caballus*. *Equus* is the genus, and *caballus* is the species. But we English speakers know it by its common name—the horse.

By using accepted scientific names, the international scientific community has standardized how animals are named. Think about the fact that in English we say *horse*; in French, the word is *cheval*; in German, it is *pferd*; in Spanish, it is *caballo*; and on and on, as every language in every country has its own word for horse. How confusing it could be when trying to discuss horses. However, if you use the scientific name *Equus caballus*, everyone in the scientific community understands that you are talking about a horse. How helpful!

CHICKENS

OK, now I ask you the age-old question, "Which came first, the chicken or the egg?" I can't answer that, but I can tell you that I have really enjoyed having chickens. Sometimes we have hatched our own, so the egg came first, but more often we have purchased the chicks first. Either way, chickens are extremely entertaining and quite comic characters that have lovely and varied feathers, but most important, they come with a bonus: they lay eggs pretty much every day. We have had chickens for the past 15 years, and caring for these cool birds and collecting and enjoying their eggs has brought my family joy and also connected us to a major food source.

Chickens can live in backyards or in large areas. They are relatively easy to care for (compared to other animals) once you've done the setup work. So, if you are interested in outdoor pets that also serve a purpose—providing food—this could be the right animal for you and your family. Let's explore deeper into the world of chickens!

Natural History

The chicken is thought to be a domesticated version of the red and gray jungle fowl found in Asia about 8,000 years ago. It is thought that chickens were the first domesticated bird. They were originally used for cockfighting, and then eventually they were raised for their eggs and meat. (Really—they were raised to fight before they were raised for their eggs and meat!) It is now known that chickens were raised in ancient civilizations such as Egypt, where there is evidence that the Egyptians even incubated their eggs. Chickens began to be bred for specific qualities, such as tameness, feather color, and egg color. Once global trading routes were established, it wasn't long before chickens were widespread across the globe and new breeds were developed. Since then, chickens have become one of the main protein sources, supplying both meat and eggs all over the world. It is thought that there are around 25 billion chickens in the world today. Now that's a lot of chickens!

KEY TERMS

POULTRY: Domestic birds, such as chickens, turkeys, geese, and ducks

FLOCK: A group of chickens

HEN: A female chicken

LAYER: A female chicken that is old enough to lay eggs

ROOSTER: A male chicken

CHICK: A baby chicken

BROOD: A group of baby chicks

COOP: A secure home for a chicken

NESTING BOX: A place for a chicken to lay its eggs

PREENING: When a bird cleans and waterproofs its feathers

ROOSTING: When chickens are resting on their perches

FORAGING: Looking for food

Communication and Behavior

Chickens spend their day looking for food. They peck around looking for bugs, cluck to communicate with one another, drink water, preen, give themselves dust baths, hopefully head to their nesting box and lay an egg, and then, as it grows dark, head to their roosts to sleep, only to get up the next morning and do it all over again. However, there is more going on in a chicken's life than meets the eye.

Body Language

Chickens do in fact have a strict social structure, hence the term "pecking order." Dominant birds chase, peck, and steal food from birds that are lower in the order. If you observe a flock, you will quickly see who is in charge and who is not. As a rule of thumb, a healthy chicken has strong, confident, and alert body language, while an unhealthy chicken tends to be lethargic and not very responsive. It is important to be aware of your chickens' behavior and observe them to make sure they are looking healthy and active. Remember, normal chicken behavior includes pecking and scratching at potential food sources, preening feathers, and taking dust baths. Abnormal behavior includes pacing, spot pecking at their own feathers, or acting aggressive. An aggressive chicken would most likely make its body big and run at you. Aggression is more common with roosters and not usually an issue with hens. If you notice a chicken that is sick or behaving abnormally, you should immediately separate it from the flock. Sadly, a chicken that may be sick will get bullied, picked on, or even killed by the other chickens.

Chicken Sounds

You can tell a lot about chickens just by listening to their many noises. As a rule of thumb, any soft peeps, clucking, and soft trilling sounds mean the birds are content and safe. Any high-pitched or insistent peeping means something is wrong. Chickens do have an alarm sound, which can range from a high-pitched siren sound to repeated, intense clucking. A mother hen protecting her chicks from a predator will make the very shrill siren sound, while a relaxed chicken should just be going about its business with a soft clucking or peeping. If you listen, you will notice that a flock of chickens is in fact constantly making some sort of noise. Scientists believe this is communication among the hens in the flock so they know where the others are, and whether they are safe or in danger. This makes sense because they are easy prey and need to always be on the lookout for predators.

Basic Chicken Care

Preparing to keep chickens does in fact take thought, care, and planning. It is a great idea to think through all the details of owning chickens before you decide to bring them home. Do you have the necessary space in your yard for chickens? Where will you build the coop?

CHICKEN SUPPLIES

- Secure coop and run
- Nesting boxes
- Clean bedding
- Perches
- Chicken feeder
- Chicken feed, including grit and calcium
- Chicken waterer

Who will build it, and how will it be built? Do you have the time for chickens? Who will take care of the chickens each day?

There is a lot to learn about chickens, and the following information will just get you started. There are many great resources out there about chickens and coop building. You can read books, ask questions at your local feedstore, or speak with folks who keep chickens. You and your chickens will be happier if you do your research ahead of time in order to understand just what your family's commitment will be. So let's see what chickens need!

Coop

Chickens need special housing called a coop. Coops can come in many different sizes, materials, and shapes. Coops must be completely secure—that means the chickens should not be able to get out and predators (such as dogs or raccoons) should not be able to get in. The coop will need to include a covered shelter for the chickens to get out of the elements (rain, wind, and sun). Your hens will also need nesting boxes inside the coop. A nesting box is a place where the chicken can lay her eggs in peace and from which you will collect them. Soft, clean bedding is needed inside the nesting boxes. Yes, your ladies want a clean and comfy place to lay their eggs. In the coop you will also need a dry, shaded spot to keep the chickens' food and water, which they will need constant access to. The coop will also need a perch—a bar above the ground where the chickens can sit and balance. Like their wild ancestors who roosted (rested and slept) in trees, chickens need a safe place to roost.

Run

It is great to have a secure area, called a run, where your chickens can safely be outside. Usually the run is attached to the coop so the chickens have constant access to the outdoors, though you must make sure the run is also predator-proof.

Free-Range Chickens

If you have the right yard, it is nice to let your chickens run free. But be warned, this is often how they are hurt or killed. If you do let your chickens out (they will be very happy if you do), make sure they are in an area with no loose dogs or other predators. Our chickens are trained to come back in when I shake the food and yell, "Here, chick chick chickies," should there be any danger looming. Also, they will help themselves to your garden and make a mess, but it can be worth it for happy chickens.

ACTIVITY

Design and draw your ideal chicken coop. Make sure to include the coop, a run, a place for nesting boxes, food, water, and a perch.

Cleaning

You must keep the chicken coop clean and dry.
This involves shoveling out the chicken poop,
which can be used for fertilizer. You can use
hay or pine shavings as bedding for the coop,
if needed. You will also need to deodorize the
coop monthly with things like diatomaceous
earth. Diatomaceous earth will help keep away
pests such as mites. Sprinkle some around the
coop, especially in the wet spots. Ask an adult
to help, and always wear a mask when handling
diatomaceous earth.

Diet

Chickens, like their wild ancestors, are omnivores.
This means they can eat both meat and vegetables.
Chickens need a wide range of food for optimal
health. Manufactured feed has most of the things
they need, but we always supplement with kitchen
scraps, garden weeds, hay, and bugs. Like us,
chickens need calcium. Calcium helps our bones
stay strong, and it also helps make strong eggshells.
Make sure your chicken feed has calcium. If not,
you can buy crushed oyster shells from your local
feedstore. And guess what else chickens need?

Rocks! That's right, I said rocks (also known as
grit). Chickens don't have teeth. Instead, they have
a strong muscular pocket along their neck called
a gizzard. It is here, along with digestive enzymes
and the grit, where their food is broken down. Cool,
huh? So remember, your chicken needs not only
high-grade food, but also calcium and grit.

Water

Chickens need access to clean water 24/7. There
are several different types of chicken waterers
to choose from; the important thing is to make
sure your chickens can always get a drink of clean
water, at any time of day or night.

How to Handle a Chicken

When handling chickens, you should treat them
with respect. It is important to know how to pick
up your chickens for health checks, bonding, or
if you need to move them. Having treats can also
help. Using treats can help train your chicken to
come to you to get a reward. When approaching

the chicken you want to pick up, go slowly, quietly, and calmly. Place your hands on your chicken's back with gentle pressure. Make sure both hands are over the wings and your fingers are wrapped around, holding the bottom of the bird's chest. If you have a good hold and are covering the wings and supporting the base of its body, gently pick up the chicken and hold it securely to your body. If needed, you can use one hand to scoop under the chicken's feet. Be careful of their wings flapping and their feet scratching you. If the chicken's wings are released, it will most likely flap them like crazy. If this happens, stay calm and again try to gently contain the wings. When you are done handling your chicken, gently bend down and release it. Never throw or drop your chicken, and never hold it by its neck.

How to Collect Eggs

You will want to collect the eggs every morning. Use a woven or wire basket to collect the eggs so you can safely carry them from your coop to your kitchen. When handling eggs, you want to be very careful. One slip, and crack! The egg will break. Make sure the chickens are out of the nesting boxes when you are collecting the eggs. With one hand, gently pick up an egg and place it in the palm of your hand, creating a cup around the egg so there is no pressure on it but it can't slip out. Then, use your other hand to place it in the basket as slowly and softly as possible.

If you do not wash your fresh eggs, you do not need to refrigerate them. If you choose to wash the eggs, you will need to refrigerate them afterward. Freshly laid eggs will keep for about 2 weeks unrefrigerated and around 3 months refrigerated. When fresh eggs are washed, the "bloom" or protective layer is removed. This leaves the egg's pores (the tiny openings in the shell that help the developing chick inside get oxygen) open, which means bacteria can get through and into the egg. And guess what? It's estimated that eggs have more than 15,000 pores.

Caring for Baby Chicks

"Look at those adorable baby chicks peeping and running around and looking so soft! Oh, can we bring them home today?" Wait a minute, did you read the previous section? Do you and your family know what you are getting into? If you have discussed raising chickens with your family, have done your research, are all set up for chickens, and are ready to take on the commitment and responsibility, then it's time for chicks! Chicks have their own special needs before they grow into chickens. Let's see what they need.

Brooder Box

A brooder is a special box for baby chicks, like a nursery, that should be their home for their first 6 weeks of life. It's a secure area where they are safe and have bedding, food and water, and a heat lamp. You can use a wooden, plastic, or cardboard box. Make sure there is room for the chicks to run and grow, as they grow quickly. Chicks also poop a lot, so make sure you are cleaning the box once a day. Otherwise, it will become quite wet and stinky, and this is certainly not good for the chicks' health.

Heat Lamp

Chicks don't have real feathers yet, only soft feathers called down, so they are unable to

---

BABY CHICK SUPPLIES

- Brooder box
- Pine shavings for bedding
- Heat lamp with bulb
- Chick feeder
- Chick waterer
- Chick feed
- Ground oatmeal
- And, of course, baby chicks

regulate their body temperature. In the wild, they would be huddling with their siblings under their mother's wing. Since that isn't available, you will need to make sure their brooder box includes a heat lamp. You can purchase one online or at your local feedstore.

Work with an adult to make sure the heat lamp is in a secure place and is out of any fire danger. You can adjust the lamp's position after watching the chick's behavior. If they are huddling under the lamp and not leaving, they may be too cold and you may need to lower the heat lamp. If you notice they are not going under the heat lamp, it may be too low, making it too hot, and you may need to raise it. Keep an eye on the heat lamp every day, as you will need to adjust it as the chicks grow. At around 6 weeks, you will begin to notice that their feathers have begun to grow. At this point, you will no longer need to use the heat lamp.

Food and Water

Make sure to get a chick feeder and waterer. Any open containers will soon be full of baby chick poop. I prefer an organic crumble starter feed for the little chicks, and I also sprinkle in ground oatmeal in order to help with digestion.

Handling Baby Chicks

Those soft chicks just make you want to hold them, don't they? But guess what? Overhandling can injure or even kill a chick, especially when they are small. As tempting as it may be, you must not overhandle your baby chicks. When you do pick them up, it should be with two hands, creating a cup with their head coming out the top. You should only hold them for a couple minutes at a time, and then gently set them back in their brooder box. You should always use caution and treat your birds with gentleness and respect whether they are newly hatched or fully grown.

Raising a Flock with Rainbow Eggs

Part of the magic of raising chickens is gathering the eggs. When choosing the breeds for their flock, Ashley's family chose chickens that would lay blue, green, pink, tan, and brown eggs. According to her children—Isla, Lyra, and Jupiter—collecting them feels a little like an Easter egg hunt! Here are the breeds they have, and the color of eggs they lay:

- **Black Copper Marans:** Dark chocolate brown
- **Easter Eggers:** Blue, pink, and greenish-blue
- **Olive Eggers:** Different shades of green, and even mustard yellow
- **Silkies:** Ivory or light beige
- **White Cochins:** Light brown or tan

Ashley's children sell the rainbow eggs to their neighbors and passersby in a little farm stand they built and set up right in front of their house. The farm stand uses the honor system, with a little box where customers can pay for the eggs or produce that they buy. That way the kids don't have to tend the stand in order to make a sale.

When they first set up the stand, they used a simple table for the food they were selling. But then crows started coming by, opening the egg cartons, and eating the eggs. To fix the problem, they built a box with a wooden roof and chicken wire walls to put over the table. That worked to keep the crows out, and there was a little door on the front that customers could open to get their eggs and fruit.

QUAIL

Ashley's family has been keeping chickens for around a decade, but they only began keeping quail in the spring of 2021. They first began to think about keeping quail after seeing a flock advertised in a mail-order catalog. They didn't know anyone locally who was raising quail at the time, so they opted to order a covey (that's another word for a flock of quail) through the catalog. Soon after, 30 Coturnix quail chicks arrived peeping in the mail.

Ashley and her family are still learning—they're not experts by any means—but they've had a great experience with quail so far. This chapter shares their story in their own words. If you are considering raising quail, maybe it will help you decide if they're right for you too.

How to Begin

The first thing we noticed when we opened our mail-order box of quail was how very tiny they were, much smaller than chicken chicks of the same age. They appeared to be very frail and weak, and many of them were lying prostrate on the ground, looking dead. Luckily, this was just the way they rested. Quail chicks will rest fully outstretched, and then hop back up to run around, eat food, and drink water.

Keeping the quail chicks at a comfortable temperature, with plenty of space around a heat lamp to warm up, as well as space to get away from it to cool down, is very important. They must always have access to clean water and food, 24 hours a day. We watched our chicks closely. Some chicks were cozied up under the heat lamp, some were running around, and some were eating and drinking. This indicated that their brooder was the right temperature. If most of the chicks had been huddled under the lamp, that would mean their brooder was too cold. If, on the other hand, most of the chicks had been piled up in a corner as far away from the lamp as they could get, that would mean they were too hot and we should raise the lamp a bit so they wouldn't overheat. It's also important not to handle the chicks more than necessary when they are very young.

When the quail chicks arrived, included in the package was gel and food. We had also ordered quail chick food and had that at the ready before they arrived. Quail and chickens do not eat the same food, so it's important to buy the correct food specific to game birds. Our chicks were also especially fond of eating the flies and spiders that flew or crawled into their brooder. The quail food we had ordered seemed to be too chunky for the chicks. We ground it down with a mortar and pestle until it was the consistency of sand. That made it easier for them to eat it while they were young. Once they were mature, after around 2 months, we didn't need to grind their food at all.

We kept the quail in a small brooder when they were tiny, but quickly moved them to a bigger brooder as they grew. We had read that Coturnix quail reach maturity at 8 weeks, and before this point the roosters (male quail) must be separated from one another, otherwise they will fight to the death. We read different opinions about the optimal ratio of roosters to hens, and most often it was somewhere around one rooster for every 10 hens.

When we noticed a little crowing, we knew it was time to start separating the roosters. Luckily, it is very easy to tell the difference between Coturnix quail roosters and hens. First, if you spend time near them and they are comfortable, the roosters will crow. Another way to tell them apart is that the hens have more spots on their chest, and the roosters have a more solid chest coloring. There is a third way of distinguishing the sexes—by turning

QUAIL SUPPLIES

- Two chicken coop heat lamps, one as a backup in case something breaks on the first one (you cannot go even a short time without a heat lamp)
- Extra light bulbs for the heat lamp
- Feeders
- Waterers
- Quail food
- Brooder box
- Larger brooder box
- Shavings for the brooder box
- Coop suitable for quail when they outgrow the brooder
- Clean, dry dirt for the ground
- Bin with a secure lid to keep the feed
- Shovel to clean out the coop and add the fresh dirt
- Quail eggshell cutter, also called quail egg scissors

them upside down and pressing the males for foam—but this felt complicated to us, and we didn't need to try it since we had a very easy time finding the roosters with the first two methods.

There is so much to consider before deciding to raise quail, but one of the biggest decisions is what you will do with all of the roosters, since they cannot safely be left together in the coop. Since we knew we did not want to try keeping more than one rooster for every 10 hens, we planned to harvest and eat the roosters we could not keep in the coop. The females we would keep for their eggs and as pets. If your family does not want to eat the male quail, it could present a problem. We knew the roosters would most likely be killed right away in the wild if they were set free, and they would surely kill one another if they were left together in one coop. But we also didn't feel they would be very happy if they were isolated, each in his own separate coop.

We felt sad about harvesting the roosters because we had grown quite attached to all of our darling quail. And I think this is why we made the huge mistake of waiting too long before separating the roosters. We went to check on them one morning, as we always did, and this time the roosters were all fighting. A few of them had been pecked in the eye and many had other injuries. The aggression seemed to have happened overnight, and we felt very sorry we had not acted sooner. We saw with our own eyes that we could not keep our covey together, and that difficult truth made it easier for us to harvest the roosters to eat.

One other thing to consider is that quail are ground birds and do not roost, so make sure they have plenty of room in their coop to run around—one square foot per bird at a bare minimum—and that the perimeter of the coop is secure. Wild animals as well as domestic ones may try to dig under the coop to get to the quail. Make sure you set up your coop so this can't happen. Our coop is fully enclosed, with a wood floor. We have to clean it out often and replace the dirt on the floor,

but we think it's worth it so we know our quail are safe. Before ordering a covey of your own, we suggest picking up at least two books from the library on raising quail. We liked having plenty of information on hand, and we learned a lot about keeping quail before we ordered them.

Why We Chose to Raise Quail

We've kept turkeys, chickens, and ducks, and have had a lot of fun taking care of our birds. When we found out quail were also available, we were curious. The more we learned about them, the more we felt they would be excellent pets for us.

One of the biggest benefits of keeping quail is that everyone in our house can eat the eggs. Some people in our family are allergic to chicken eggs, but we heard that many people who can't eat chicken eggs can eat quail eggs. In our case, this proved to be true. Now we can make eggs, omelets, frittatas, and French toast that everyone in our family can eat. (If you have a chicken egg allergy, please check with your healthcare provider before ingesting quail eggs to make sure they are a safe option for you.)

If you're going to eat quail eggs, it's a good idea to buy a quail eggshell cutter, which is an inexpensive tool that makes it very easy to open the eggs. Quail eggshells crack very easily, but unlike chicken eggs, which have a thin membrane under the shell, quail eggs have a tough membrane that is harder to break without the tool.

Why Not to Raise Quail

Because quail roosters cannot be kept together, and are generally harvested for food when they reach maturity, vegetarian families might not want to raise quail. A way around the rooster dilemma would be if you knew someone locally who would give or sell your family a flock of only hens. In that case, you'd be able to raise and care for quail hens, have delicious eggs, and not have to worry about what to do with the roosters.

Some Problems That Can Arise

We have had some challenging issues with our quail and have learned from them, so we'll share some here to help you learn how to deal with them or, ideally, how to avoid them altogether.

The first problem, which we mentioned earlier, is that roosters fight one another quite aggressively once they reach maturity. This can be avoided by separating them out and harvesting them for food by 8 weeks old, or as soon as you hear the first crow.

The next problem we encountered was poop balls on their feet. One day when we went to check on our birds, we noticed that one of them was hopping around in a strange way. We saw she had a big brown ball of poop and mud on one of her toes, and a couple of smaller balls on two other toes. When we inspected the rest of the covey, we found three other hens with poop balls on their toes. This happened after a big rain, and some water had gotten into their coop. It looked like the mud and poop had mixed together and stuck to their toes, making a ball that was as hard as cement.

We filled a shallow basin with warm water, and, one by one, we soaked each quail's feet until the balls softened and cracked off when we squeezed gently. This took a long, long time—more than half an hour per bird. Patience is key here; if the balls are pulled off too soon, they will also pull off the quail's toenail.

The best thing would be to avoid this issue. From what we've heard from other families who raise quail, there are several ways to do so.

First, some people keep their quail on wood shavings rather than dirt. Other people keep their quail in wire cages so the poop falls through the bottom. Last, for families like ours who like to keep their quail on dirt, it's really important to clean out the coop often and make sure the dirt you add is completely dry. We only had the poop ball problem when the dirt in the coop got wet. Now that we make sure it is always dry, we haven't had the problem again.

Another problem that can arise is bird mites. Bird mites are tiny parasites that live on birds. They are oval-shaped and light gray in color. We haven't had any mites on our quail so far, but our chickens have had mites two times over the years. Both times it happened after days and days of rain, when the chickens were not able to give themselves dust baths in dry dirt. We discovered the mites because we saw them on the walls of the coop, and when we collected the eggs, we saw the little parasites walking on them. The mites were easily managed by dusting each bird with diatomaceous earth and sprinkling diatomaceous earth on the floor of the coop and in the nesting boxes.

Last, chickens will peck at quail and could easily kill them. You'll need to keep your quail separate from your chickens and other animals to make sure they are safe and happy.

The Verdict

Quail are gentle and quiet, beautiful to look at, and entertaining to watch. We especially love watching them when we add a big scoop of fresh dirt to their coop. They get so excited to explore the dirt, hopping around and fluffing up their feathers. All in all, raising our covey has been a lot of fun, and we will probably continue to keep quail for many years.

HORSES

This section is for both parents and children who are intrigued by the magnificent and majestic creature we call the horse. I encourage all of you, no matter your age, to explore the world of horses, and perhaps you too will be inspired to become actively involved with them. You will need your parent or guardian on board for this adventure, so talking to them about taking this journey with you is a great place to start. Many barns offer lessons for both adults and children.

The topic of horses is so incredibly vast that I will only be touching the tip of the iceberg here. If, after reading this chapter, you want to continue learning, you'll need to find a professional who can mentor you. Horses can only truly be experienced by being around them. Taking professional lessons is a great starting point to learn about horses under supervision. There are also many wonderful and detailed books and local resources to help you continue on your journey.

The most important aspect of being around horses is safety. I will be going over some of the basics here, but know first and foremost that in everything you do around horses, safety considerations have to be followed. From what you wear and how you move around the horses to the knots you tie and so much more, safety is always first.

My Experience with Horses

Horses have captured my imagination ever since I can remember. Like so many other young girls and boys, I dreamed of having my own horse to care for and to gallop with through the fields behind my childhood home. After much begging, pleading, and writing up an actual contract—which spelled out exactly how, without question, excuses, or prodding, my sisters and I would keep the stall immaculate, stack the needed hay, and water, groom, and exercise the animal—the horse that we were so hoping to have finally became a reality. My parents got a beautiful chestnut Morgan horse named Duchess that I shared with my sisters. We kept her at our house, where we had a barn and enough land that we could ride out into the fields and woods. This was the start of my preoccupation with horses. Many of my best childhood memories are with this very sweet-tempered and willing horse.

Both of my sisters have owned horses of their own, and one of my sisters has even gone on to become a professional dressage rider, managing her own barn and breeding horses as well.

KEY TERMS

EQUINE: Related to horses

EQUESTRIAN: Related to horseback riding

MARE: An adult female horse

GELDING: An adult castrated male horse (without testicles)

STALLION: An adult male horse (with testicles)

FOAL: A young horse

COLT: A young male horse

FILLY: A young female horse

PONY: A small horse under 13 hands tall

MULE: A hybrid offspring of a female horse and a male donkey (mules cannot breed)

MANE: The coarse hair that grows from the crest of a horse's neck

HORSESHOE: A U-shaped metal plate nailed into the underside of a horse's hoof

FARRIER: A person who takes care of horses' hooves, including trimming and horseshoeing

GAIT: How a horse moves

TROT: A gait that is faster than a walk, in which the horse lifts each diagonal leg alternately

GALLOP: The fastest gait of a horse

CORRAL: A pen used for confining livestock

PADDOCK: A small fenced area used for horses

PASTURE: A large fenced area used for horses

TACK: The equipment needed to ride a horse

BIT: The piece of equipment (usually metal) that goes into the horse's mouth and attaches the bridle and reins to control and steer the horse

BRIDLE: The headgear that goes around the horse's head and attaches to the bit and reins to steer the horse's head

REINS: Long straps attached to the bridle and bit of a horse that are used to control and steer it

SADDLE PAD: Material placed between the horse's back and saddle to prevent any rubbing or injury to the horse's back while absorbing any sweat (they can be made of different materials and thicknesses)

SADDLE: A seat for a human set on the back of the horse and held in place by a cinch or girth

GIRTH: A piece of equipment that goes around the horse's belly to attach the saddle to the horse's back; usually has buckles on both ends to attach to the saddle and to tighten or loosen as desired

CINCH: A piece of material that goes around the horse's belly and attaches at both ends to the saddle to secure it for riding

SPUR: A prod on the heel of the rider's boot used to direct the horse from its side

I currently own three horses, one pony, and one mini mule. Horses are part of my family's daily rhythm, and though they require a lot of work, time, and money, for us the reward is worth the effort. Seeing them running the fence line for the sheer joy of running, hearing them nicker and whinny when they see us coming to feed them, or just watching them graze peacefully fulfills part of my soul.

I grew up riding English (no saddle horn, smaller saddle, and two hands holding the reins), but after moving out West in my 20s, I transitioned to Western-style riding (a larger saddle and one hand holding the reins), which I, along with my husband and children, currently ride. The cowboy way of life and working cows while on horseback has always captured my imagination, and now I am lucky enough to work with friends on some of their cattle ranches, riding the hills and gathering and branding cattle.

My children have always had horses in their lives, so they are comfortable and natural around them. Chores, including daily feedings before and after school, are just a way of life to them. From an early age, they have learned safety on the ground when around the horses, as well as safety when they are riding. There are many subtleties of having relationships with these large beasts, and it truly takes a lifetime of learning.

Natural History

To understand a horse's behavior, it is important to study the natural history of horses. It is by observing herds of wild horses that we humans were able to begin to understand more about equine behavior. By learning about the behavior of horses, we can modify our own behavior in order to stay safe when around them and enable us to build understanding and trusting relationships with them.

Wild horses lived (and still live) in herds, which consist of many individuals living together. Within a herd there are many complex relationships, but each horse learns its place. This system is called a hierarchy. Herds of horses are usually led by a lead mare or boss mare. She protects her herd through instinct and cunning, and in turn she demands complete obedience from the lower-ranking members. The survival of the herd depends on her, and in order to make sure she is trustworthy in that position, other mares in the herd challenge her. This behavior makes sure the strongest, most capable leader is in charge. When we begin a relationship with a horse, we must fulfill the role of that leader. Much like a boss mare, we too need to show the horse that we are trustworthy and safe to be around. We must be the one to take charge!

Another very important component of a horse's natural history for us to understand is their instincts. Instinct is a pattern of behavior that is mostly genetic, but can also be learned to some extent. When faced with danger, some animals instinctively turn and face the approaching danger, other animals flee as quickly as they can, and some animals simply freeze. This is called the fight, flight, or freeze instinct. This instinct depends on whether an animal has evolved as predator or prey. Can you guess which one horses are—predator or prey? And which instinct they follow—fight, flight, or freeze?

If you guessed that horses are prey animals, you guessed correctly, and their instinct tells them to take flight and run from danger. In a herd, if danger approaches—for example, a pack of wolves—the lead mare makes the decision about which direction is the safest to flee and the rest of the herd follows her. Because of the horse's natural instinct to flee if startled or frightened, whether we are on the ground or riding, we must always be aware of what the horse's body language is telling us.

Horse Breeds

There are hundreds of breeds of horses, each with its own history and characteristics. All breeds have been bred for certain reasons, such as speed, beauty, or strength. Before I share some of my personal favorite breeds with you, let's discuss the five broad categories horses can be broken into: ponies, draft horses, light horses, gaited horses, and warmbloods.

Ponies are not as tall as horses. Any horses under 14.2 hands (about 4½ feet) are considered ponies. Ponies were bred for jobs such as riding, pulling carts, and carrying loads. Today, they are still used for those purposes, as well as for kids to ride and enjoy. Their small size makes it easy for children to learn how to groom, be on the ground with, and ride a horse, but ponies can be ornery and not very well trained (though they sure are cute—trust me, I have one).

I bet you can guess what draft horses were bred for. Yes, work, and lots of it. Their large size and massive strength meant they were great at carrying heavy loads. Historically, draft horses were used for farming, logging, and even for military battles.

Light horses are a diverse group ranging in color, size, and build. These breeds were historically bred for riding and can be used for all different types of sport and work, from ranching to showing. This group shares speed, endurance, high energy, and agility.

Gaited horses have been bred for riding and are known for their smooth gait. They are also called saddlebreds. They always have one foot in contact with the ground, which means less bouncing around for the rider. Historically, they were ridden long distances, and they are still popular today.

Warmbloods originated in Europe from the breeding of a draft horse with a light horse. What did they get? A midweight horse! This crossbreeding gives warmbloods good bone mass and strong muscles, yet they also have incredible speed and agility. Today, they excel at most things, especially dressage and jumping.

Now that you know the five types of horses, let's discuss my favorite specific breeds.

Thoroughbred

The Thoroughbred horse is known for its speed. In horse racing, they are considered the fastest horses in the world. They are also known for their agility and are high-spirited. It is this intensity that makes them want to run fast and compete, which can make them difficult for the average person to handle. Thoroughbreds can be a variety of colors, but are usually black, chestnut, gray, or bay. They are known for their long, lean, muscular, athletic build. Thoroughbreds are not only used for racing, but also for other disciplines, including show jumping, polo, and dressage.

Clydesdale

The Clydesdale is a large draft breed that originated in Scotland. They are massive horses, on average more than 6 feet tall! They can weigh around 2,000 pounds when fully grown and weigh more than an adult human male when born. When their feet are fully grown, they are the size of a dinner plate. You surely don't want your foot stepped on by one. Clydesdales are often reddish brown, bay, or chestnut in color, with some white, and always have feathering, which is hair coming off the lower quarter of their legs. Can you guess what Clydesdales are used for? If you guessed that they are workhorses, you are correct. Historically, they plowed fields and pulled heavy loads. They are known not only for their strength, but also for their willingness and gentle nature. Today, Clydesdales are occasionally ridden, but are mostly used to pull carts and wagons. Other popular large draft breeds are the Percheron, the Shire, and the Belgian draft horse.

Morgan

The Morgan horse was one of the earliest breeds developed in the United States. They are known for their compactness, strength, good temperament, and versatility. They usually have solid coats in dark colors. They are a relatively small breed, but with strong legs. They are well muscled, compact, and have a muscular, arched neck. They are used in a variety of activities, including Western and English riding, driving, endurance events, and pleasure riding. Because of their friendly, easygoing personalities, they are known as a great family and beginner horse. Morgan horses are known for the Morgan stretch, a stance where the horse stands with its front legs stretched out in front and back legs stretched out behind it. (As mentioned earlier, my first horse was a Morgan named Duchess!)

Arabian

Arabian horses are known as the oldest of all known horse breeds. They originated in the Arabian Peninsula and are one of the most easily distinguishable breeds in the world. They have a relatively small head and compact body. They are known for their gentleness and stamina. They have a "floating," graceful trot. Today, Arabian horses are used for endurance events, jumping, polo, and pleasure riding. In fact, the Arabian horse was used in the development of the Thoroughbred, quarter horse, and Morgan breeds!

Hanoverian

The Hanoverians are the oldest and most popular of the warmblood breeds. They originated in Germany and are known for their size, grace, and power. Originally used for farm work, this athletic breed can now be seen in the Olympics, winning sporting events such as jumping and dressage. Their well-proportioned, muscular bodies give them a ground-covering walk, a floating trot, and a powerful, rhythmic canter. Though they are known for their size and strength, they are also known for their calm disposition.

QUARTER HORSES BY MILLY

The reason I love quarter horses is that I have a lot of personal experience with them, they are good for ranch work, and I know a lot about them.

Quarter horses are good working horses. They work hard and stick with it. A quarter horse got its name because it can run a quarter mile very fast without stopping. Quarter horses are also calm. People use quarter horses for many jobs on a ranch, including fixing fences and corrals and gathering, roping, and sorting cattle. Quarter horses are very good at gathering cattle. They are sturdy and fast. They are interested in the cows. You have to have a speedy quarter horse that loves to run and do tight turns when you gather cattle.

I have my own quarter horse named Peaches. I run barrels on her at the rodeo. I also gather cattle on her and am learning to rope off of her. Peaches loves to run, and she is really, really fast!

Horse Colors

Horses come in different colors and can have many different markings. I love seeing all the different varieties of colors and patterns. The four basic colors of horses are bay (a warm brown-colored horse with black legs and mane, which may or may not have a stripe of white on its face), brown, black, and chestnut. The coloring of all other horses is simply a variation on these four colors, often with accents of white.

Why is white not listed as one of the primary horse colors? Well, a truly white horse is very rare indeed and will probably have very pink skin, a pink nose, and lighter eyes. Gray horses are actually born dark gray or even black, and they get lighter with age, while truly white horses are born white. Perhaps this is where the saying

"a horse of a different color" actually came from. White markings on a horse at birth usually stay white. Here are a few of the more common colorings of horses:

- **Bay:** Dark brown to a lighter brown body, but the mane, tail, and legs are black
- **Black:** Black eyes, hooves, skin, and coat
- **Brown:** Dark brown coat that can look almost black
- **Chestnut or Sorrel:** Reddish-brown with no black; the mane and tail are the same color as the body
- **Pinto:** Multicolored horse, usually with white and black or brown
- **Roan:** White hairs eventually intermix with the other colors, but the heads stay the original color

Communication and Behavior

You might have heard of horse whispering. Does this mean actually whispering to a horse? No. It is about deeply understanding a horse's body language, then using your own body language to effectively communicate with the horse.

A Horse's Senses

Because horses are prey animals, they have very acute senses in order to detect and escape potential danger and communicate with one another and their world. Like us, horses use their sense of sight, smell, hearing, touch, or taste to make decisions about their bodies.

SIGHT

Horses have eyes eight times larger than ours, which are set along the sides of their heads, whereas ours are facing forward. We can see directly in front and are slightly aware of things beside us, but a horse can see clearly almost all the way around itself, except directly in front of or directly behind itself. This is why one of the safety rules is to never approach from directly in front of or behind the horse; it might not see you, which could scare it and cause it to react.

SMELL

Horses have an acute sense of smell that is better than humans'. They use this sense to detect and identify other horses, humans, approaching predators, and, of course, food. It is said that horses can smell fear. Could that really be true? Yes, it is. When we experience emotions, we sweat, which releases certain chemicals that horses can detect. For this same reason, horses can identify individual humans and remember them by their smell. Wild, huh?

HEARING

Some humans claim to be able to wiggle their ears. Well, horses can actually turn their ears forward and backward. Their large, pointed ears express how they are feeling and what they are focusing on. Their ears are incredibly flexible, large, and open, enabling them to detect possible danger sounds and hear what is going on in the herd. If a horse's ears are facing toward you, it is focusing on you, knows you are there, and is curious about you. Conversely, if a horse's ears are pinned backward against its head, it means do not approach. This is the horse's nonverbal warning to stay away.

TOUCH

The horse's sense of touch is one of its most developed senses. A horse can feel a fly land on a single piece of hair on its body. The most sensitive parts of the horse are the nose, mouth, whiskers, lips, and ears. Touch is important not only between horses, but also between horses and humans. In fact, this highly developed sense of touch is perhaps the most important piece of communication in the human and horse relationship. Touch is the primary sense used in horse training. When we are riding, we are using our seat (yes, our bum), our legs, and our heels, along with the reins that are attached to the bit inside the horse's mouth, to let the horse know what we want it to do. It is through specific touch and pressure that we tell the horse to move forward, move left, move right, or stop.

TASTE

A horse's sense of taste is closely related to its sense of smell. Like us, horses have taste buds that detect sweet, salty, bitter, and acidic tastes. Their taste buds are located mainly on the roof of their mouths and the back of their tongues. Having these taste buds helps horses detect what they should and shouldn't eat. This sense was most likely developed to prevent them from eating large amounts of poisonous plants when grazing in the wild, which are often bitter and do not taste great. If you watch a horse eat, you will observe it picking and choosing what grass or hay it prefers to eat and avoiding what it does not like.

Body Language

Reading a horse's body language is one of the most important parts of learning about these animals. Horses use their body language to show us how they feel. We can read it to see if it is safe to approach or not. How is the horse's overall body language? Is it calm with its head down? Does it appear relaxed? Or does it look tense and anxious, throwing its head around, pawing at the ground, or seeming threatening?

Pretty much all of our communication with horses happens without vocalizing. In fact, for the most part communication between horses happens silently too. Therefore, if we learn to understand a horse's body language and tune into its natural behavior, we will be much better at understanding what the horse is trying to communicate to us.

Each horse communicates slightly differently, but there are basics to help you understand if a horse is relaxed, happy, in pain, or anxious. Let's take a closer look at some basic emotions and how a horse may communicate its feelings.

I'M NOT FEELING WELL

A horse that is not feeling well can often be standing alone, away from other horses, with its head hanging low. It may seem lethargic and not bright or alert. Its facial expression can be almost like a grimace with its eyes downcast. A sick or injured horse may be laying down and reluctant to get up. It can show pain by being aggressive or pawing or kicking at its belly. Should you notice this abnormal behavior, take precautions and call your vet.

I'M HAPPY

Horses can certainly express contentment and happiness. You can tell a lot by looking at your horse's head. A content horse has relaxed nostrils and lips, and a horse's mouth can curve in a way that is almost like a subtle smile. A horse's ears will always be pointing up. Their direction will change depending on what it is listening to, but in general, if relaxed, the ears will not be pinned back or rigidly pointed forward. When a horse is relaxed, its body should be calm, with no pawing or anxious movements. Even a horse's tail can indicate if it is content. A content horse's tail will swing freely or just be hanging straight. A back foot may also be folded under.

I'M STRESSED

A stressed horse usually communicates its emotion through clear body language. An anxious horse likely has its head held high, with flared nostrils and rigid, forward-facing ears. Horses often poop when stressed, and may also pace restlessly, run, neigh, snort, and paw at the ground with their front legs.

I DON'T LIKE THIS

A horse that doesn't like something will let us know through its body language. Swishing its tail aggressively, shaking and raising its head, pursing its lips, opening its eyes wide, tensing its body, stomping its feet, and shifting its weight are all indications that the horse doesn't like something.

Our Behavior

Now we need to look at our own behavior around horses and what we are communicating to them whether we mean to or not. Our own natural history has prepared us to be predators, and that is how horses see us. We hunted, gathered, and were more or less at the top of the food chain. Our eyes are at the front of our heads, our ears are small, and our hands move quickly and randomly, which can startle a horse who is looking for any reason to be frightened. When we are around horses, it is our responsibility to help them understand we are not dangerous. This is why we must be extremely aware of our own behavior and what our movement and body language is communicating to the horse.

Now that you know horses can be easily frightened, it is important to know just how to reassure them. When first approaching a horse,

remember they see more clearly sideways so that is how you should approach, from the side, moving slowly and calmly while talking to them in a soft voice. You can then hold your hand out below their nose so they can smell you. This is the very first step in communicating and building a trustworthy relationship with a horse.

Disrespectful or Dangerous Animals

Horses like to constantly test humans just as they would test their herd hierarchy in the wild. Horses exhibit a few common behaviors when trying to test or disrespect their human counterpart. These things must be disciplined and corrected in order to show the horse that the human is the boss. Working with a professional teacher will help you identify and work with the horse to correct these behaviors. Horses that are misbehaving can do things like crowd your personal space, walk too slow or fast while being led, try to graze while being ridden, bump into you, refuse to be tied up or loaded in a trailer, become aggressive when eating, or not listen to direction while riding.

Though horses aren't predators and don't eat humans, they can be extremely dangerous. Much of the risk can be mitigated with proper equipment, proper management, and safety protocols. However, no matter how many precautions we take, or how well the horse is trained, horses can still be unpredictable and accidents can happen. In fact, recent studies say it is more dangerous to ride a horse than a motorcycle because there is always the risk of being thrown from the horse and getting a head injury. For this reason, you should always wear a helmet, and learn horse safety with a professional.

This section about communication and behavior has given you a lot of information to process, but it is important that you understand it thoroughly. This information is the foundation of your relationship with any horse and will affect and influence every aspect of the interactions you have with horses throughout your life. This is just the start of learning the subtleties of your body

BASIC SAFETY TIPS

- Wear sturdy boots with a heel and long pants.
- To begin with, only approach a horse when supervised or with a professional.
- Pay attention to your own movements and the horse's movements at all times.
- There should be no running, screaming, or fast movements around a horse.
- Always be calm and use a friendly, soft voice.
- Always alert the horse to your presence by talking to it.
- Never stand directly behind a horse, as that is its blind spot.
- If your horse gets spooked, talk to it in a calm manner. If you are calm, it will feel safe.
- Always stay standing around a horse (no squatting, kneeling, or sitting down).
- Unless you are interacting with the horse, stay 10 feet away in case it moves quickly.
- Never approach a threatening horse.
- Remember that some horses may never learn to respect humans, and these horses can be incredibly dangerous. They are only for experienced professionals to handle.

movements and those of your horse to enable you to more easily communicate with one another. Like people, each horse is different, and every situation is different, so learning to properly respond to the horse takes a lifetime of practice and learning.

Basic Horse Care

Caring for a horse is labor-intensive and can be costly. Caring for horses takes a lot of time, patience, energy, and dedication. Horses need to be fed twice a day and their water checked daily.

They need to be exercised regularly, their stalls need to be mucked, they need to be groomed and fly sprayed when needed, their hooves need to be cleaned and checked—and this is just the beginning of their care. Due to the time and energy horses take, people say owning a horse becomes a lifestyle or a way of life. This basically means that owning and caring for a horse will, in fact, change your life. So, before you even think about getting a horse of your own, be sure to learn as much as you can about horses through books and by taking riding lessons. Let's explore what horse ownership entails!

Suitable Living Conditions

Horses need a large, safely fenced area and a shelter or barn where they can escape the heat, sun, rain, snow, wind, and even bugs. There should be a flat area for the horse to stand and rest. The area where your horse stays must be kept clean and dry.

Suitable Feed

Horses need a regular supply of food and clean water. Their food consists of hay or grass and sometimes grains, which are given two times a day.

COST OF HORSE CARE

Studies show that the average cost of owning a horse is approximately $4,000 a year, with costs only going up. Of course, this can vary from place to place based on whether you board your horse or keep it at home.

Maybe there are ways of getting creative in order to keep costs down. Perhaps you could find a local horse barn and work there in exchange for lessons or horse boarding. Or you could lease a horse, which means sharing the cost and care with someone else. Do you have a big field with grass? If so, you could cut down feed costs because you already have a pasture.

A full-grown horse can eat around 20 pounds of food a day and drink at least 8 gallons of water. Surprisingly, horses have sensitive digestive tracts and basic horse-feeding knowledge must be learned and practiced in order to maintain the horse's proper weight and nutritional needs.

Suitable Routine

Your daily routine will depend on many factors, such as where your horse is kept, whether inside at night or let out during the day, but a proper routine of care is a must. This includes exercise and attention for your horse. Horses need anywhere from 20 minutes to 2 hours of movement a day. Remember that in the wild, horses would be moving the majority of their day, looking for food, following the herd, and interacting with other horses within the herd. Like humans, a healthy horse needs to be physically and mentally stimulated.

Grooming

Grooming certainly helps your horse look nicer, but, more important, it is a crucial and pleasant way to bond with your horse. While grooming your horse, you may notice something you didn't before, perhaps a cut, a rub mark from the saddle, or a stone in its shoe. Grooming is an important part of your horse's overall health.

Picking a horse's hooves is very important in order to clear out any rocks or debris. It is also important to clean the hooves in order to detect any abnormalities like cracking or a loose horseshoe. You should start doing this with a professional until you get the process down to avoid hurting yourself or the horse.

Equipment

In order to have a safe situation with your horse, you will need proper equipment that fits your horse correctly—a halter, lead line, feed tub, fly mask, and possibly a fly sheet, and if you live where it is cold, a warm, waterproof blanket, brushes and hoof equipment, and riding equipment, including a helmet, saddle pad, saddle, and cinch and bridle with reins and a bit properly attached.

Health

Your horse's health is a priority, and there are many great books on this topic alone. There are some things you can do, and some only your vet

---

GROOMING TOOLS AND INSTRUCTIONS

Tools

- Curry comb
- Hard brush
- Soft brush
- Mane and tail comb
- Horse hoof pick

To Groom a Horse

1. Use the curry comb to loosen dirt and remove shedding hair by brushing in circles.
2. Use the hard brush to remove excess dirt and hair on your horse's body by using strokes going in the direction of your horse's hair where you already brushed in step 1.
3. Use the soft brush to smooth your horse's hair by using strokes going with your horse's hair after doing steps 1 and 2.
4. Gently brush your horse's face with the hard or soft brush.
5. Use the mane and tail comb to brush through your horse's mane and tail. Always stand to the side of your horse, holding its tail, while brushing it.

To Pick a Horse's Hooves

1. Stand directly next to your horse facing toward its back end. Stand next to the horse's shoulder when cleaning its front hooves and its hip when cleaning its back hooves.
2. Run your hand down along its leg. Depending on how cooperative your horse is, you may need to lean your shoulder into the horse (not too hard) and assist in picking up the hoof.
3. As the horse lifts its hoof, hold right above the hoof at what is called the coronary band.
4. Use the hoof pick to remove debris from around the hoof but not on the "frog," which is the fleshy triangle in the middle of the hoof. Make sure you are always picking away from yourself.
5. When dirt, rocks, and any other debris have been removed, gently help place the horse's hoof back on the ground.

Making Horse Treats with Olivia

Olivia, Emma's daughter, loves to make animal treats because she can reward her animals when they have done something good, especially during training. Plus, she likes to bake, so that's a bonus. Just don't give your horses too many treats because they can sometimes be sugar bombs. Even though the treats described here contain only the natural sugars found in plants, it's not great for your horse to have too many at once. The following treats were created with Olivia's mini pony and pygmy goat in mind. She hopes you enjoy making them too!

CARROT AND APPLE ICE LOLLIES

Makes 1 ice lolly

Carrot and apple ice lollies are perfect for summer days. They're super easy to make, and ponies (and goats) love them!

1 apple
1 carrot
Apple juice
Filtered water

1. Cut up the apple and carrot. Place them in a freezer-safe container, like a small Tupperware bowl or ziplock bag. Pour in enough apple juice to cover the cut-up apples and carrots, then top with water and freeze.
2. Give one to your horse or pony on a hot day!

CARROT AND APPLE COOKIES

Makes 15 (2-inch) cookies

These cookies are a fun treat and animals love them!

1 cup shredded carrots
1 cup rolled oats
½ cup applesauce
2 tablespoons molasses
½ cup ground flaxseed
1 tablespoon coconut oil
1 teaspoon ground cinnamon
1 teaspoon sea salt

1. Preheat the oven to 350°F. Add all the ingredients to a large bowl and stir until well combined.
2. Form the dough into small 1-inch balls with your hands. Place the balls on a parchment-lined baking sheet and bake for 20 to 25 minutes, until they are golden brown.
3. Let the cookies cool completely before giving them to your horse or pony.
4. Store in an airtight container in the fridge.

can do, to ensure your horse stays healthy. Your horse must see a vet at least two times a year for vaccines and checkups. The vet will not only help prevent your horse from getting diseases, but also check its overall health. Horses also need to be wormed once a month to help reduce any parasites. Knowing your horse's healthy weight and making sure it is not overweight or underweight is also very important for its health. Horse owners learn quickly that if a horse can hurt itself, it probably will, so be prepared for your horse to injure itself, hopefully not seriously. Realistically, I expect at least two emergency vet visits a year.

Horseshoeing

Yes, horses wear shoes, and they even need their toenails clipped. A person who trims horses' hooves and puts on their shoes is called a farrier. First, the farrier trims the horse's hoof wall and then makes a shoe to fit on the bottom of the hoof to protect it while the horse is walking. Horseshoes are usually made of metal and nailed into the hoof wall. Trimming its hooves and putting on shoes does not cause the horse any pain when done correctly. Horses need to be shoed approximately every 6 weeks. If you live where there is ice and snow, you may need to have winter shoes put on your horse. Like snow tires, they have studs. Not all horses need shoes, but all horses do need their hooves trimmed.

Companions

Horses are social and need companions. Remember, in the wild, horses live in herds. These social interactions are very important for a horse's mental health and well-being. If you can only have one horse, I recommend that it have a friend that is another species, like a sheep, goat, or even a mini horse. Yes, horses can definitely bond with these other species.

Growing up, we started out with one horse, and we had a companion sheep. The horse and sheep were so bonded that the sheep would follow us when we rode in the fields behind our house. They were basically inseparable.

Horses who spend time together can become so deeply bonded that they do not want to be separated. This is called herd-bound or sour-buddy behavior. When this happens, it helps to separate the horses so they are still able to see one another but aren't together. You can then slowly move the horses farther from each other if you have the room. When you ride, you need to be the boss and get the horse's mind focused on the task at hand instead of on the fact that it is missing its buddy. This behavior can be frustrating or even dangerous if the horse is experiencing intense separation anxiety. Always stay patient and calm, and ask a professional for help if needed.

Next Step

So you want your own horse? I hope this chapter has given you some basic information to begin, or continue, your horse journey. These magnificent creatures can change your life. I recommend taking consistent horseback-riding lessons for at least 2 years before even considering getting your own horse.

As you can see, horses take a lot of care, dedication, and financial commitment. Before getting a horse, it's a good idea to make a list of everything you would need to take care of it and a list of daily chores you would have to do, and then carefully consider the decision. Owning a horse is a very big responsibility, and you want to make sure the choice is right for you and your family. Please see the Resources list in the back of this book for recommended reading, and please find a professional to help if you want to begin riding. Happy trails to you!

Ranching

STEPHANIE MATHIS

Stephanie Mathis seems superhuman. She is one of the grittiest, toughest, yet kindest people around. It is with her heart of gold and incredible work ethic that she—along with her husband, Jeff, and their children, Lewie (14) and Zane (12)—manages two ranches totaling more than 26,000 acres. Together they have lots and lots of cattle to manage, as well as a dozen horses and eight dogs to feed every day. Can you imagine what running such a big ranch is like?

Stephanie has been a cattle rancher her entire life (39 years). She was born into a cattle-ranching family and has been living and working with cattle since the cradle. Her family on her mother's side has been cattle ranching for more than 150 years, ever since the gold rush in Northern California. Her husband is also from a multigenerational ranching family, and they hope their children will carry on their families' tradition.

A day in the life of a rancher is very hard to pin down because it changes daily. During the busy times, when the ranch is branding and shipping cattle, Stephanie's day involves getting up at 4:00 a.m., making breakfast for her family, and prepping lunch for the entire working crew. Then she saddles a horse and, by sunrise (sometimes earlier), rides out to gather cattle with the crew, which could mean anywhere from 2 to 6 hours of intense horseback riding. Once the crew brings the cattle into the corrals, they sort, rope, brand, deworm, and vaccinate them, which is very intense physically. Stephanie is also in charge of feeding the work crew. Depending on the circumstances, this could be a casserole at her house or grilled steaks with a couple of sides and dessert if they're eating in the field. After eating, everything has to be cleaned up and the cattle have to be put away or loaded on a truck. Once the cattle are managed, Stephanie heads home to clean, put everything away, and prep for dinner. Her children are then picked up and taken to their various activities, and chores are done. Dinner is served, and then Stephanie falls into bed.

When it is not branding or shipping season, her schedule is a lot more flexible, but living on a ranch means there is always something more to do. She gets up at 5:00 a.m., mostly so she can get a few minutes to herself. After getting her kids to the bus at 7:15 a.m., her workday starts. Generally, Stephanie and her husband discuss which job is the highest priority the night before, and then they figure out how to get it done. She is also in charge of maintaining all

the mowing and fire abatement, wild artichoke and weed abatement, slash pile burning, helping with fence building, and general odds and ends. Her kids' schedules, grocery shopping, and house chores play into how much she is able to accomplish each day, but at least she is never bored.

Stephanie says the best thing about her job is that she loves what she does. She loves to be outside and to work with the animals. She loves that no two days look the same. She loves that she gets to raise her two boys in the ranching lifestyle. The physicality and challenge of this lifestyle really appeals to her, and she knows she is contributing a quality food product to the world.

Conversely, the hardest part of her job is that the volatile beef markets are really difficult to manage financially and emotionally. The vilification of their product (beef) and lifestyle are sometimes difficult to endure. Her family works really hard for not a lot of money and holds open wild space in the world, and right now a lot of people are blaming them for greenhouse gases. While everyone can do their part to improve, she dislikes feeling like the scapegoat.

If anyone is interested in becoming a rancher, though, she says go for it! If possible, get an internship with a rancher or anyone who has livestock. If this is unavailable, take a class or read up on animal husbandry. Ranching can be a difficult industry to break into, but it is not impossible. Finding ground to lease is often done by word of mouth, so networking is really important when you're beginning to buy and run cattle. Remember, many days do not look like the glamorous version of ranching we see on television, so just persevere and keep working hard.

MULES

I have always loved mules. Their big ears, small feet, and the fact that they are a mix of two species have always fascinated me. When I was about 10 years old, we rode mules into the bottom of the Grand Canyon. The way they moved and were so stable on the narrow rock cliffs made them even more interesting to me. A few years later, my family and I headed into the mountains of Montana on a guided pack trip with a string of mules carrying all of our goods. This trip solidified my love of mules and my passion for the Wild West.

We currently have a mini mule named Darla. She is as cute as she is stubborn, but once she is on a job, she is focused and ready. We have a miniature pack set up for her, and once it's strapped on and loaded up, she is ready to head into the mountains. My dream is to get a mule to ride and then train it to be just as good as, if not better than, a horse. I hope you enjoy learning more about these awesome creatures in this chapter.

Natural History

As Charles Darwin once said, "The mule always appears to me a most surprising animal. That a hybrid should possess more reason, memory, obstinacy, social affection, powers of muscular endurance, and length of life than either of its parents seems to indicate that art has here outdone nature." It is thought that mules were the first-ever domesticated hybrid animal. A hybrid animal means that it is the offspring of two different species. In the case of the mule, it is the offspring of a male donkey and a female horse. Mules are unable to reproduce, so a mule cannot give birth to another mule. Their exact history is unknown, but we do know they were bred in ancient times. There are even archaeological records of paintings and carvings of mules in ancient Egypt. The mule was highly valued in ancient Greece and ancient Rome.

Mules are known for their incredible endurance and strength, and this is why they have historically been used as a beast of burden. They can carry heavy loads on their backs for long trips and were used to pull heavy equipment in fields and in mines.

In fact, the history of the United States is intertwined with mules, as the animals were instrumental in opening up the American West to colonial settlers. Mules were used not only for exploration of the West, but also in warfare, helping soldiers by pulling cannons and moving equipment. They hauled loads of rock, dirt, and building supplies to build roads, towns, and canals. They even helped build the railroads.

Because mules are half horse and half donkey, they often display the best traits of both animals. They are known to be hardier and more surefooted than horses, while being tamer, less stubborn, and smarter than donkeys. The mule is said to be hardy because it can withstand the elements—rain, snow, cold, and heat—better than a horse. Mules are thought to be more disease resistant than horses, and can even survive with less nutritious and rougher forage.

Mules can be a variety of colors. Their size can range from draft cross mules to mini mules and everything in between. In general, mules have shorter, thicker heads, narrower legs and hooves, and much bigger ears than horses.

Today, mules are less common in the United States than they used to be, but they are still used for the similar disciplines of farm work, riding, and packing.

Packing

Packing is when mules are used to carry goods on their backs. A mule train is when there is a line of mules tied together for a designated use, like to carry loads or riders. This can also be referred to as a string of mules. In a mule train, there is a head rider, either on a mule or horse, who is leading the string of mules. The head rider determines the order in which the mules are tied, which depends on each mule's personality, experience, and herd hierarchy.

Packing loads on a mule may sound easy, like you just throw the load up and tie it down tight, but in fact it is challenging, and there is quite an art to it. Special equipment is needed to ensure the mule stays comfortable and the packs don't slip.

KEY TERMS

MULE: Hybrid offspring of a male donkey and a female horse

HINNY: Offspring cross of a female donkey and a male horse

HYBRID: Offspring of two different species

JACK: A male donkey

JENNY: A female donkey

MARE: A female horse

The pack saddle, also known as a sawbuck, is a structure that goes on the mule's back. It has two wooden Xs and is attached to the mule by cinches. Panniers are hung on the sawbuck Xs and where the loads are packed. Loads can then be secured with canvas and rope. Specific knots and methods are used for tying the loads down, which is why it is necessary to learn these skills from a professional.

It is very important that load weights are balanced on either side of the mule. If not, this could throw the mule off-balance and cause it to fall and get injured. As they say, "May your load stay straight."

Packing and Horseback Riding

GRAHAM GOODFIELD

Los Padres Outfitters (LPO) is the premier packing and horseback-riding business in California's Santa Barbara County. This family-run business is led by Graham Goodfield, whose passion and knowledge of horses, mules, and packing is evident the moment you meet him. His wife, Hannah, and their two children, Darla and Hugo, are also involved in the daily operations of LPO. Together, they care for between 30 and 40 pack animals.

LPO offers not only beach and trail rides for beginners through experienced riders, but also full-service packing experiences into the Los Padres National Forest and beyond. Yes, you and your friends and family can head into the backcountry

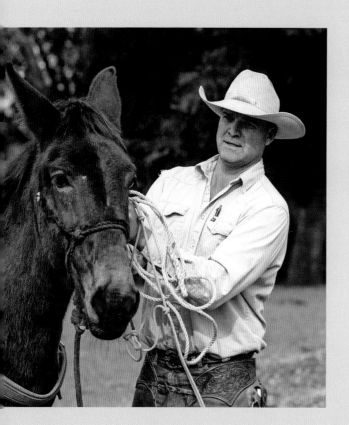

on horseback with a string of mules packed with your necessities—sleeping gear, clothes, water, and food—for days on end. Sounds like a fun and life-changing experience, right?

Graham took over LPO in 2005 after the company lost its founder, Tony Alvis, in the La Conchita landslide. Tony had started the outfit in the early 1970s. In the early 1990s, Graham began working for him on the ranch and riding with him into the backcountry. Tony taught him about how to pack mules, shoe horses, guide trips into the mountains, and basically just a lot about life in general. After high school, Graham decided to attend a packing and horsemanship school in Montana, and he ended up packing and guiding hunts and fishing trips in Idaho for 4 years. He attended college, then came home after graduation to go right back to work for Tony.

Graham's favorite part of his career is sharing the things he has learned about horses and showing folks the magic of the wilderness. He finds it truly rewarding to teach folks about horses and for them to see the horses working hard and being treated well. The horses and mules need a job; it's not a fair life for them otherwise. They're bred to work and have a purpose, and they deserve to be cared for accordingly.

Other than running a business in California, the hardest part of Graham's job is keeping the western traditions alive and surviving in an environment that doesn't always appreciate the work he does with horses and mules. Keeping access for equines is a constant concern. They're an important part of the history and foundation of not only our country, but also the world. Too many people have forgotten that part of our history. Also, Graham's job can be a logistical challenge that requires constant problem-solving 24 hours a day. Every day LPO has 40 or

more horses and mules to feed and attend to, phone calls to answer, rides to organize and pack for, and, finally, rides to take folks on. The job is certainly tough physically and demands a ton of time with the animals and equipment, trucks, and trailers, but Graham doesn't consider those factors work. If all he had to do was sweat, bleed a little, break a finger here and there, pack mules, and ride good horses all day long, that would be easy.

The good thing is that Graham has lots of good help, and he says when you ride off from the trailhead and into the mountains with a string of mules loaded with only the things you need for the next several days, all of those problems just fade away. Graham's favorite things to hear are all the great stories from people, especially kids, who have been on trips with him. Many of them return year after year. He has been told that these riding experiences are life

changing and have helped many people have a new appreciation for their family and friends.

If you're interested in learning how to pack, start from the bottom, and if you love it enough, you'll end up on top. There are lots of opportunities for those who want to learn; you just need to find them. The Sierra Nevada Mountains, for instance, are full of outfitters looking for eager help. You can find outfitter jobs in other states too, or you can go to a packing school to get a head start and get your boots in the door. No matter what, by working in the backcountry and with the animals, you'll learn something that will be useful in whatever path you choose.

If you'd like to book a pack trip with LPO, please visit lospadresoutfitters.com for more information. Graham would love to show you what you're missing and let you and your group of family or friends see the beauty of the California wilderness.

PIGS

Pigs are some of the funniest animals we have ever had. The way they move, squeal, love food, and run around always makes us laugh. Milly and June spend hours with our piggies, walking them, scratching them, feeding them, and playing with them. It is true—pigs spend their entire days wallowing in the mud or looking for food! Pigs are often raised as a food source—pork, bacon, ribs, and ham are all pig products. But pigs can also make great pets, and I have heard they can even be potty trained. Pigs are smart, dynamic creatures, each with its own personality and temperament. Some studies say pigs are even smarter than dogs.

No matter what your reason for wanting a pig, there are many things to learn before becoming a pig owner, including basic pig behavior and how to care for your piggies. There are many different pig breeds, and they come in a range of sizes and temperaments. If you are raising pigs as pets, you probably want to get a smaller breed. If you are raising them for meat, you probably want to get a big, fast-growing breed. I hope this chapter helps you understand more about pigs and whether they might be right for you and your family. Like they say, "A pig is good for the soul." Actually, I have never heard that saying, so I will claim it as my own!

Natural History

Scientists believe that pigs were domesticated about 10,000 years ago from wild boar. Our ancestors probably corralled the wild boar and eventually bred them for favorable traits like tameness and size, and that is where the more than 180 recognized pig breeds all originated. Pigs have stout bodies, short legs, thick skin, and usually bristles on their skin. Pigs have a great sense of smell but poor eyesight. They have split hooves and usually have tusks that help them dig and fight. Their snouts are sensitive and help them dig for food and root around. If you are interested in getting a pig, I urge you to learn more about pigs to see if they will be a good fit for you and your family. There are many great books and resources available. This chapter will hopefully help you understand pigs and their needs a bit more.

KEY TERMS

SWINE: A descendant of a wild boar

PIG FARMING: Raising and breeding of domestic pigs

HOG: A domesticated pig

SOW: An adult female pig

BOAR: A male pig

FARROW: A litter of piglets

PIGLET: A young pig

WATTLE: A finger-sized outgrowth of skin that can grow below the neck of certain pigs

WALLOW: When a pig creates an area, usually with water and mud, to roll around and cool off in

ROOTING: The instinctive pig behavior of using their snouts to find food, regulate their temperature, and communicate

Pig Breeds

You definitely need to know about pig breeds before selecting a pig that is right for you. A breed is defined as the animals (or plants) within a species that have specific characteristics and appearances, which have been selected over time through breeding. I think all piglets are adorable, and I usually want to take all of them home with me, but guess what? Pigs can range from around 50 pounds to around 2,000 pounds when full grown. You really wouldn't want to get the wrong breed and have your backyard pig outgrow your yard. Looking at a breed's origin (where it came from), its history, and what it has typically been used for will tell you a lot about what your pig will look like, how big it will be, and what its temperament will most likely be. Most pigs are bred either to be pets or for their meat or lard. I have had experience with a few different breeds and will share my favorites here.

Vietnamese Potbellied Pig

Perhaps the most common pet pig, these cuties can live between 12 and 18 years, and that is a long time! Potbellied pigs can range in size from 60 to 100 pounds when fully grown. The size of the adult parent pigs should be taken into consideration when determining how large a pig will be. Potbellied pigs are intelligent and need lots of social interaction; in fact, some people even litter train their pigs!

Kunekune

We love our Kunekunes. They are a small heritage breed that originated in New Zealand. They are known to be easy keepers and have short snouts, which means they root less. They can be black, white, brown, or ginger and can grow to be about 200 pounds. They make great pets, but they can also be used for lard and meat.

Hampshire

The Hampshire is a medium to large pig that is usually raised for meat. They are black with a white stripe around their bellies. They have long snouts and ears, and can grow to be 600 pounds. I wouldn't recommend this breed for a pet.

Red Wattle Pig

An American breed, the red wattle is named for its red color and for its wattles, which are finger-sized pieces of skin hanging off its face. These pigs are known for their docile temperament, but they can grow up to 1,000 pounds. They are great for meat, but not so great for a pet.

Communication and Behavior

Pigs have a complex communication system and social behaviors. Like other animals we have studied, pigs use their body language, voice, and scent to communicate with one another and with us. We cannot smell or recognize the meaning of their scent markers, so we rely on watching their body language and listening to their vocal cues to understand them.

A pig's body language, like a dog's or a horse's, can tell us many things. An upset or aggressive pig tends to have a stiff, upright body and may even be swinging its head from side to side. A happy pig will have a more relaxed body position, will usually be moving slower, and is often quieter. In general, a relaxed pig has lower vocal sounds, like grunting or snuffling. A stressed or unhappy pig has a higher-pitched scream. Have you ever heard a pig scream? It sounds like a crazed alien!

Basic Pig Care

When you bring a pig home, you want to make sure you are ready. Pigs have specific needs that must be met in order for them to feel comfortable and thrive. For example, did you know pigs can't really sweat, so they roll in the mud to keep themselves cool? Read on to learn more about how to take care of pigs.

Food and Water

A pig's day is based around food—finding it, eating it, then looking for more! They are usually more active in the mornings and evenings when, in the wild, they would be foraging for food. And yes, pigs do love to "pig out." They take much joy in eating and also in grunting and snorting while they eat. They are omnivores that can, and will, eat most things you feed them. They are surely the perfect garbage disposal.

Pigs need access to clean water at all times, but if their water tub is too big, they will try to climb into it and make a big mess. We have waterers where the pigs have to bite at a button and then water squirts into their mouths. Pigs are so smart that it only takes showing them where the water is coming out a few times before they do it themselves.

Shelter

Pigs need to regulate their temperature since they cannot sweat like we do. When it is hot, pigs wallow in mud in order to drop their body temperature. The mud not only helps them stay cool, but also keeps them from getting a sunburn or bitten by insects. Pigs also have to work to stay warm. If chilly, they need to huddle together to keep warm, and they often build nests out of hay to stay even warmer. Because of their temperature-regulating difficulties, it is important that pigs have good shelter and bedding, like hay, to help keep them out of the elements, whether it is too hot, too sunny, or too cold. Of course, they need a mud puddle too.

Fencing

Pigs use their incredibly strong snouts to root up soil when looking for food in the wild. This strong snout can also dig below the fence that is enclosing your pigs, and, believe me, pigs do love to roam free, especially through your garden. For this reason, you have to make sure you have appropriate and strong fencing when keeping pigs.

Attention

Pigs are social by nature, so you should have at least two pigs, have other animals nearby, or spend lots of time with your pig. Most pigs crave attention, and the more scratching, the better. We often scratch our pigs' backs with rakes, and they really love that. Pigs can also bond with other species. We had a pig that we raised with our dogs. He would go for walks and sleep with the dogs, and he seemed to love playing with them.

Vet Care

Like the other animals we have discussed so far, pigs need regular checkups and vaccinations by a vet. If you want a pig, call around to make sure there is a vet in your area who works with pigs.

Pig Farming

Pigs are actually very friendly and can be raised as pets, but the majority of pigs are raised for meat and lard. (Some are also raised for medicines, leather, and even fertilizer.) Obviously, the life of a pig on a large commercial farm is nothing like a pig raised as a pet or on a small farm. A commercial pig farm's primary purpose is to fatten the animals and keep breeding them. There are two types of commercial pig farms: factory farms and free-range farms. Factory farms usually have a

FUN PIG FACTS

← Pigs are among the smartest of the domesticated animals. Scientists say they are even smarter than dogs, and it is said that they are more trainable than dogs and cats. It has been proven that they have an incredible sense of direction and a very good memory. I have seen their great sense of direction firsthand and trained my pigs to come when they are called, which isn't too hard to do, especially if you have food.

← Pigs are relatively clean compared to other barnyard animals. If given enough room, pigs will go to the bathroom in an area away from where they spend most of their time, and even away from where they roll in the mud. Piglets even learn to do this just hours after being born.

← Pigs love belly rubs and scratches.

← Pigs are social and love being together.

← Pigs have dreams.

← Pigs have the best sense of smell of any barnyard animal.

← Some pigs are even used by law enforcement officers to sniff out drugs and weapons.

massive number of pigs that are kept indoors and fed mainly grain. Mothers and babies are usually confined to very small enclosures, and antibiotics are fed to the pigs regularly to prevent diseases caused by overcrowding.

A free-range farm allows the pigs to go outdoors and have room to roam. This means mothers and babies can lead a much more natural life. Free-range pigs are often fed a wider variety of foods and are able to root and exhibit natural pig behavior.

I am not a vegetarian. Since I do choose to eat pork, I either eat our own raised pigs or purchase local or free-range pork so I know the pigs have had a more natural life. I think it is important when buying pork products to know where the pork is coming from so you can be sure the pigs were raised humanely. Farmers markets are a great place to find small-farmed pig products and to be able to talk directly to the farmer who raised the pig. In stores, look for products that say "Certified Humane" or "Certified Animal Welfare Approved."

Next Step

Pigs are fun to have around, but they do require special care, management, and time. If you are interested in owning a pig of your own, see the Resources list in the back of this book for more reading material or, even better, find someone who owns a pig and ask them questions.

Goat and Sheep Care

RUBY WITCHER

Ruby Witcher is 15 years old, and she began working with animals when she was just 9 years old. Taking care of sheep, goats, and other animals is part of her daily routine, and she knows more about them than most adults. With the help of her mentor, Larry, Ruby has learned to shear sheep, castrate ruminants, milk animals, trim hooves, administer medicines to the whole herd, lead young llamas around the pasture, and even build fences and pens.

The daily care of goats and sheep is pretty similar. The most important job is feeding the animals, which Ruby says is pretty satisfying, as they get so excited when they see someone coming to the gate. Ruby feeds them alfalfa hay twice a day, and the sheep get to graze the pasture between hay feedings. She also makes sure they have plenty of clean, cool water to drink. She cleans their pens once a week and trims their hooves twice a year.

Ruby fell in love with farm animals as soon as she was introduced to caring for them at school. Her

kindergarten teacher, Miss Sally, brought a baby goat to school for the students to bottle-feed. Her love for animals has been growing ever since. She especially loves goats and sheep. She loves the goats' quirky, silly, and curious temperaments. South African Boer goats are her favorite farm animals because they are so goofy and loving. When they are kids, they are so cute and sweet. She loves to watch them jump, dance around the pen, and climb on their moms or even on her. They have so much personality, and they are so clever. Some of Ruby's sheep are more timid, but if they were bottle-fed, they will eagerly come to the gate for some affection.

A big challenge when it comes to caring for animals is the commitment. The animals are reliant on Ruby and her family for food, so even if she feels tired and wants to sleep in on the weekend, she needs to help feed them. But the biggest challenge is predator control, which includes keeping the goats safe from coyotes trying to catch an easy meal. Ruby thinks it is really sad to lose an animal to coyotes.

When she was in fourth grade, Ruby joined the Santa Ynez 4-H program, where she learned to show a market goat, dairy goat, and market lamb at the county fair. For young people interested in learning how to care for farm animals, she recommends joining a 4-H program in your area. She learned a lot through the opportunities 4-H offered, such as doing presentations for school groups and showing animals at the expo and county fair. Plus, it was fun to learn about animals from other kids her age, as well as from experienced adults. Watching other kids handling farm animals helped her realize she could do it too. She loves competing for ribbons, but she loves learning how to care for the animals even more. As for the future, Ruby dreams of one day having her own ranch where she can work with all of her favorite animals.

DOGS

I was lucky enough to grow up with a black Labrador named Sam. He had to be one of the world's best and most loyal dogs, and he followed us wherever we went. He always stayed by us on our many adventures in the woods behind our house. When our cat had kittens, Sam would go into the barn and "babysit" by letting the kittens play all over him while the mom cat slipped away to take a break. When she came back, he'd head back outside.

When Sam passed away of old age, it was a pain I hadn't yet experienced, but I was so lucky to have those years with him, and those memories helped ease the pain of losing him. I have always had a dog in my life, a buddy to be there through thick and thin, who never judges me and is always overjoyed to see me. I am incredibly thankful for the dogs in my life.

Natural History

It has been scientifically proven that every single dog that exists today descended from the wolf. It's hard to believe that little Chihuahuas are related to wolves, right? In fact, it is believed that wolves were the first animals to be domesticated by humans, as well as the only large carnivore ever domesticated. There is some debate about exactly when the wolf began buddying up to humans, but science points to about 14,000 to 29,000 years ago. It is believed that wolves followed nomadic peoples and ate the scraps and carcasses left behind by hunters. Eventually, the tamer wolves became a very important alarm system for early humans. The wolves' highly sensitive hearing and sight allowed them to see and hear things before the humans could, and their barking alerted the humans to possible danger.

Eventually, through trial and error, humans bred specific traits in the animals, choosing which traits were most important to them. For example, when humans began farming, the dogs that had the strongest instincts to herd and guard were bred together. Once humans figured out they could pick specific traits, they were off to the races, creating every kind of dog from the Chihuahua to the Great Dane and so many in between. Some dogs were bred to hunt and retrieve, some to guard and protect, some (like terriers) to help get rid of small pests like rats, and some to look regal and be pampered. Today, there are about 350 recognized breeds in the world, all with their very own characteristics and traits.

Dogs have worked their way into human lives and hearts. Though many dogs still have very important jobs to perform, today the sole purpose of most dogs is to be a faithful, adoring companion, and many people have very meaningful relationships with their dogs.

Dog Breeds

When you are considering getting a dog, the natural history of the breed or mix of breeds must be considered. Is it a herder, a hunter, or a dog who needs a job? Knowing this information will give you an idea about the general behavior of the dog, and then you can figure out if that type of dog fits

KEY TERMS

CANINE: Relating to dogs, the group of carnivorous mammals that includes the wolf, domestic dog, jackal, fox, and coyote

CARNIVORE: An animal that eats primarily meat

PREDATOR: An animal that hunts other animals for food

PACK ANIMAL: An animal that lives and hunts in a group

BREED: A stock of animal that has been bred and selected for certain distinguishable qualities

PEDIGREE: A register that records a dog's breeding and ancestry

MUTT OR MIXED BREED: A dog descended from several breeds that is unidentifiable as a certain breed

WORKING DOG: A breed of canines that has a specific job and the instincts to do the job

FERAL DOG: A dog that has not been raised by humans, does not live with humans, and finds its own food; feral dogs are usually scared of people

STRAY DOG: A dog that is not currently being cared for by a human

BEHAVIOR: The way a dog acts and reacts

OBEDIENCE: Submission to authority, or how well one listens to authority

AGILITY: A sport in which a trainer asks a dog to move quickly and easily through a set of obstacles

TEMPERAMENT: A person's or animal's habitual behavior

SCENT CELLS: The basic building blocks of life; specific scent cells are used for smelling

WHELPING: A female dog giving birth

Border Collie

A working breed known for its intelligence, endurance, and herding skills, the border collie is a great dog if you have animals you need to herd, or if you have a very active lifestyle. They were developed in England and Scotland for herding sheep, and they love to work. They are medium-size dogs, weighing around 45 pounds. They are amazingly loyal dogs, but they do require lots of mental and physical stimulation, care, and appropriate training.

Greyhound

Found in the hound group, greyhounds are bred for their speed in dog racing. Greyhounds are intelligent, quiet, and loving, and make great family pets. They have short hair and long legs, and weigh around 65 pounds. They become very attached to their owners and can have separation anxiety when left alone. They have little body fat, so they do require some extra attention. Check a local greyhound rescue if you are interested in this breed.

Labrador Retriever

Labs are in the sporting group and are known as affectionate, loving, and great family dogs. They are very active and athletic dogs; they originated in England and were used to retrieve animals when hunting, which means they like to run. They are intelligent and trainable, but you must put your time in to train them properly. They can weigh around 65 pounds, and their colors include black, yellow, and chocolate brown.

Shih Tzu

A toy breed known for its long hair, big eyes, and short snout, this little dog is also beloved for its sweet personality. They make great pets, as they are friendly, calm, and able to adapt to different environments. They average about 12 pounds. They are social dogs that need lots of attention and care, and they are not known for their obedience. The breed originated in Asia.

your lifestyle. Making an educated decision on the breed, type, size, and temperament of a dog can help ensure it is the right dog for your family.

Bernese Mountain Dog

A working dog, the Bernese mountain dog originated in the Swiss Alps and was used as a farm dog. They are a large breed and often weigh more than 100 pounds. They have specific markings, and generally have long black hair, a white blaze and chest, brown eyebrows and feet, and brown around the mouth. They are known for their sweet, loving personalities and make great family dogs. They are very social dogs that need lots of human attention.

Dog Types

Dogs can be broken down into seven basic categories. Of course, there are so many different and unique dogs, from purebreds to mutts, but this is a place to start.

Working, Service, and Herding Dogs

This group covers many different kinds of dogs that can be trained to perform many different jobs. These dogs enjoy their jobs. Within this group are dogs that were bred for herding animals, helping farmers round up sheep, cattle, and other farm animals. The border collie and the Australian cattle dog are two of the many types of herding dogs. Other dogs, such as the German shepherd, were bred to be guard dogs, and now are often used by law enforcement. This group also includes guide dogs for the visually impaired, such as Labrador retrievers and other service dogs. Also in this group are rescue dogs, such as the Saint Bernard, the breed we often see in pictures of snowy mountains with a cask under its neck. Bernese mountain dogs are included in this group too, as they were bred to pull carts, and huskies, as they pull sleds over difficult snow terrain.

Sporting Dogs

These dogs are generally used to hunt and retrieve. Dogs in this group include setters, such as the Irish setter; retrievers, such as the golden retriever; and pointers, such as the German pointer.

Hounds

These dogs could actually be part of the sporting dogs group because they, too, are used for hunting. They hunt by scent or by sight. This group includes beagles, greyhounds, and even dachshunds.

Terriers

These dogs are very active. They are usually smaller dogs who are natural hunters, and they were bred to find small animals and remove them from their dens. This group includes Airedales and other dogs with "terrier" as part of their name, such as cairn terriers and Jack Russell terriers.

Toy Dogs

These dogs are sort of like living stuffed animals. They are bred more for companionship than anything else. They can be as small as 1½ pounds, and they are very alert and responsive to their owners. This group includes Pekingese, pugs, and Chihuahuas.

Non-Sporting Dogs

These dogs are bred mainly for companionship and don't show any of the purposes listed in the other groups. This group includes poodles (thought to be one of the smartest dogs), bulldogs, and bichons.

Miscellaneous

When you can't fit a dog into any other group, it belongs to this group, which includes the Havanese, Korean Jindo, and many others.

Communication and Behavior

Dogs use their bodies to express and communicate their feelings and intentions. They use their posture, ears, tails, voice, and facial expressions to communicate to one another and to us. Understanding a dog's body language is very important, not only for your safety, but also as the first step in building a healthy relationship with a dog.

Stance

The way a dog stands and positions itself and how it distributes its weight can tell you what its mood or intention is. A dog that tucks its ears and tail and lowers its body to the ground is frightened, while a dog standing upright and getting ready to move forward could simply be curious or could be feeling aggressive.

Hair

Raised hackles (hair standing up on the dog's back) clearly means that the dog is excited. This paired with a growl or an aggressive stance means the dog is feeling protective or angry.

Voice

Dogs, like their wolf ancestors, are pack animals, and communication within the pack is incredibly important. As dog owners, we become part of the pack, so we must be able to "speak dog." There are many different types of vocalizations dogs use to communicate with one another and with us. A whine is a puppy's distress call when it's hungry or alone, but a whine from an adult dog usually expresses fear or pain. A yip usually means a dog is feeling excited and playful. A bark can mean a dog is bored and trying to get your attention, and a loud, persistent bark can be a warning of something out of the ordinary. A howl is a dog's way of saying it is lonely and trying to connect to other dogs. And last, a growl is a sign that a dog is feeling tense, scared, or aggressive.

Tail

You can learn a lot about how a dog is feeling by watching its tail, but not all tail wagging is happy. Yes, a happy dog wags its tail from side to side or even in a circle, but an unsure or anxious dog will bring its tail close to its body and wag its tail between its legs. When a dog is curious or possibly sensing danger, it puts its tail upright and high, and may wag it back and forth slightly. You see? Not all wags are the same.

ACTIVITY

Head to your local dog park with a notebook and record all the different types of tail-wagging dogs you see.

Basic Dog Care

Dogs are a huge commitment. When thinking of getting a dog of your own, there are many things to consider. You may have the desire to have a dog, but do you have the time, the patience, and the funds to meet your dog's emotional and physical needs? Dogs need food, clean water, a safe and healthy environment, vet checkups, basic supplies, regular exercise, attention, and training. Let's dive deeper!

DOG SUPPLIES

- Sturdy collar
- Leash and identity tags
- Grooming supplies
- Water and food bowls
- Bedding

Food and Water

A nutritious diet will help your dog live a long, healthy life. High-quality dog food with high protein and a good balance of nutrients is best for your pooch. Dog food costs money, and the amount of dog food you need will depend on the size of your dog. Of course, smaller dogs need less food than bigger dogs. Adult dogs need to be fed twice a day (puppies need to be fed four times a day) and must have access to clean water all day, every day.

Safe, Healthy Environment

Indoor dogs need a safe, warm, and quiet place to rest and regular access to the outdoors. Dogs who live outdoors need a place to shelter out of the sun, wind, rain, and snow. Having clean bedding or a crate is ideal. Like their ancestors, dogs like a place that feels cozy, like a den. Dogs need a safe area that is either suitably fenced or away from roads and other hazards where they can run and play.

Attention

Most dogs thrive on human attention. Petting, grooming, and just spending quality time with your dog is very important for its overall well-being. From the beginning, kindly let your dog know that you are the "top dog" and leader of the pack. This is an important first step. Start training your dog early in basic behaviors, as this is an extremely important aid to helping socialize your dog. Training takes consistency and time. Sometimes a professional is needed to help. There are even puppy classes in most areas.

Vet Checks

Dogs need annual health checkups and vaccinations, and all dog owners should be prepared for an unforeseen emergency.

Regular Exercise

Dogs need daily exercise, not only to burn calories but also to stimulate their minds. The amount of exercise varies depending on the breed and age of your dog. Boredom and lack of exercise can lead to destructive behavior, such as chewing and aggressiveness.

Training

Training is an essential part of owning a dog. If overlooked, it can be detrimental to both the owner and the dog. Much like in a wolf pack, dogs must learn boundaries and have a clear leader (yes, that should be the owner). Through training, dogs not only learn which behaviors are accepted and which are not, but also build confidence. Training your dog helps with their own safety. An unruly dog can hurt itself, you, or others. Dogs who are properly and consistently worked with tend to be more bonded with their owners, less aggressive, more social, and less stressed. Depending on the dog and the situation, training a dog can be overwhelming, but don't worry. There are many wonderful resources and dog trainers to help you, your family, and your dog with the process.

Dog and Human Bond

Scientists have long studied the intense bond between dogs and humans to try to understand the how and why of the relationship. Have you ever been sitting with a dog who continually nudges or paws at you for more attention? Is this love, or is the dog using you to get what it wants? Recent studies indicate that a specific part of the dog's brain lights up when it hears human voices, especially its pack leader's, and this happens to be the same part that lights up in our brain when we like something. This study suggests that our presence is pleasurable for the dog. We don't know how their emotions work, but this exciting new area of research is just the tip of the iceberg.

ACTIVITY

If you ask me, dogs can love one another, not just humans. I once had two dogs, Taj and Sheila, who were best buds. Sheila always slept in my laundry basket. I had never seen Taj sleep there, or even try to. One day, tragically, Sheila was killed by coyotes. My heart was broken, and so was Taj's. From that night on, he slept in the laundry basket. Think about some animals you have known. Do you have a similar story about an animal experiencing a deep emotion?

Animal Shelters

An animal shelter—or a pound, as they are sometimes called—is a place where abused, neglected, surrendered, or stray animals are taken in, cared for, and potentially adopted out to new loving homes. The first animal shelter was opened in 1869 in Philadelphia, Pennsylvania, by Caroline Earle White and a group of female activists. Today, there are shelters and dog-rescue programs all over the world. It is estimated that six million pets enter shelters every year in the United States.

Animal shelters mainly take in dogs and cats, but they can house other species as well. There are many unforeseen circumstances that could cause a dog, cat, or other pet to end up having to be rescued. These reasons may range from owners deciding that they no longer want the animal to an owner who can no longer afford to properly care for it, or is physically unable to do so. Sometimes dogs or cats do wander away and get lost. Sadly, some animals are neglected or abused by their owners and need to be rescued. There are also some dogs who become too difficult to handle, making their owners no longer feel safe. They too will end up in the shelter. Whatever the reason, animal shelters give these sad animals a second chance.

If you'd like to help, adopting an animal from a shelter is a great place to start. Spaying and neutering your animals is another way to help. Shelters usually have spay and neuter days to

FUN DOG FACTS

- Dogs live an average of 10 to 14 years.
- Dogs' noses contain approximately 220 million scent cells, which is 40 times more than humans have.
- Dogs can hear sounds four times farther away than we can.
- The most common registered breed of dog is the Labrador retriever.
- Dog urine is so acidic that it can corrode metal.
- Dogs don't sweat, so they have to pant to cool themselves.
- The fastest dogs are greyhounds, which can run up to 45 miles per hour.
- Female dogs are only pregnant for about 58 to 68 days. That's only about 3 months!

help prevent any unwanted pet pregnancies. This reduces the number of unwanted animals who need homes and therefore reduces the number of animals coming into shelters. Shelters also always need volunteers. Call your local shelter to see if you can help. I know our local shelter looks for dog walkers and cat petters.

And last, since we don't want dogs to end up at the shelter, making an educated commitment is important. Dogs take time, energy, and money. Being educated about dog behavior, knowing the breed history, and understanding what a lifetime commitment means before you take a dog home are all critically important considerations.

Dog Training

BARBARA MACKIE

Barbara Mackie is a dog and horse trainer who has more than 30 years of experience. She is a no-nonsense, straight-to-business type. Her expertise runs deep. When you're around Barbara and her horses and dogs, you can immediately tell not only the bond they share, but also their mutual respect. Watching Barbara work cattle from horseback by commanding her dogs is a thing of beauty. Four different species working together to complete a task is profound and takes incredible skill.

Through her training business, Barbara offers a host of opportunities to help folks achieve their goals for themselves and their dogs. She teaches an array of skills, including basic obedience, problem-solving, agility, and specific skills for working dogs. Barbara helps dog owners and their dogs gain a

clearer understanding of and a more gratifying relationship with one another.

Barbara was born in Puerto Rico. She grew up in Santa Barbara, California, and at the age of 21 moved to the Santa Ynez Valley, where she still lives with her family and animals today.

Her love of animals goes as far back as she can remember, starting with a parakeet named Squeaky she had when she was 6 years old. This was the beginning of a lifetime of owning, caring for, and training animals. Around the age of 10, she began helping her neighbors with their dogs and taking them on walks. She did it to be helpful, but mostly she just wanted to be around the dogs. She would teach them how to walk on a leash without pulling and then began to teach them other simple tricks. That was when she realized she enjoyed communicating with dogs and her love of dog training truly began.

Eventually, she ended up working at the local sheriff's department. It was through that department and a German Schutzhund dog club that her formal training began. She learned professional training techniques in obedience, tracking, protection, and exactly how to intensively handle working dogs. After that, she went on to work with the Guide Dogs for the Blind. She worked with puppies and puppy handlers to get them ready for formal guide dog training. Barbara thinks it is important to train dogs because they like to know their boundaries, just as they would in a pack. Dogs are, for the most part, people pleasers. By teaching them basic manners and obedience, everyone is in harmony, and your life together is more enjoyable. When your dog is under control, not causing chaos or problems, it's better for both the dog and you.

Barbara's favorite dog breed is the border collie, which is a working and herding breed, because of its intelligence. Right now, Berni, her border collie, is her

number one cattle dog. Berni follows her commands when she is on horseback, helping Barbara gather and move cattle. If the dog didn't follow her exact instructions, things could go very wrong.

As for whether she thinks dogs feel love, Barbara's answer is definitely yes. She says dogs love their people, but they must also learn respect for their handlers through good training practices. If you'd like to learn more, please visit barbaramackietraining.com.

Barbara's Training Tips

- Dog obedience is more than just commands; it is about the relationship you have with your dog going into training.

- Finding a dog that fits your lifestyle is a must. It's important to understand that owning a dog takes commitment.

- Feeding, cleaning, and training are important. When training, plan what it is you want your dog to learn and why. Is it obedience, tricks, tracking, agility, or cattle work?

- Make sure your dog has the natural instincts to do what you are asking it to do.

- Find a good trainer or some informative books to help you properly train your dog.

- Don't use treats. Dogs want to make you happy. A simple pat and verbal "good dog" is the reward they really want.

- When working with your dog, always be patient and firm but never mean.

How to Teach "Sit"

1. Pull up slightly on a flat collar and repeat the word "Sit."
2. When your dog sits, release the pressure.
3. Reward the dog by saying, "Good dog."

How to Teach "Down"

1. Pull down slightly on a flat collar and repeat the word "Down."
2. When your dog lies down, release the pressure.
3. Reward the dog by saying, "Good dog."

CATS

The cat is one of the most beloved house pets in the world. These elusive creatures are incredible to watch as they jump and play, and they can even make us feel special when and if they choose to grace us with their presence. Today's house cat can at times be like having a miniature wild cat in your home. This is because they still display many of the same qualities their wild counterparts do. Cats can offer us companionship, and this can be an extremely rewarding relationship. Studies have indicated that having a cat can help relieve stress, reduce loneliness, and even improve some people's health and well-being. Cats can also help keep places free of rodents, are relatively low-maintenance (they even bathe themselves), and simply bring us joy. I have always had a cat in my life, and I believe I always will. Let's learn more about these creatures that have, with their wit and intrigue, taken over our homes and our hearts.

Natural History

It's believed that cats were domesticated in Egypt around 10,000 years ago. Once humans began farming, they had to store the grains they harvested, which probably attracted mice, and you know what likes to hunt mice, right? Today's cats evolved from a wild ancestor that roamed these ancient farming towns, much like feral cats do today, and eventually found their way into our homes and hearts. Cats still display behaviors they share with their wild ancestors. For example, wild cats like to hunt at night when it's cooler. They have great nighttime vision. Many domestic cats also sleep all day and are up all night. Cats are usually solitary animals and prefer to be independent. Knowing this fact may help us understand why cats are so elusive. Studying the natural history of the wild cat's behavior and then observing our domestic cat's behavior can help us understand these creatures a little better.

Communication and Behavior

Cats are constantly communicating with us. They use behaviors such as vocalizations and body language to tell us things. (Are you seeing a pattern among all the different species?) Watch their tails, ears, and backs, and listen to their sounds to try to understand what they are feeling.

Like people and all other animals, cats all have different personalities. Some cats are more social than others, some cats love attention, some prefer to be alone, some are more talkative, and some are more active than others. Learning what is normal for cats as a species can help you better understand your own cat.

Vocalizations

Some cats vocalize more than others, but no matter how often they "talk," when cats make a sound, they are communicating something. What

---

KEY TERMS

FELINE: Relating to cats

DOMESTIC CAT: A cat that was raised with humans

HOUSE CAT: A domesticated cat that lives in a house

KITTEN: A young cat

FERAL CAT: A cat that was not raised with humans and that finds food and water on its own; feral cats are usually scared of people

STRAY CAT: A cat that has been raised around humans but has lost its caregiver

HISS: A sharp vocalization resembling a "hssss" sound

PURR: A low, vibrating sound

---

if we could speak their language? Well, I'm not sure how to do that, but we can analyze some of their meows and other sounds to learn what they might mean.

MEOWING

A meow can mean many different things. It can be a greeting or a command. Cats can meow to us, other cats, other animals, or even themselves.

CHIRPING

Have you ever heard your cat chirp? This vocalization is usually used by mama cats when they'd like their kittens to follow. Is your cat trying to get you to follow it?

HOWLING

If your cat is making a long, drawn-out meow, it can mean it is in distress or pain. Make sure to check on your cat if it is making this sound, and bring it to the vet if needed.

PURRING

Purring usually indicates that your cat is feeling relaxed, content, and happy. It can be a form of self-soothing too, like a baby sucking

its thumb. What a delight to be curled up with a cat while it's purring.

HISSING OR GROWLING
Cats make it pretty obvious when they are mad. They hiss and make a low growl when angry, threatened, or scared. Leave this cat alone. You do not want a cat bite!

Body Language

Let's take a look at the body language of cats. Cats are some of the most graceful animals on the planet. Their sleek bodies allow them to be incredibly agile, their ears are like satellites picking up any little sound, and their long tails help them balance even in the most precarious situations. Cats use their bodies to jump, run, hunt, and play, but what other things are their bodies and body positions trying to tell us? Let's explore.

Tail

A cat's tail can tell us quite a bit about what the cat is feeling, but we need to look closely. If the tail is up and it seems relaxed, then the cat is content. If the cat is holding its tail straight up and seems tense, this can mean that it is feeling threatened or scared. If the cat has a quivering tail, something certainly has excited it. A tucked tail usually means the cat is afraid, while flicking the tail back and forth can mean the cat wants to play or, just to confuse you, might mean your cat is annoyed and may pounce or bite at you soon.

Ears

Even your cat's ears are expressive and communicate its feelings. A relaxed cat's ears are usually facing forward, and this is a good time to interact with the cat. Ears that are standing tall and moving around usually mean the cat is listening intently. Twitching ears mean your cat is on a mission. When your cat's ears are low and pinned back, beware and back off.

Back

A cat with an arched back that is yawning is probably just waking up and stretching. A cat purring and putting its back up to you means it wants attention, maybe a scratch at the base of its tail. But a cat with an arched back and its hair standing up is a threatening cat, trying to make itself as big as possible. This is not a happy cat.

GAINING YOUR CAT'S TRUST

Here are a few tips to help you gain the trust of your cat.

- Be patient with your cat.
- Talk quietly to your cat.
- Use food to reward your cat.
- Use play and cat toys to interact with your cat.
- Let the cat come to you instead of grabbing the cat.

Basic Cat Care

These creatures that live among us have certain needs that must be met in order for them to be healthy and happy. It's true that their wild cousins that live in the jungle don't need toys or our affection, but our companions just might. Read on to learn how to take care of your cat's needs.

Food and Water

As all animals do, cats need access to food and clean water at all times. Cats need taurine, an essential amino acid, for their overall health, so choosing a high-quality, well-balanced cat food that includes taurine is necessary.

CAT SUPPLIES

- Food
- Water
- Bowls
- Cat house or bed
- Cat brush
- Cat toys
- Litter box
- Kitty litter
- Litter scoop
- Scratchers

Making Cat Toys with Jupiter

Cats and kittens love to play with toys. Even just a piece of string or yarn can entertain a kitten for a long time. Ashley's son, Jupiter, made this toy for their family's kittens when they first got them, and the cats still love it now that they've grown up.

Scissors or knife
Cork
24-inch piece of twine or yarn
Stick
Pushpin
Feathers

1. Ask an adult to help you cut a thin notch ⅓ inch from one end of the cork all the way around. Tie a piece of twine or yarn around the cork right where the cut is, so that the twine goes into the cut a little bit. This will keep the twine from sliding off the cork when your kittens or cats play with it.

2. Next, tie the other end of the twine to a stick, toward one end.

3. Stick a pushpin in the center of the bottom of the cork. This will make a little hole so it's easier to stick the feathers in. For the final touch, stick a few feathers in the little hole you made with the pushpin.

4. To play, shake the stick a little in front of your kitten so it can see the feathers move. Then, drag it slowly along the floor and that cat will pounce on it!

Housing

Cats are the ultimate creatures of comfort and will find a warm, dry, clean place to rest. Cat beds can be covered or open. Even when given comfy beds, cats will often find a place they prefer on their own. It may even be on your favorite pillow!

Grooming

Most cats do not need baths. They are the consummate self-groomers. Brushing your cat regularly helps keep it clean and helps with your bonding. Longhaired cats need more brushing than shorthaired cats.

Vet Care

Your cat will need a vet for yearly checkups and vaccinations, as well as unforeseen emergencies.

Attention

Make time to give your cat attention. A cat needs attention and stimulation or it can become destructive, especially an indoor cat. Ever heard of the game cat and mouse? Cats like to play and love to hunt. It is especially essential for young cats to be stimulated and play. You can buy cat toys or you can make them. Making your own cat toy is easy and fun (see page 281).

Kitty Litter

If you choose to have an indoor cat, you will need to litter train it. This means the cat is taught to go to the bathroom inside a designated litter box. For most cats, this is not a problem. They are generally persnickety about cleanliness, although some cats have a tougher time learning. The kitty litter must be cleaned daily. If not, your cat may find another place to go to the bathroom. Before getting a cat, think about who will clean the litter box every day.

Scratchers

Cats love to scratch. Cats actually need to scratch in order to remove the outer part of the nail called the husk, as well as to exercise the muscles in the front part of their legs. Cats tend to scratch when they are happy and relaxed. Outdoor cats scratch at trees or other hard surfaces. If your cat lives indoors, providing scratchers will certainly help prevent furniture, rugs, or even curtains from being damaged.

How to Pick Up a Cat

Always treat your cat with respect, and calmly and quietly approach it. It helps to give it a treat before picking it up. To pick up your cat properly, place one hand under its front legs and the other under its hindquarters. Hold the cat to your chest area so it feels secure. The more points of contact between you and your cat, the safer and more secure it will feel. Some cats like to be picked up and cuddled; others do not, and will use evasive tactics or even scratch you. Judge how much your cat likes to be held by reading its body language. If the cat is scratching or biting, put it back down. Never drop your cat or throw it down.

Adopting a Cat

There are so many cats that need homes. If your family is thinking about getting a cat, make sure to check with your local Humane Society or animal shelter first. Read on to learn about more things to consider when choosing a cat.

Humane Society

When you get a cat from the Humane Society, it has already been spayed or neutered and has received its first shots. The Humane Society usually requires you to keep your cat indoors.

No Declawing!

Declawing is when the last bone of each of the cat's toes is removed in order to remove its claws. It would be like us removing the top bones on our fingers at the knuckle. Ouch! Cats that are declawed have a high chance of living in constant pain. After the claws are removed, they try to grow back inside the paw, which causes excruciating pain, along with a high chance of infection and constant limping. Declawed cats have a higher risk of aggression issues and can have trouble using a litter box. Many cities in the United States have outlawed declawing cats and many vets now refuse to declaw.

Indoor vs. Outdoor Cats

Cats that live indoors tend to live much longer. Outdoor cats face many more risks, including injury or death by cars, dogs, coyotes, and even diseases. Indoor cats can be destructive and will definitely need to be litter trained. Some people believe that outdoor cats have a better quality of life and live a more natural existence, but in addition to the greater risk factors, outdoor cats can also kill birds, which can be unfortunate for some native species. It is important to understand the pros and cons of indoor and outdoor cats and weigh your options to make the best choice for your family and your kitty.

Feral Cats vs. Stray Cats

Feral cats are cats that have not been socialized with humans. Stray cats are cats who were at some point living with humans but have lost their home and caregiver and are now living on their own.

Can a feral cat become a pet? Feral cats act much differently than socialized house cats. With patience and time it is possible to tame a feral cat, but some feral cats are impossible to tame. If a feral cat is a kitten when caught, and it is raised with humans, it has a better chance of becoming social with humans. An older cat is much harder to tame, and many times would prefer to hide from humans and live on its own.

Consider the Commitment

Before getting any animal, it is important to think about the downsides. Cats can make great pets, but they can also be destructive when indoors, scratching furniture and knocking things over because they acrobatically spring and can (and do) go basically anywhere they want, including on your food, counters, and kitchen table. They shed cat hair and dander, which can cause allergies; they can disrupt your sleep; and they vomit hairballs occasionally.

When living outdoors, they can hunt and kill birds and small animals like mice and moles, and they will often leave these animals as a "present" on your doorstep. Cats need constant care, so consider who will take care of the cat if you go on vacation.

Cats are incredibly interesting creatures, so it is no wonder that hundreds of millions of cats are kept as pets all over the world. Cats do have special needs though. Should you choose to get a cat, you must remember that you are responsible for its health and well-being, not only when it's an adorable kitten, but also as it ages. Please see the Resources list in the back of this book to learn more about cats.

Wildlife Rescue

RUTH DOVER

Sam and Ruth Dover began the Channel Islands Marine & Wildlife Institute (CIMWI, pronounced "sim-wee") in 2006. CIMWI is an organization with the goal of positively impacting conservation through marine mammal rescue, rehabilitation, and release, as well as research and education to promote ocean and human health. It rescues, cares for, and releases marine mammals back into the ocean. How cool is that? CIMWI is made up of an all-volunteer staff. Every day dedicated folks help with the entire operation, from answering the

hotline to rescuing animals off the beach, from feeding, cleaning, and caring for them to preparing them to be released back into the Pacific Ocean.

Ruth grew up having a family dog, but she wasn't around a whole lot of animals as a kid. She went from having a Pekingese poodle to an English springer spaniel, so she was comfortable around both small and large dogs. Her true love of animals came with starting the nonprofit organization, and it came in the form of marine mammals. CIMWI's core work is the rescue and rehabilitation of seals and sea lions, with the goal of returning them to their ocean home for a second chance at life in the wild. Ruth's husband, Sam, is a veterinarian who has been practicing marine mammal medicine for 34 years, so it was only fitting that Ruth's love for animals grew with her relationship with Sam and this very special organization.

Ruth's favorite marine mammals are humpback whales. They have a charismatic, gregarious, and inquisitive nature, and they are truly majestic to listen to and watch. Male humpback whales are the masters of melody, and they sing beautiful, complex, and evolving songs. Their songs can be heard more than 20 miles away and last up to 20 minutes. Plus, if you're looking for a show in the ocean, humpback whales are the ones to watch. With their spectacular breaches, powerful peduncle throws, pectoral fin slapping, splashy lobtailing, and curious spyhopping, they can be quite flamboyant and acrobatic in the ocean.

CIMWI was Sam's life dream that then became Ruth's passion, and together they are making it come true. It all started with a 5-year-old boy living in St. Louis, Missouri. Sam wanted to save animals, and he loved the water. He was also a smart, curious, and adventurous kid with an easy smile and gregarious laugh. As he grew up, so did his passion for making a difference. He worked hard to create a career

where his work was his play and his play was his work. He built a successful international veterinary consulting practice specializing in marine mammal medicine and endoscopy and laparoscopy. Ruth's background is in hospitality and consulting—very different from animals, medicine, and science—but when Sam told Ruth about his dream to build CIMWI, it felt so tangible she could touch it.

She was all in. They've created an amazing grassroots nonprofit that makes a difference in the health and well-being of marine mammals. They are also passionate about encouraging their volunteers to give and do more in the world, as well as inspire future generations of ocean stewards.

CIMWI helps an average of 125 marine mammals in need each year. The highest number

of animals it helped in a single year was 359. Ruth believes it is important to help wildlife because everything is connected. Animal, plant, and marine biodiversity (the variety of life on earth) keeps ecosystems healthy and functional. When we protect animals and plants, we also protect the ecosystems that are the foundation of our well-being. Biodiversity conservation is the practice of protecting and preserving the health and variety of species, habitats, ecosystems, and genetic diversity on the planet. CIMWI helps do this with marine mammals. As indicator and sentinel species, the health of these marine mammals and the reasons they strand are indicative of the health of our oceans. Following these trends can determine the relative state of ocean health, which impacts our health. Ocean, environmental, animal, and human health are all connected under the One Health approach. Each of us has the ability to make a difference. Take the time to learn and find a way to be a positive force in protecting wildlife.

If you'd like to get involved with CIMWI, you can do so by supporting the work it does. You can tell your friends how to report a marine mammal in distress, you can donate or raise money to support its mission, you can volunteer if you're at least 18 years old, or you can be an ocean steward and make a difference for the health of our oceans and marine mammals in your own way. If you're interested in learning more, please visit @cimwi on Instagram or CIMWI.org.

What Should I Do If I Find an Injured Animal?

If you encounter a marine mammal that is sick, injured, malnourished, entangled, deceased, or oiled, please follow these steps:

1. Do Not Touch It!

Do not touch, feed, harass, cover, pour water on, coax, drag, push into the water or out of the surf zone, allow dogs near, or take selfies with the animal. These are wild animals, and they may bite!

2. Observe the Animal

Observe the animal from a minimum of 50 feet away. Keep people and pets away from the stranded animal. Note the animal's physical characteristics and condition.

3. Determine the Location

Determine the exact location of the animal. Be as accurate as possible, and note any landmarks so a rescue team can easily find the animal.

4. Call Your Local Animal Rescue Hotline

CIMWI serves the counties of Santa Barbara and Ventura in California. If you live there, call the CIMWI rescue hotline at 805-567-1505. If not, call an animal rescue hotline specific to your area. Provide your name, phone number, and specific information about the animal and its location.

How Can I Get Involved in Helping Injured Wildlife?

You can get involved with helping injured wildlife by being a good steward of the environment! Here are two easy tips you can incorporate into your daily life.

← Clean up trash and dispose of it properly. Some things can be recycled and some will need to be put in the trash. Be sure to use safety precautions when picking up trash. You can wear gloves or use trash pickers, and be sure to ask an adult for help if needed. Look for trash on your way to and from school, in your neighborhood, at the beach, or in the park. You can do it on your own or organize a family or group cleanup.

← Think of ways you can reduce your family's use of single-use plastic. You can find a lot of ideas on the internet or through conversations with your family. Pack your lunch and store your food in reusable food-storage bags and containers instead of plastic bags like ziplocks. Use washable cloth napkins, towels, and rags instead of paper napkins and paper towels. Use reusable straws or drink directly from the cup or glass. Use a reusable water bottle instead of single-use plastic water bottles. Look for items with less packaging or plastic-free alternatives when you are buying things at the grocery store or shopping in general. Even small actions like these can have a big impact.

BUNNIES

Emma's children, Olivia and Liam, first learned to take care of a bunny rabbit at their preschool. Together with their classmates, they learned what to feed the bunny and how to care for her. They also learned that rabbits are really quiet, have sweet personalities, and can easily be trained to use a litter box and do tricks. As you can imagine, the bunny made quite an impression on Olivia and Liam. Who doesn't love the soft, cuddly feel of their fur? So when Olivia and Liam were a little older and could really understand how to care for a rabbit, Emma's family decided to get one.

Instead of going through a pet store or a bunny rescue, they ended up adopting one from a friend who could no longer care for it. The bunny, named Sespe, was about seven months old when they took him in, and right from the start, it was apparent that he had been well loved and handled daily, as he enjoyed being cuddled continuously and smothered with lots of kisses. Sespe is now an adult rabbit and has become the center of attention among the animals at Emma's house. He gets along well with the chickens and cat, though the family had to separate him from their pygmy goat and mini pony because Sespe thinks he is just as big as them, which can get him into trouble.

This chapter shares the story of their journey with a bunny in their own words. If you are considering getting a rabbit, maybe it will help you decide if it's right for you too.

Why We Chose to Raise Bunnies

Our family chose to keep a bunny rabbit for two reasons: friendship and fertilizer. Olivia and Liam wanted a pet bunny rabbit they could play with and hold, and we knew the bunny poop would make great fertilizer for our garden. Yes, it's true, bunny poop can work wonders around the garden. It's full of nitrogen and phosphorus and can be placed directly around your plants in the garden without burning them. Although some families raise bunnies for meat, our family did not have that as our goal.

Will Bunnies Be a Good Fit for Your Family?

Bunnies are super cute and furry creatures, but it's important to note that bunnies all have different personalities and some can be outright mean. Although we have not experienced this with our bunny, we know friends whose bunnies seem to be territorial and often bite. Our bunny rabbit is more like a puppy dog, and he is friendly and mellow. This could be attributed to the fact that he is a Mini Rex, a breed that is known for its calm and friendly disposition and also for being good around children and the elderly. Still, we have found that by gently handling our bunny and talking to him in a calm way early on, we might have influenced him to be more forgiving and friendly and less easily startled.

Another consideration to make when thinking about keeping bunnies is that they are sensitive. One loud noise, sudden jerk, or even being held too tightly might send a bunny into a panic. For this reason, bunnies might not be best for families with really young children. Olivia and Liam were 10 and 7, respectively, when we introduced a pet rabbit.

Last, we live near the coast of sunny Southern California, where the weather is quite moderate

> **BUNNY SUPPLIES**
>
> - Bunny hutch (indoor or outdoor, depending on your needs)
> - Hay
> - Bunny feed
> - Extra veggies
> - Waterer
> - Exercise pen or run

and comfortable year-round. For this reason, we choose to keep our bunny outside in a hutch. However, bunnies do not do well in extreme temperatures, especially heat, so if you live in a very warm climate you might want to consider that before getting a bunny. I remember keeping a bunny at my childhood home, which was inland, and even though I lived on a farm where there was plenty of outdoor space, I kept him in my bedroom in a hutch and even potty-trained him because the temperature could easily reach above 100°F for long stretches in the summer. During the day, if I left him out, he would cuddle with the stuffed animals on my bed. In fact, he even looked like one of them until his nose twitched.

More Considerations

Before deciding to rescue (in our area, you can adopt a bunny from a local shelter) or purchase a bunny rabbit from a local breeder, we suggest picking up at least one or two books on raising bunnies. We liked having plenty of information on hand, and we learned a lot about keeping bunnies before we decided on one for our family. As a side note, before saying "yes" to a bunny, we also recommend spending some time with several bunnies to see which would be the best fit for your family.

Bunnies are very social and don't do well in isolation. If you get a bunny, you have to play with it daily, or have same-sex bunny friends for it to play with. Because we only have one rabbit, when we go away, we make sure Sespe has a buddy (Olivia's best friend's bunny) so he gets the attention he needs.

Another consideration is that bunnies are really great escape artists—at least our bunny is. He has escaped from our yard multiple times, and since he is such a sneaky bunny we now have an extra-tall exercise pen for him.

The Verdict

We are of course biased, but we have to say Sespe has been such an awesome pet and we are smitten with him. He loves following us around, giving kisses (little licks that mean "I love you"), and will do anything for a treat. Plus, our garden is loving the extra nutrients that the rabbit poop provides. So, if you're willing and able to work together as a family with patience and gentleness to train the bunny, keeping a rabbit can be rewarding and fun.

Bunny Treats

Rabbits love treats and our bunny is no different. The problem with most rabbit treats sold in pet stores is that they have too much added sweetness or filler ingredients (such as wheat and corn) that aren't great for bunnies to eat. When you make treats from scratch, you'll know exactly what is in each bite, and your bunny (and its belly!) will thank you for it.

VEGGIE AND FRUIT ICE LOLLIES

Makes 8 lollies

Veggie and fruit ice lollies are perfect for hot summer days. They're super easy to make, and our bunny really loves them. If you'd rather use vegetables only, you can substitute them for the fruit. (Fruit should only be given to bunnies in moderation.) Our rabbit loves carrots and carrot tops, as well as fennel and apples.

¼ cup chopped vegetables, such as carrot or fennel

¼ cup chopped fruit, such as apples, blueberries, or pears (optional)

Filtered water

1. Place the cut-up veggies and fruit (if using) in an ice cube tray, cover with water, and freeze.
2. Give one to your bunny for a treat on a hot day!

BUNNY COOKIES

Makes 20 (2-inch) cookies

Bunny cookies are a fairly simple treat to bake, and our bunny, Sespe, loves them.

1 apple, cored and chopped into 2-inch pieces

1 banana, peeled and chopped into 2-inch pieces

2 medium carrots, peeled and chopped into 2-inch pieces

½ cup rabbit pellet food

¼ cup rolled oats

1. Preheat the oven to 325°F. Place all the ingredients in a food processor, close the lid, and pulse until the mixture is smooth and comes together to form a dough.
2. Roll the dough into 1- to 2-inch balls with your hands. Place the balls on a parchment-lined baking sheet.
3. Bake for 30 minutes, then turn off the heat and allow the cookies to sit in the warm oven for about 1 hour.
4. Serve one of these cookies to your rabbit, and store the extras in an airtight container. They will stay fresh in the fridge for up to 7 days.

MAKE

Creating Beautiful Things

ASHLEY

MAKING BEAUTIFUL AND USEFUL THINGS BY HAND IS A COMMON THREAD THROUGH every culture around the world. The techniques of art and craft are passed down from grandparents to parents to children, and every new generation either adds something new or finds connection in staying true to tradition. I think both ways are inspiring. I have much appreciation for quality craftsmanship that has remained true to its roots for hundreds and hundreds of years, and I am also impressed to see how the younger generation can take something their relatives once made and enhance the technique or style in some way to truly make it their own.

The techniques I've learned have been handed down to me by many people over my lifetime. As a little girl, I learned the art of origami and painting from my stepmother, who was Japanese. As a young adult, I learned to make herbal medicines and skincare from my teachers and mentors, including herbalists Rosemary Gladstar, Marlene Adelman, Susun Weed, and local Renaissance man Lanny Kaufer. I owe my love of gardening and foraging to my dad, and my love of flowers and beautiful things to my mom. I'm grateful to my stepdad, who bought me my very first sewing machine—the same one I use today, 25 years later! And I learned how to knit and crochet from my grandmother. She was an avid crafter, a master at knitting, sewing, and making beautiful needlepoint art, to name just a few of her hobbies.

Learning to make something is wonderful, but the real gift is being able to pass on all you've learned so the next generation can take it up, make it new, or celebrate the tradition and become part of it. In this section of the book, I offer many of the techniques, skills, crafts, and recipes that have been so generously shared with me by those mentors, friends, and relatives I love and admire. I hope you find inspiration to take up something new, make it your own, and, in time, pass it on to the younger generation yourself.

My three children—Isla (13), Lyra (11), and Jupiter (7)—enjoy crafting and herbalism and have started teaching others already. Isla is an artist and illustrator, and she kindly helps her siblings and friends learn to draw people, plants, and animals. Her favorite animal is the horse, so she often draws horses galloping, prancing, and standing. Isla also has a close relationship with the plants growing around her, and she teaches her friends how to know which plants can be eaten, which are toxic, which can be made into herbal medicines, and which make the prettiest dyes.

Lyra is the only one in the family who has mastered spinning wool. She uses a drop spindle well and makes lovely weavings with the yarn she makes. When we sheared our sheep, she helped process the wool, including cleaning, washing, carding, and, finally, spinning it into yarn. She also loves to dye clothing with plants like indigo, wood sorrel, onion skins, and eucalyptus, and she even crocheted a beanie for me using yarn she spun herself, which she had dyed with fennel, onion skins, and marigold.

Jupiter helps me in the Waldorf parent-child class I teach. When he gets out of school, a few minutes before my class ends, he comes in to sit with the parents and help them learn to knit. He is a patient and kind teacher. He also loves to help me forage for edible weeds, berries, and roots, and he can't wait to get home and bake them into cookies, pies, and frittatas. He was very excited to teach the first step in knitting or crocheting—finger knitting—in this book.

All three of my children do much to feed, clean, and love the 40 animals we care for on our half-acre homestead. They help grow, harvest, and preserve the produce we eat; mend, dye, and knit some of the clothing we wear; and prepare the herbal remedies we use to stay healthy through the seasons. You can learn to do these things too, and maybe you'll teach your parents how to do something new.

Some of the crafts I really enjoy are beyond the scope of this book—knitting sweaters, crocheting blankets, mending clothing, and doing needlepoint. For some of these crafts, I'm including a short introduction to inspire you, but I feel each deserves a full book dedicated to the topic, so I've listed some suggested titles in the Resources section in the back of this book. If you take a serious interest in a craft, go ahead and learn as much as you can about it. Books are very helpful, but the best way to learn is from a person. If your parents and grandparents aren't able to teach you the crafts or skills you want to learn, maybe they can help you find a mentor who can. Friends can also be great teachers. It's fun to learn a new skill from a friend, or learn something new together.

GARDEN AND HERBS

Most of us usually enjoy gardening the best when we pick our own plants to grow. There is extra enthusiasm when the plants can be eaten, made into a dye, or have some other hands-on use.

When planning a garden bed, consider what your favorite vegetables and fruits are, and which plants grow well with them. The gardeners at your local nursery will be able to tell you which plants make good companion plants with the ones you have picked out. Suggested books on this subject are also listed in the Resources section in the back of this book. A favorite combination that grows well together is pumpkins, corn, and beans. A garden with these three vegetables is known as a Three Sisters Garden, named for an Iroquois legend about three sisters who grow and thrive together. The beans add nitrogen to the soil, feeding the corn and pumpkins; the prickly leaves and stems of the pumpkins protect the beans and corn from bugs and bunnies, who might otherwise love to eat the young plants; and the corn pops up first, giving the beans something to climb.

An important word of caution for this chapter is that you should always be sure of what you grow and pick. Some flowers, berries, and even leaves can be very toxic to humans, so it's important to always check with your parents or guardians before you eat or even touch any plants that are new to you. When you buy plants or seeds from a nursery or farmers market, you'll be able to talk to the experts there, and they can tell you which plants are safe to plant, grow, and eat.

Simple-As-Can-Be Dye

Besides growing food, another great idea is a dye garden—a garden full of plants you can use to make natural dyes. Some flowers that make great plant dyes and stains are wood sorrel, which is also known as sour grass (bright yellow), marigold (golden tan), viola and black pansy (purple), coreopsis (yellow to orange or salmon), and lobelia (cornflower blue). Berries such as blackberries and elderberries (both magenta) can also make great dyes.

Dyeing with these plants can be as simple or as complex as you'd like. Beginning simply still gives wonderful results, and with just a few supplies you can get started right away. Lyra enjoys making coreopsis dye with the flowers she has grown. She fills a jar with a handful of blossoms, pours just-boiled water over it, and then adds the napkin she wishes to dye. Silk or wool fabric is ideal. Cotton will also work, but the color will not be as rich. If you enjoy dyeing with plants and are ready for more, our first book, *The Women's Heritage Sourcebook*, has more advanced techniques that will give you even richer, longer-lasting colors.

1. First, choose your dye plant. Maybe you've chosen to grow coreopsis and you have a dozen or more blossoms on your plant, or perhaps you have a handful of black pansies you could pick. Maybe you've grown more blackberries than you can eat. Whatever the case may be, pick a handful of the blossoms or berries and fill a mason jar at least halfway with them. Next, add rainwater or filtered water up to the top, screw on the lid, and set the jar out in the sun. (If you'd like to speed up the dye-extraction process, you can use just-boiled water rather than room-temperature water. If you use boiled water, you can start dyeing the fabric after a couple of hours instead of having to wait 2 days.)

2. After a day or two, strain out the solids, then put the fabric in the jar, along with the alum powder (if using). This is optional, but it will help the color last longer. Put the lid back on and set the jar outside in the sun again, this time for 2 to 3 days.

3. Take the fabric out of the jar and let it dry (without rinsing it). If you will be washing the fabric (if you made a napkin, for example, you likely will want to be able to wash it), give it a good rinse after it is completely dry. Then hang it to dry again.

Dye plant of choice

Mason jar

Rainwater or filtered water

Small piece of silk or wool fabric, such as a napkin or play silk, small enough to easily fit into the jar

1 teaspoon alum powder (optional)

Bundle Dyeing

ALYSIA MORENO

Alysia Moreno is an herbalist and natural dyer whose love for plants has naturally evolved into a thriving business. She is a crafter and creator by nature, making and selling beautiful yarns that she spins and then dyes with plants; botanical clothing bundle-dyed with flowers she grows and forages; herbal skincare; and many other items inspired by the plants and land around her. She is passionate about working with plants, creating, and helping others connect more deeply with the earth, and she has found a way to incorporate her interests into her business. One of Alysia's favorite ways to dye is bundle dyeing, and she has graciously agreed to share her process here. To learn more, you can find Alysia on Instagram at @magnolia.and.oak or visit magnoliaandoak.net.

Floral bundle dyeing, also known as eco-printing, is a wonderful way to capture the colors of the season. Alysia particularly enjoys this method of natural dyeing because it is simple, it encourages connection to the earth, and it is a craft that even the littlest of children can participate in. All sorts of plant materials can be used, from flowers and plants growing in your yard to ethically wildcrafted local plants or even food scraps. This is a project where you can get as creative and as experimental as you want.

100 percent cotton bandanna

Large pot, for steaming

Rainwater or unfiltered water

2 tablespoons aluminum acetate (optional)

Plant material, such as dyer's coreopsis, sour grass, marigold, hollyhock, nasturtium, rose petals or leaves, eucalyptus, rosemary, blackberry leaves or fruit, onion skins, avocado skins, nettle, hibiscus flowers, or Hopi black sunflower seeds

Plant powders or extracts, such as cochineal, indigo, madder, turmeric, or logwood (optional)

String or yarn

Scissors

Iron (optional)

1. Before you begin the dyeing process, you will need to prepare the bandanna by washing it with a natural laundry detergent. Machine washing works well.
2. This step is optional, but to ensure that you get the brightest and clearest colors possible from the plant, it is highly encouraged that you mordant the fiber after washing. To do so, fill a large pot with water. Add the aluminum acetate, stir, and add in the cotton fabric. Place the pot on the stove and turn it on low heat. It is best to keep it on low for at least 1 hour. You can then turn the heat off and let the bandanna sit overnight.

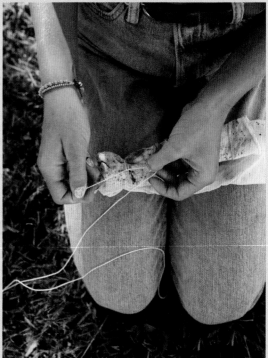

THE CHILDREN'S HERITAGE SOURCEBOOK

In the morning, hang the bandanna out to dry. Once it is dry, you can use it immediately or you can store it for a later date when you are ready to dye. I often prepare many bandannas at once and keep them on hand for whenever I come across beautiful dye plants.

3. After the bandanna has been washed (and preferably mordanted), gather all of the dyeing materials. Once you have everything prepared, dampen the bandanna. It is easier for the botanical color to move through wet fabric.

4. Lay the bandanna fully open on a flat surface.

5. Place the plant material on half of the bandanna. Get creative with it and make a mess. There is no right way to do this, and the beauty of natural dyeing is that you never know what you are going to get. You can place the plant material in a pattern, design, or simply scatter it.

6. If you are using plant powders or extracts, sprinkle them on top of the plant material. A little goes a long way, so you do not need much.

7. Now that you have half of the bandanna covered in plants, fold the empty half on top of the plant material, then carefully fold it in half again so you have a square shape. Now, begin rolling the bandanna as tightly as you can so you end up with a tubelike shape.

8. With the string or yarn, tie a knot at one end of the bandanna, leaving a 2-inch tail. Then wrap the string tightly around the bandanna, going up and down the tube and ending back where you tied the knot. Now tie the end of the string in a knot with the 2-inch piece that you left. The bandanna should now be wrapped in a tight coil.

9. You are ready to begin steaming the bandanna. Fill a pot with 3 to 4 inches of water and place the bandanna on the steaming rack inside the pot. Place the lid on the pot and turn the stove on medium-low heat. Allow the bandanna to steam for 1 hour. After the steaming is done, turn off the stove and let the bandanna cool completely.

10. Now for the most exciting part! Once the bandanna has completely cooled (I know it's hard to wait, but waiting is important for color development), take it out of the pot, cut the string with scissors, and begin to unroll it. Remove any large plant material. Rinse the bandanna with cool water and allow it to air-dry. The color will continue to oxidize as it dries. Once it is dry, use an iron to smooth it out if you'd like, and then you are ready to wear it.

11. To ensure the longevity of the bandanna, it's a good idea to wash it with a natural soap and only as often as needed. Some natural dyes can be fleeting, while others can last a very long time.

Botanically Dyed Easter Eggs

It's fun to dye eggs any time of year, not just at Easter. We like to make these colorful hard-boiled eggs for spring and summer picnics.

Medium pots, one for each color you will make

Filtered water

Dye plants, such as red or yellow onion skins, red cabbage, or blueberries

A few small herbs, flowers, or weeds, such as rosemary, sour grass, or fennel

White or very light eggs

Cheesecloth

Rubber bands or twine

Vinegar or baking soda (optional)

Mason jars (optional)

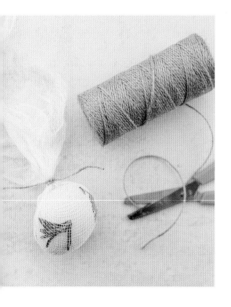

1. Fill a medium pot halfway full of water, then add a few handfuls of onion skins, 2 cups chopped red cabbage, or a large package of frozen blueberries. (If you want to make multiple colors, you can use different pots, putting one type of dye plant in each pot.)

2. Keep the lid on the pot and boil the plants for 10 to 20 minutes, until the water turns a rich color, then strain out the solids and pour the liquid back into the pot.

3. Place a few herbs or flowers on an egg, then cut a piece of cheesecloth and wrap it around the egg to hold the flowers on it. We like using sour grass the best because the flowers will dye the egg a bright yellow, making a beautiful contrast on a blue or brown egg. Secure with a rubber band or twine. Prepare the next egg in the same way, and continue until you have six eggs, or however many will comfortably fit in the pot. Repeat until you have the desired number of eggs in the pot, making sure the liquid fully covers the eggs. (You can add a little more water if it does not.)

4. Pour a few tablespoons of vinegar or baking soda (if using) into the pot and boil for 15 to 20 minutes, as you would for preparing hard-boiled eggs. (Vinegar and baking soda will change the pH of the dye liquid, so we like to do some pots with vinegar or baking soda, and some without, to achieve different colors.)

5. If you'd like, leave the eggs to cool in the dye bath for another 20 minutes to darken in color. Carefully remove the eggs from the pot, let them cool a little, then remove the cheesecloth and herbs or flowers.

6. If you want very rich colors, after the eggs have finished cooking, add each one to its own mason jar. Cover each with the dye liquid. Let cool, and refrigerate overnight. Carefully remove the eggs from the dye the next morning and remove the cheesecloth. Remove the herbs or flowers carefully, and against the colorful background you should see a white print where they were (unless you used sour grass, which leaves a yellow print). Beautiful!

Slugs and Snails

Nothing is more frustrating than putting time and care into growing a garden and waking up in the morning to find it has been devoured by slugs and snails. To help keep the slug population down, we go on nighttime slug hunts. Each of us brings a flashlight, and before bed we walk down to the garden with a big jar. As we find slugs and snails, we put them in the jar. Wanting to be as respectful as possible to the slimy creatures, we don't feel right about just killing them and throwing them away. But keeping them alive on our property would mean the end of our gardening adventures. So, we decided the best thing we could do was save them until the morning, then feed them to the chickens. That way, the chickens would get nourishment, even if it was a sad end for the slugs.

The first time we did this process, after we put at least a dozen slugs and snails into a jar, we put the lid back on and went to bed. In the morning, we woke up to find silvery snail trails all over the kitchen and floor, and we could only find a few of the snails. They were lost all over the house! The next time, we put the jar in a pan filled with salted water. In the morning, we found that they had, once again, twisted the lid open themselves. But instead of being all over the house, they were crawling around the rim of the jar, not wanting to go into the water. Now we've found an easier solution, which is to use a Weck or similar canning jar that has a clamp-down lid. These they can't open. In the morning, we feed them to the chickens and ducks.

Another way we keep the snail and slug population at bay is by making slug traps. They are simple to make, nontoxic for us, and very effective. All you have to do is go to the garden in the evening with a shallow tray or pie tin (we have separate ones reserved for this purpose that we do not use for baking) and a can of beer. Slightly bury the pie tin in the ground near your plants so the rim is basically level with the ground, then fill the tin with beer. We think it looks like a little swimming pool. You can leave it there for several days, and each day you will find slugs, snails, and earwigs in the beer pool. We make several traps and place them all around the garden.

Grapevine Wreaths

Our grapes are one of the most useful and beloved plants on our property. At the end of each summer, we harvest the fruit. Some we eat right off the vine, some we make into jelly, some we juice and can, some we dehydrate into raisins, and some we freeze for snacks. In the spring, the fresh grape leaves are delicious pickled and used to make dolmas (see page 124). In the late fall, we cut back the old, bare branches and twist them into wreaths.

It is easier than it sounds to make grapevine wreaths, but you must use freshly cut vines. Otherwise, they will be brittle and break easily. If all you have are old, dry vines, you can soak them for a few hours in warm water until they are supple enough to bend without breaking. Very dry vines can be soaked overnight.

To make a wreath, first take one long vine. Bend it into the shape of an O, and either use twine to tie it in place or wrap the thinner side around and around the thicker side so that it stays on its

own. Next, take a second vine. Wrap this vine around and around the O shape you made with the first vine. Continue this process with as many vines as you'd like, securing any parts that try to pop free with a little twine if needed.

These wreaths look beautiful on their own, but they're especially lovely when decorated with dried flowers. Lyra grew strawflowers in her garden and saved hundreds of their colorful blossoms. We arranged these blossoms around the wreath, along with some dried safflower stems and statice flower stems. The long stems we tucked and wove in between the layers of grapevine. The strawflowers we carefully glued into place with a glue gun. Wreaths made with dried flowers have the benefit of lasting for years, not drooping or fading like fresh wreaths.

But you can also use fresh plants for your wreath. Some plants that hold up well for wreath making are eucalyptus, pine, and juniper, to name just a few. It's nice to experiment. And you can tuck new plants in to replace the old ones once they get too dry or fall out.

Another method of decorating your grapevine wreath is making little bouquet bundles out of the plants you are using. The bundles can be secured with a rubber band. The number of bundles you'll need will depend on how big they are and the size of the wreath you are decorating. First, make around a dozen little bouquet bundles. Attach one to the wreath with twine or wire, then layer another one on top, going the same direction, so that the top of the second bundle covers the bottom third of the first bundle. Secure the second bundle, then layer a third bundle on top of that one in the same way. Continue until the entire wreath is covered, or for a different look, you can stop after just a few bundles, leaving the rest of the grapevine wreath exposed.

Flower Crowns

Flower crowns are like a little wreath you can wear. This project uses a wooden embroidery hoop as the base, but you could also make one by braiding together small handfuls of 3-foot-long strands of raffia or yarn, securing with knots at the ends, and tucking in dried or fresh flowers.

Wooden embroidery hoop large enough to fit around your head comfortably

Flowers or leaves

1. Embroidery hoops have an outer hoop that can change sizes, and an inner hoop that cannot. Twist the screw on the side of the hoop to loosen it. This widens the outer hoop so the inside hoop will slide out. Keep twisting the screw so the outer hoop is a little larger. The outer hoop has to be large enough to allow the flowers to fit between the two hoops when they are put back together.

2. Arrange flowers or leaves around the inside of the outer hoop, then press the inner hoop back down into the outer hoop. The flowers or leaves should be sandwiched between the two hoops. You may need to adjust the width of the outer hoop to make it larger or smaller by twisting the screw. Once it's all together, your crown is ready. If you need to adjust the flowers or leaves, you can loosen the screw, arrange the flowers, and tighten the screw again.

Flower Essences

Flower essences, also called flower remedies, were developed nearly 100 years ago by Dr. Edward Bach. You can find them at health food stores and many grocery stores, often near the homeopathic remedies and essential oils. Flower essences, however, are not homeopathic medicine or essential oils; they are something completely different.

Herbal remedies are medicine for the physical body, but flower essences are medicine for the etheric or emotional body. People who use flower essences intend to restore balance when their emotions or sense of well-being are out of whack. Some people find them to be very effective, and other people don't believe they work any better than a placebo, but either way, everyone agrees that they are completely safe for adults, children, and animals to use. Will flower essences work for you? Only you will be able to tell. They are simple, and you can easily make your own.

1. Go outside around 9:00 a.m. on a sunny day in spring with a small glass bowl filled halfway with rainwater or filtered water. Pick the flowers using two leaves of the plant over your fingers so they don't directly touch the flowers. Cover the surface of the water in the bowl with the flowers. Leave the bowl outside next to the plants you are using for a few hours, then use a plant part such as a stem to remove the flowers from the water. It is said that flower remedies work best when we touch them as little as possible.

Small glass bowl
Rainwater or filtered water
Flowers of your choice
2 (1-ounce) dropper bottles

CHOOSING AN ESSENCE

Different flower essences support different imbalances. Some are chosen to use long-term to support your life lesson or purpose; others are chosen to address short-term imbalances and transitions. Here are some flower essences to make and explore.

BORAGE: When you want a little more courage

CALIFORNIA WILD ROSE: When you want to feel more loving toward others

LAVENDER: When you want to calm down or sleep more deeply

ROSEMARY: When you want to feel comfortable in your own skin and improve your memory

SAGE: When you want to tap into your own inner wisdom

VIOLET: When you are moving or going to a new school and want to feel friendly and comfortable

YARROW: When you want to protect yourself with healthy boundaries

2. Next, fill a dropper bottle half full with the water you've made, then fill it the rest of the way with fresh rainwater or filtered water. Fill the second bottle nearly all the way with rainwater or filtered water. Add a few drops of the essence from the first bottle to the second bottle. This second bottle is the flower essence. The usual dose of flower essence is four drops under the tongue three times per day.

3. Because there is nothing in it to preserve the essence, it will only last a few days. You can wash the dropper bottle and make a new batch when you are ready. (Flower essences are traditionally made and preserved using brandy, but this rainwater technique feels best to me when children and teens are making the essences.)

Lavender Wands

Lavender wands are sweet-smelling sachets that began as a tradition a few hundred years ago in France, where they were woven with ribbons and given as good-luck tokens to brides. They can be used to give a subtle fragrance to small rooms, or they can be tucked into sock drawers or closets. The scent of lavender is said to repel moths, keeping them away from wool sweaters and other natural materials in your closet. Although lavender wands are traditionally made with ribbon, you can use yarn or twine instead.

7 lavender flowers on long stems

3 feet ribbon, yarn, or twine

1. Gather the lavender together and tie the ribbon just below the base of the flower heads. Use a square knot if you know how; otherwise, just knot the ribbon twice. One end of the ribbon should be very short and the other end quite long.
2. Now, carefully bend each of the stems down over the group of flowers. Try to arrange the stems evenly around the flowers like a cage. Don't let the flowers pop out of this little cage, and try to keep it in place as you begin to weave.
3. To begin weaving, take the long end of the ribbon and weave it over, then under, then over, then under, all of the stems. Keep going around and around, gradually moving the ribbon down the flowers as you go, so that you can see a little of the lavender blossoms inside. To keep everything in place, hold each stem down as you finish weaving it.
4. If you miss a stem by accident, you'll notice the pattern of over-under is not right. No worries. You can just pull out the ribbon until you get to the place where you accidentally did two overs or two unders in a row, then continue on.
5. Once you get to the end of the flowers, wrap the ribbon around a few times. Tie a knot and trim the excess.

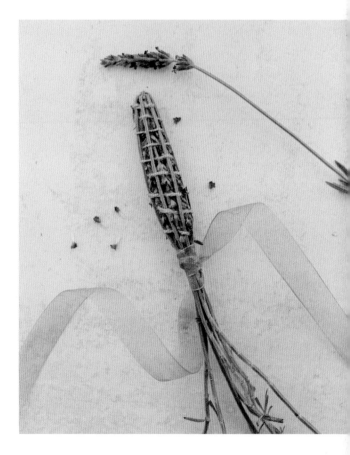

Comfrey Poultice
for Twisted Ankles

Comfrey (*Symphytum officinale*) grows readily in many gardens. It has large, hairy green leaves and beautiful purple flowers that hang together like bells. Comfrey is used by herbalists to treat bruises and sprains. When one of us twists an ankle, we make a poultice out of comfrey leaves and put it on the area to help it heal.

To make the poultice, put a large comfrey leaf in a small bowl and pour just-boiled water over it. Let it sit for a few minutes, until it has cooled some, then wrap the wet leaf around your twisted ankle. Dip a long, thin rag or handkerchief in the liquid remaining in the bowl, and wrap that around your ankle to secure it. You can tie a knot to keep it on.

This is best done outside, since comfrey can easily stain surfaces it is in contact with for too long, such as countertops or floors. You can repeat this poultice a few times a day, leaving it on for at least 20 minutes, until your ankle feels better.

Calendula-Plantain Salve

Comfrey is not recommended for use on broken skin, so for cuts and scrapes, we use a salve made from calendula (*Calendula officinalis*) and plantain (*Plantago lanceolata* or *Plantago major*) instead. Calendula is used by herbalists to treat many skin imbalances, and plantain is a great weed for healing, as it has a drawing quality that is excellent at pulling out splinters or dirt that might be in the cut. To identify herbs, we recommend a minimum of two good plant identification books. They will tell you to look for the long ribs that run the length of the plantain leaves, and show you pictures of the flowers so you can be sure you are using the right plants.

1. First, you will need to make an herbal oil. Fill a mason jar one-third of the way full with a mix of dried calendula and plantain.
2. Pour olive oil over the top until you get to about 1 inch from the top of the jar.
3. Put on the lid, and give the jar a shake. Set it in a sunny window, and be sure to turn it upside down and then right side up at least twice a day. This will keep the herbs covered in oil so they don't get moldy.
4. After 3 or 4 weeks, the herbal oil is ready, and you can strain out the solids.
5. Now, you will use this infused herbal oil to make the salve. Put a couple inches of water in the bottom pot of a double boiler. Be sure not to get any water in the top pot because water can spoil the salve.
6. Turn the heat on low, and pour 1 cup of the herbal oil into the top pot.
7. Add the beeswax pastilles to the oil, and stir.
8. Heat on low until the wax has melted. Turn off the heat, and add a few drops of lavender essential oil (if using). This will give the salve a nice scent, even more healing properties, and act as a preservative so it stays fresh longer.
9. Carefully pour the mixture into clean small jars or salve tins. You may need to wipe the bottom of the top pot of the double boiler so that water does not drip into the salve. Fill the containers nearly to the top with the mixture.
10. Sometimes we put a dried calendula flower right on top for beauty, which also helps us remember what the salve is.
11. After the salve has dried, put on the lid and label the salve. Labeling is very important so you don't forget what is in the salve.
12. To use the salve, rub a little on small cuts and scrapes. You can even use it on your cuticles, or to moisturize dry elbows and knees.

Mason jar with lid

Dried calendula flowers

Dried plantain leaves

Organic olive oil

Double boiler

¼ cup beeswax pastilles

Lavender essential oil (optional)

Small jars or salve tins

Folded Paper Seed Packets

Saving seeds to give to friends or plant the following year is easy if you keep them organized and labeled. You can make your own seed packets with square kite paper or even just regular printer paper.

Before you can save seeds, you'll need to make sure they're at the proper stage. For flower seeds, this usually happens once the flower has died, turned brown, and feels a little crunchy in your hands. Different plants have different signs when the seeds are ready to harvest. We recommend checking out a seed-saving book for detailed advice, or if you don't mind possibly making a few mistakes along the way, you can learn from experimenting yourself.

Square piece of paper, around 6 by 6 inches, or a piece of printer paper

1. If you are using printer paper, you'll need to cut off a little bit so that you have a square. To do this, fold the paper diagonally, then cut off the little rectangle bit at the top. Now you have a square folded in half to make a triangle.
2. Arrange this triangle so that the long side is closest to you, with the point at the top.
3. Now, take one of the two points at the base of the triangle and fold it over so that the tip touches the other side. Try to keep the line this makes across the top parallel to the base of the triangle.
4. Take the other point at the base of the triangle and fold that one across the top, on top of the first one.
5. There is a front piece and a back piece of the point at the top. Take the front piece and tuck it into the space between the second side you folded over. This will keep it together, making a little cup so you can add the seeds.
6. Once you've put a handful of seeds inside the packet, fold the remaining point at the top into the same place the first one went. Now the packet is closed.
7. Label the outside of the packet with the name of the seeds you have put inside and the date. Each type of seed should go in a different packet, and you can store them in a basket or bowl for easy access when you are ready to plant.

IN THE KITCHEN

We seem to be going back and forth from the garden to the kitchen most days because many of the things we make in the kitchen are first grown in the garden. And unless we are eating food right off the vine (which, of course, we often do), we bring it to the kitchen to wash, prepare, can, dry, or otherwise preserve in order to enjoy it later.

What we grow in the garden inspires what we make in the kitchen. We love finding new uses for the edible flowers we grow, the fruit on the trees, and even the edible weeds we gather. Once you have a little garden growing, it's fun to explore and be imaginative with all of the edible plants you harvest and find new ways to eat or prepare them.

Our kitchen is probably the most creative and fun room in our home, where we experiment with making new types of teas, colorful foods, and plenty of crafts. We even keep a miniature garden in our kitchen, growing microgreens and sprouting seeds. Of course, we make our meals in the kitchen as well, but there are so many other exciting things to do in this lively room.

Beeswax Wraps

Beeswax comes from the hard work of bees who busily visit all the flowers in our garden. Beeswax wraps are used to keep food fresh in the fridge or in your lunch. They can replace single-use ziplock bags, foil, and plastic wrap in many instances.

Baking sheet

Parchment paper

Piece of cotton cloth, 10 by 10 inches or larger

1 tablespoon beeswax pastilles, plus more if needed

Old paintbrush

Tongs

1. Line a baking sheet with parchment paper, and preheat the oven to 225°F.
2. Place the fabric on the lined baking sheet and sprinkle the beeswax pastilles on top. The amount you use will depend on the size of your fabric. For a 10-inch square piece of fabric, start with 1 tablespoon of beeswax pastilles.
3. Put the baking sheet in the oven to warm until the wax melts. You will need to stay in the kitchen and keep an eye on the wrap. It should be taken out right when the wax melts. Use the paintbrush to smooth any spots that have too much wax.
4. There will likely be some bare spots at this point. Sprinkle more beeswax pastilles over any spot that hasn't been covered with wax and return the tray to the oven.
5. You may need to flip the fabric and sprinkle more beeswax pastilles on it. Once it is uniformly coated, you can remove it from the oven. Pick it up with a pair of tongs and wave it in the air for a few seconds until it is cool enough to touch. Now it's ready to use.
6. To use, wrap the beeswax wrap around a piece of food you'd like to keep fresh, then warm it in your hands for a few seconds to help soften the beeswax. This will help the wrap stay closed around your food. Now, you can put the wrapped food in the fridge or your lunch.
7. After using, clean the beeswax wrap with soap and cool water. (Washing it in warm or hot water will melt the wax.) Then, drape it on a dish dryer or faucet to dry. Once it's dry, it's ready to use again.

Growing Microgreens

With just a few supplies, you can garden in your own kitchen, growing yummy microgreens to wrap up in sushi rolls, put in salads, or eat as is for a healthy snack. *Microgreens* is the word we use when we are talking about seedlings of vegetables and herbs. If you have already studied botany in school, you may remember that when you plant a seed, the embryo inside sprouts and develops. This nutritive part of the seed that develops as the first one or more leaves of the plant is called the *cotyledon*. Plants have either one or two cotyledons, and botanists use the number of cotyledons to classify plants. Those that have only one are called *monocots*, while those that have two are called *dicots*. There are a few veggies, like corn and leeks, that are monocots, but most vegetables and herbs are dicots. Some of our favorite dicots to plant for microgreens are kale, red clover, peas, radishes, and sunflowers. These seeds all make tasty microgreens.

1. In a bowl, mix some potting soil with water so it is evenly moist but not soggy. You should be able to gather a handful of soil and squeeze it in your hand and it will hold its form. If it crumbles apart, add more water; if it drips through your hands a bit, add more soil. Next, fill a shallow bowl nearly to the top, leaving about ½ inch of space, with the moist soil.

2. Now it's time to plant the seeds. You don't want to have so many seeds that you can't see the soil. An approximate rule of thumb is around 12 to 18 small seeds per square inch, while large seeds like pea and sunflower will only need around three to six seeds per square inch. You will want to have the seeds much closer together than if you were planting them to grow into mature plants. Don't worry too much about making this number exact. After your first round of microgreens, you'll be able to tell if you'd like to try more seeds for the next batch or fewer seeds.

3. For small seeds, sprinkle an even layer over the soil, as if you were adding seasoning, then gently press them down just a bit into the surface of the soil. For large seeds, press them down into the soil so they are nice and secure, but also make sure they don't go completely under the surface.

4. Now, use a spray bottle to spray the seeds a bit. They only need a little water; try not to make the soil soggy.

5. The last step is to cover the bowl with a kitchen towel or cloth to keep it dark (this simulates being under the earth for the little seeds) and set it away from the sun on the kitchen counter.

Large bowl

Potting soil

Rainwater or filtered water

Shallow bowl

Seeds, such as kale, clover, pea, or sunflower

Spray bottle filled with water

Kitchen towel or cloth

Scissors

You can check the seeds each day to see if they've sprouted. Keep the surface from drying out by giving it a little mist every once in a while. Once the seeds have begun to sprout, you'll notice two little "leaves" on each plant. Those are the cotyledons. Now you can remove the towel and watch the little microgreens grow.

6. Each type of plant takes a different amount of time to sprout, basil perhaps taking the longest. When the microgreens are a few inches tall, they are ready to harvest. Use scissors to carefully cut the amount you will be using.

7. Microgreens should be eaten pretty soon after they have reached a height of 3 to 4 inches. If they are left too long, they could get a little moldy. Also, when the seeds are beginning to sprout, you may see some white hairs on them. This may look like mold, but it is almost always just the little root hairs. If you are worried it might be mold, you can use the spray bottle to spray them. If they are root hairs, they will somewhat disappear when wet.

SOAKING SEEDS

Before planting microgreens, you may need to soak the seeds. To do so, fill a mason jar up to one-quarter of the way full with seeds, then fill to the top with water. Leave in a shady spot on the counter for the recommended amount of time, then drain the seeds so they are ready to plant in the bowl. If you have purchased sprouting seeds, you will find soaking directions on the back of the package. If you have packets of seeds without soaking directions, you can use the following as a guide for soaking time:

KALE: 0 to 4 hours

CLOVER: 0 to 4 hours

PEA: 8 hours

SUNFLOWER: 8 to 10 hours

Some seeds, especially the smaller ones, don't need to be soaked. If you are using radish seeds, for example, you do not need to soak them at all. They are ready to use just as they are.

Sprouting Seeds

Another way to garden in the kitchen is to sprout seeds. Sprouts are packed with nutrients and make a yummy snack. They're easy to make. First, choose some seeds to sprout. We like to use chickpeas, peas, and lentils the most, but there are many others you can try, such as buckwheat, radish, broccoli, and wheatgrass.

8-ounce mason jars, one for each type of seed you'll sprout

1 to 2 tablespoons vegetable, herb, or grain seeds

Filtered water

Cheesecloth

Rubber bands

1. Fill a mason jar with the seeds. You can combine seeds of similar size if you'd like. For example, if you have peas, chickpeas, and lentils, you can use a mix of all three.
2. Next, fill the jar with filtered water. Cover the jar with a square of cheesecloth and secure it with a rubber band. Let the seeds soak for 8 hours, or overnight.
3. Once they're finished soaking, drain the water and fill the cup up again about halfway. Give the seeds a swirl to clean them, then drain the water again. You will need to rinse them this way at least twice a day to keep them fresh, hydrated, and free of mold.
4. They are ready to eat as soon as they begin to sprout a little "tail" (note that split lentils will not sprout, but unsplit lentils will). You can let them grow until they are the size you like, then give them a rinse and eat them.

From Grapes to Raisins

Have you ever left a handful of grapes outside and come back a few days later to find they've turned into raisins? Making raisins can be as simple as that. If you want to make sure you get to eat your harvest, and that ants or other bugs don't get to your raisins before they're finished, you can make them inside in a dehydrator or the oven.

Freshly picked seedless grapes

Toothpick

Food dehydrator tray or oven drying screen

Mason jar with lid

1. Pull each grape off of its stem. Next, wash and dry them well. To avoid any exploding in the oven, you can poke a little hole at the bottom of each grape with a toothpick. Arrange the grapes on the dehydrator tray or oven drying screen in a single even layer. It's OK if some of the grapes are touching others, but try not to put so many on the screen that they're all pressed together. They need a little space to dry evenly.

2. If you are using a food dehydrator, put the tray back in it, put on the top, and set the temperature on low. If you are using an oven drying screen, preheat the oven to 200°F, then place the screen in the oven. (We do not leave the oven on when we aren't home or when we are sleeping. We only have it on during the day.) Grapes will usually take a few days before they've fully dried into raisins, but be sure to try them once or twice each day. The larger grapes will take longer to dry, so you can remove the ones that are ready and store them in a mason jar, adding to it as the others become dry enough.

3. Another way of making raisins is to dry the grapes out in the sun. This can be as easy as setting the washed and dried grapes on a plate and putting it outside in a sunny spot. Depending on what kind of critters you have nearby—birds, squirrels, flies—you might end up sharing a lot of your raisins whether you want to or not. One way to keep your drying grapes safe from interested wildlife is to use a food tent (a mesh tent made to keep flies out of food at picnics). To keep them safe from crawling critters that cannot swim, like ants and snails, you can put yogurt containers filled with water under the legs of the table the grapes are sitting on. (If the table has wooden legs, the water could damage the wood, so the yogurt container trick is really only for tables with plastic or metal legs.)

4. Once the raisins are dried to your liking, they can be stored in a mason jar with a lid until ready to enjoy.

Preserving Persimmons

If you have a persimmon tree, you've probably noticed that the persimmons often get ripe all at once, much faster than they can be eaten by just one family. We love to share our persimmons with neighbors and friends, and we also love to dry them so we can enjoy them all year long. Luckily our tree is so huge that we have plenty to share, as well as plenty to keep us busy for a few weeks while we peel, hang, slice, and dry our fruit.

There are many different types of persimmons, but the most commonly known varieties here in Southern California are Hachiya and Fuyu. Hachiya persimmons are full of tannins that make them very astringent if they are eaten before they're fully ripe. They are very soft when ripe, and much sweeter than Fuyu persimmons. They're more oblong, with a little point at the bottom; their shape reminds us of a giant acorn. Fuyu persimmons are squat and hard. They're crunchy and less sweet than Hachiyas, but they don't have the astringent tannins, so they're not bitter.

Because Fuyu persimmons don't have the bitter tannins, they have a much longer shelf life. Hachiya persimmons have a very small window of time they can be eaten fresh. They aren't ripe until they are incredibly squishy, so they don't last more than a couple of days after that. For this reason, we really like to preserve our Hachiya persimmons.

The easiest way to dry persimmons is to pick them before they are ripe. If you dry them when they are even a little ripe, they will be brownish in color and taste bitter. We pick ours when the top third is still green, and they are very hard. Then, carefully cut them crosswise into ¼-inch-thick slices. They remind us of little suns. Last, arrange them in a food dehydrator and set it on low, or dry them in the oven at 200°F on baking sheets lined with parchment paper.

When the persimmons are fully dry, they can be stored in large mason jars with lids. They make sweet snacks and last until the next round is nearly ready to harvest.

Hoshigaki

Another way to dry Hachiya persimmons is hoshigaki style. Hoshigaki are a Japanese delicacy, and although they take more time to make, they're really delicious and worth the effort.

Hachiya persimmons

Vegetable peeler

Twine

Laundry rack or other place to hang the fruit

Old towel

1. To make hoshigaki, pick the Hachiya persimmons while they are unripe and still very hard. We've found the best timing is to pick them when the top third or so is still green. Leave at least a 1-inch stem on the persimmons when you pick them. Next, carefully peel the persimmons with a veggie peeler, leaving the stem and the top portion of the persimmon unpeeled. If you nick them, or peel more than just the skin, they could rot before they are fully dry and fall on the ground with a splat.

2. Next, tie the twine around the stem of the peeled persimmon, and tie it to the laundry rack. The rack should be indoors in a sunny, warm spot. You may want to put an old towel down on the floor in case one of the hanging persimmons falls while drying.

3. Continue until all of the persimmons are peeled and hung on the rack. Be sure to leave enough space between them; otherwise, they will rot at all the places where they are touching. Leave them there until they are dry, but the last step is to gently—very gently—massage each persimmon every day. This shouldn't take long, just a few seconds per piece of fruit.

4. After a while you will notice some white on the persimmons. At first, it may look like mold, but if you look closely, you can see tiny sugar crystals on the fruit. (Blue or gray furry spots mean the persimmons have gone moldy and should be composted.) When the persimmons feel like dried figs, they're ready. Slice one crosswise and try it. When they are all dry enough, they can be stored in a mason jar with a lid. If they aren't quite dry enough, they could rot in the jar, so we often leave our hoshigaki on the laundry rack and cut them down as we eat them. If they dry out too much they can be a little tough, but that never bothers us because they're still tasty.

Picking and Drying Herbs

Once you've made raisins and hoshigaki, drying herbs will seem like a cinch. We dry herbs and flowers in hanging bundles and on drying screens. No matter which method you choose, be sure to gather the herbs in the late morning. In the early morning or evening, there will often be dew on the plants. If you gather them when they are wet, they are prone to mold, which will ruin the harvest. Flowers and fragrant leaves are best gathered in the late morning, after the dew has dried, but before the afternoon sun has carried much of their fragrance away.

Drying Herbs in a Bundle

To dry herbs in a bundle, you will need garden shears to cut the herbs, rubber bands to hold the bundles together, a hanger to attach them to, and some string to tie them to the hanger.

The first step is to cut a bunch of herbs. Peppermint, spearmint, lavender, catnip, and sage are all great choices. Separate the herbs by type into bundles that are easy to grasp in your hand. If the bundles are too big, the herbs may not dry all the way where they touch. Large bundles also have a tendency to drop sprigs of herbs as they dry out.

Once you have a good-sized bunch of herbs, secure them 3 inches from the bottom of the stems with a rubber band. We use rubber bands rather than twine or string because as the plants dry they shrink in size. The rubber bands stay nice and tight around the herbs, even as they shrink, so usually none fall out.

Slip a 2-inch-long tail of a 12-inch piece of string under one part of the rubber band securing the herbs, then tie it to the long tail of string. Use the long tail to tie the herb bundle to the hanger. Continue adding more bunches of herbs to the hanger until you can't add any more without the bundles touching one another. Hang the hanger up somewhere there is good airflow and not a lot of light. Attics are great for this purpose. Try to hang it so that the herbs aren't touching anything, including the wall, so they are able to dry evenly.

It's advisable to check on the drying herbs every few days, to see if the bundles need adjusting. You will know when they have completely dried because they will be brittle and crumble when you crush a leaf in your hand. If the leaves bend rather than crack, that means

they still have some water in them, and they need more time to dry.

Once the herbs are fully dry, you can strip all the leaves and flowers from the stems. Add the stems to the compost pile and store the leaves and flowers in mason jars with lids, away from direct sunlight. Remember to write the name of the plant you have dried on the jar so you know what it is.

Drying Herbs on a Screen

Plants like rose petals, calendula blossoms, pansies, and rose hips are all easier to dry on a screen rather than in hanging bundles. We dry peppermint, catnip, sage, and lots of other plants on screens as well. Color, fragrance, and flavor are best preserved if the screens are indoors and kept out of direct sunlight.

To dry rose petals, simply pick fresh petals off of roses in the late morning and sprinkle them on the screen. A single layer of petals is best; if there are too many piled on the screen, they won't dry evenly and they could mold. They are fully dry when they've become small in size and dark in color, and when they feel a bit crispy when crushed in your hand. They won't crumble as easily as peppermint leaves, but they will feel quite dry.

To dry calendula flowers, pluck the flowers off of the stem, leaving the petals attached to the center. Lay them facedown on the screen in a single layer. They take a while to dry, and because they are so resinous, they will not become crumbly. When they are completely dry, the petals will be skinny and make a crinkling sound when you crush them.

To dry pansies, violets, and Johnny-jump-ups, pick the flowers and lay them on the screen. Sometimes laying them facedown helps the flowers keep their shape as they dry. They will shrink quite a bit in size and be wrinkly, not soft, when they are completely dry.

To dry chamomile, snap the flower heads off of the plant and arrange them in a single layer on the screen. They will crumble in your hands when they are dry.

To dry herbs like plantain, catnip, sage, and peppermint, arrange sprigs of the herb in a single layer on the screen. They are fully dry when they crumble in your hands.

Flowers and herbs can be kept, separated by type, in mason jars with lids. Edible herbs like peppermint make great tea. We like to make tea from fresh peppermint whenever possible, but we always keep a jar of dried peppermint leaves for times when the fresh herb is scarce. Try making a delicious herbal tea by mixing dried peppermint with rose petals and steeping them in hot water. Use a tea strainer to strain out the solids before drinking.

Calming Lemon Balm
Herbal Tea

One of our favorite teas is lemon balm. Lemon balm (*Melissa officinalis*) is a lemony-tasting plant in the mint family. It looks similar to spearmint (*Mentha spicata*) and it's known for its calming and soothing quality. We make it whenever someone has a tummy ache, or feels like they need help relaxing. Growing lemon balm is easy, but it is a good idea to grow it in a big pot rather than in your garden bed.

Otherwise, like all varieties of mint, it will take over the whole bed.

To make lemon balm herbal tea, fill a teapot about halfway with lemon balm leaves (stems are OK too). Pour just-boiled water over the top, stopping about an inch away from the top of the teapot. Let steep for anywhere from 2 to 15 minutes, add a spoonful of honey if you'd like, and enjoy.

Blue Viola Tea and Pink Viola Lemonade

Viola is the name of the large genus of flowers in the violet family. Violets (*Viola odorata*), pansies (*Viola x wittrockiana*), and Johnny-jump-ups (*Viola tricolor*) are all violas. Your local nursery can help you choose the best edible violas to plant in your garden, and depending on where you live, if you have good plant guidebooks and a parent to go with you, you might even be able to harvest violets in the wild.

We grow violets, pansies, and Johnny-jump-ups in our garden, and they make a wonderful tea. Depending on the colors of your flowers, the tea will likely be blue or purple. More flowers will make a darker tea.

To make blue viola tea, put a large handful of violas in a teapot and pour just-boiled water over them. The amount of violas and water is up to you. Using more flowers and less water makes a stronger and darker tea, while using more water and less flowers makes a milder tea. Strain out the flowers and pour the tea into a clear heat-safe glass cup so you can enjoy the color. Add a spoonful of honey if you'd like.

After you've made the tea, you can easily turn it into lemonade. The fun thing about this drink is that it changes color. It starts out blue, but adding lemon juice turns it pink! To make it, squeeze a lemon wedge into the cup of blue viola tea, and wait a few seconds. More lemon juice will brighten and lighten the pink color.

Why does this happen? Different foods have different pH levels—in other words, different levels of acidity. Changing the acidity of certain foods can change the color. Lemon juice is acidic, so adding it to the blue tea will change the color to pink. Red cabbage will turn blue when boiled and left in water, but will stay red or pink if it is cooked with something acidic, like lemon juice or vinegar. Many cooks use this trick to keep their cabbage from turning blue when they cook it.

After you've tried experimenting with turning your blue viola tea into pink viola lemonade, try making color-changing rice (see page 352) by cooking some rice in red cabbage water instead of regular water.

Color-Changing Rice

Making color-changing lemonade is fun, and you can do a very similar trick with rice. Even more impressive, your bowl of rice can stay two different colors right up until it's eaten. When you first make the rice, it will be purple because of the cabbage water you cooked it in. Then, wherever you squeeze the lemon juice on it, it will turn bright pink! If you don't put lemon juice on all of the rice, the parts without any juice will stay purple, so your bowl of rice will be purple and pink. And if you let it sit for a while, about 10 minutes or so, the pink will become even more vibrant.

Red cabbage

Large pot

Filtered water

Rice

Lemon juice

1. Cut up a red cabbage and add it to a large pot.
2. Add water to cover the cabbage, bring to a boil, and let it simmer until the cabbage is tender. The cabbage can now be eaten, fed to chickens, or put in the compost.
3. The remaining water will be purple. Use this water to cook the rice instead of regular water, and you will have purple rice!
4. When it is done, squirt some lemon juice on top. Everywhere the lemon juice touches will turn pink!

SKINCARE AND HAIRCARE

You have probably heard the term *self-care* before. Self-care simply means taking care of yourself—your physical health as well as your emotional health and happiness—by making healthy choices. Some of these choices include taking care of your body by eating nourishing foods, drinking plenty of water, getting enough sleep, and spending time outside. Taking care of your body helps you feel good about yourself.

Many of the products you see in stores that are made for skin and hair are full of ingredients that are not good for you. This may be hard to believe, but it's true! The good news is that you can make sure the products you put on your body are healthy for you by making them yourself out of clean ingredients.

Basic Skincare

As you get older, changing hormones will cause your skin to change. You might notice that acne, oily spots, or dry patches start to appear. Keeping your skin clean, moisturized, and balanced will help keep it clear and healthy. Healthy skin is not only for girls. It's just as important for guys to care for their skin. Following are steps to a healthy skincare regimen.

Cleanse: Washing your face at night will remove the dirt, sweat, dead skin cells, sunscreen, and any makeup that might be on your face from the day. Many face washes can be too irritating, stripping, or drying, and skin will react by getting dry patches or producing extra oil, which causes acne. To avoid this outcome, make sure to use a very gentle face wash that does not contain any soap.

Tone: A simple rosewater spray works well to tone the skin, although you can skip this step if you wish, or if you don't have any on hand.

Serum: A few drops of an oil serum will nourish and hydrate the skin. If your skin is prone to acne breakouts, a serum with sea buckthorn oil will help clear up any acne.

Moisturize: Depending on how much serum you use, and your skin type, you may not even need to moisturize. If you feel like your skin is a little dry, a gentle moisturizer that will not clog your pores is a good choice.

Mask: Once every week or two, a face mask is a special treat for your skin. After cleansing, apply the mask. After you rinse it off, you can apply serum and moisturizer.

Sunscreen: Sunscreen and a hat during the day will protect your skin from sunburn and, when you are older, age spots and wrinkles. It sounds strange to worry about it now, but trust me, when you're older you'll be glad you took good care of your skin.

The first four steps of this regimen are done at night. In the morning, simply wash your face with water, and use a little rose water and moisturizer if needed. A sunscreen formulated for the face is the final step in the morning.

Gentle Honey or Olive Oil Face Wash

The first step in caring for the delicate skin on your face is to wash it every night. The two best ways to wash your face are very simple, and you can usually find the ingredients right in the kitchen cupboard.

The first option is a honey face wash. Tie your hair back away from your face, and spread ½ teaspoon of honey over your skin. Splash a little water on your face so you can massage the honey with your fingertips in little circles. Rinse well with warm water, and gently pat dry with a clean towel. This is a sticky face wash, so often the best time to do it is when you are taking a bath or shower. That way you won't be left with any honey on your face or hair.

Another option is an olive oil face wash. Tie your hair back and gently massage 1 teaspoon of olive oil onto your face. Get a washcloth wet with warm water, squeeze it out, then hold it over your face until it cools. Once cool, gently wipe away the olive oil with your washcloth.

Calendula Sea Buckthorn Face Serum

This serum is balancing for skin, especially acne-prone skin. It has an orange tint to it, so it's best to use it at night rather than in the morning. If you'd like to use it in the morning, you can add a little olive oil to dilute it and make it less orange. You may also notice a little orange on your pillowcase from the serum rubbing off of your face while you are sleeping. It should wash out easily in the laundry.

1. Add the dried calendula flowers to the mason jar. The jar should be filled around one-third full with the flowers. Don't pack them in tightly; you want the oil to be able to cover all parts of the flowers, and they should move easily in the oil once the lid is on and you turn the jar upside down.

2. Next, pour the sea buckthorn oil over the calendula flowers. Fill the jar with the olive oil or sweet almond oil, leaving about 1 inch or so of space at the very top. Put on the lid, and give the jar a gentle shake. Put it near a sunny window so the warmth from the sun coming in warms the oil. Shake the jar gently once a day for at least 2 weeks. (You can let it infuse for up to 4 weeks if you'd like.)

3. Once you're finished infusing, remove the calendula flowers from the serum. If little bits of the flower are still in the oil, don't worry. We even like to leave a couple of petals floating in the serum for fun. Now, use the small funnel and carefully pour the serum into the dropper bottles. Make sure you label the bottles so you remember what's inside.

4. To use the serum, after washing your face at night and spraying a little rose water on, massage three to seven drops of the serum onto your face with your fingertips. Massage your face for about 30 seconds to help the serum absorb.

Handful of dried calendula flowers

8-ounce mason jar with lid

2 ounces sea buckthorn oil

4 ounces olive oil or sweet almond oil

Small funnel

1-ounce dropper bottles

Sensitive Skin
Face and Body Lotion

Using a lotion that is noncomedogenic (meaning it will not block or clog your pores) and made with clean ingredients makes all the difference in any skincare routine. When skin is too dry, usually from using a face wash that is too harsh, it responds by creating extra oil to moisturize itself. This can easily cause acne breakouts and oily skin. Using nonstripping, gentle cleansers and a noncomedogenic moisturizer will help your skin retain its natural moisture, keeping it from becoming dry or flaky.

I've been making my own moisturizers for more than a decade now, and using them has made a big difference in keeping my skin clear. I first learned how to make a good face lotion from one of my teachers, herbalist Rosemary Gladstar, and that very first lesson has inspired every lotion I've made since. How wonderful it is to have a skilled, experienced mentor sharing her hard-won knowledge! I'm grateful for Rosemary's generous spirit, and I try to offer the knowledge and skills I've gathered in the same openhearted, unselfish way. I think you will love this recipe, the first step of which is to make some herbal oils. It will make enough lotion for you to share with family and friends.

This lotion makes a great gift, but remember, it's totally natural, without any chemical preservatives, so it will last longer if you keep it cool (inside your house is fine, but it may spoil in a hot car) and use clean hands when applying it. Once opened, it should stay fresh for around 3 months. If bacteria gets in—from dirty hands, for example—it could spoil. You will know if it has gone bad because you will see little blue or greenish spots on the top or around the rim. If this happens, it's time to throw it out and make a fresh batch.

TO MAKE THE HERBAL OILS:

1. Fill both of the mason jars about one-third of the way full with the dried calendula flowers.
2. Pour the olive oil into one jar, until it is about ½ inch from the top.
3. Pour the sesame oil into the other jar.
4. Put the lids on the jars and set them in a sunny window.
5. Shake the jars once a day to keep the flowers covered in the oil.
6. After 3 to 4 weeks, strain out the flowers.

TO MAKE THE LOTION:

1. Fill the bottom pot of a double boiler about one-fifth of the way full with the water and set it on the stove over low heat.
2. Carefully pour both herbal oils into the top pot of the double boiler.
3. Add the coconut oil.

FOR THE HERBAL OILS:

2 (8-ounce) mason jars with lids

Dried calendula flowers

Olive oil

Sesame oil

FOR THE LOTION:

Double boiler

Filtered water

6 tablespoons calendula-infused olive oil

6 tablespoons calendula-infused sesame oil

4. Add the beeswax pastilles and stir slowly until the ingredients are melted together.
5. Remove the top pot of the double boiler and carefully wipe the water off the bottom.
6. Pour the rose water into a blender and turn it on.
7. Pour the vitamin E oil into the blender while it is going.
8. Keep the blender going, and add the melted beeswax-oil mixture.
9. Once blended, pour the lotion into the clean mason jars. Once it has cooled, carefully wipe any spilled lotion off the sides of the jars and put on the lids.
10. Don't forget to label the lotion. You can make a simple label on a small piece of paper and tape it to the lid, or write directly on the jar. It's also a good idea to put the date on the jar so you know when it was made.
11. To use as a face lotion, massage a small amount on your face after cleansing, toning with rose water, and using serum. To use as a body lotion, massage onto clean, damp skin. Using it just after you towel dry after a bath or shower is ideal. If your skin is very dry but you don't have time to take a shower, just spray a little rose water on your dry skin first, then massage in some lotion.

⅓ cup coconut oil

5 level teaspoons beeswax pastilles

1 cup rose water

Blender

1 teaspoon vitamin E oil

2-ounce mason jars with lids

Honey-Rose Exfoliating Face Mask

Once a week, treat your face to a mask. This mask nourishes the skin and exfoliates dead, dry skin away, leaving your face soft and fresh.

1. If you have an herb grinder, you can grind a handful of very dry rose petals into a fine, even powder. You will most likely have to run it through a few times. If you don't have an herb grinder (or a coffee grinder used only for the purpose of grinding herbs), you can buy rose petal powder.

2. Put 1 teaspoon of the rose petal powder in a small bowl. Add a spoonful of honey and a few drops of olive oil, and mix until the whole thing is the consistency of slightly runny honey. Add a few more drops of olive oil, if needed, to thin out the mixture. When it is a nice, spreadable consistency, set the bowl aside and rinse your face with warm water.

3. To use the mask, gently massage it all over your face with your fingertips, avoiding your eyes and mouth. Leave this mask on for 10 to 20 minutes, then use a warm, wet washcloth to gently wipe it away. Rinse your face with warm water until the mask is completely gone, then splash a little cold water over your face.

Big handful of dried rose petals and an herb grinder, or 1 teaspoon store-bought rose petal powder

Small bowl

Honey

Olive oil

Herbal Body Wash Soap

Melt-and-pour soap base is available at most craft stores, as well as online craft shops where soapmaking supplies are sold. It's too drying to use on your face, but it makes a great body wash. This recipe calls for a glycerin soap base because it's transparent, which makes the bar of soap look like a work of art when you add nature confetti or dried flowers. Silicone molds come in many different shapes and sizes, so choose your favorite shape for this soap.

FOR THE NATURE CONFETTI:

Dried leaves

Hole punch

FOR THE SOAP:

Silicone molds

Rubbing alcohol

Small bowl

Paintbrush

Nature confetti or dried flowers

1 pound melt-and-pour glycerin soap base, cubed

Double boiler

Lavender essential oil

Chopstick

TO MAKE THE NATURE CONFETTI:

1. Go outside and find some pretty dried leaves. It's important that they are dry. Otherwise, they might get moldy in the soap.
2. Making nature confetti is as easy as using a hole punch to punch holes in leaves. We like using ones that make star-shaped or heart-shaped holes for fun. Empty the hole punch and you will have a little pile of confetti made from the leaves.

TO MAKE THE SOAP:

1. Set the silicone molds on a flat surface. (A baking sheet works well.) Make sure they are clean and dry. Pour a tiny bit of rubbing alcohol into a small bowl, dip a paintbrush in the alcohol, and brush the inside of the silicone molds.
2. Sprinkle some nature confetti or a few dried flowers into the molds. Set aside.
3. Put the soap base in the top of a double boiler. (Make sure the bottom pan has water in it.) Heat the glycerin on low, stirring every so often, until every cube is completely melted. Once the soap base has melted, turn off the heat, add approximately 20 drops of the essential oil, and stir.
4. Carefully pour the melted soap base into the molds, stopping just before the liquid reaches the top. Dip the paintbrush in the alcohol again, and tap it above each mold so that each one is sprinkled with a little alcohol. This will help prevent bubbles from forming on the surface. Let the soap completely cool before removing it.
5. You might find that all of the nature confetti or dried flowers rise up to the surface when you pour in the soap base. Giving a quick stir with a chopstick can help keep them below the surface. Another way to make sure they stay inside the soap is to only fill each mold halfway with soap at first. The confetti or flowers will rise to the top

of that first layer, where they will stick. Let the soap cool for a bit, then add more melted soap base to fill the mold to the top, remembering to sprinkle with alcohol at the end. The confetti and flowers you added should stay right on top of that first layer, so when you add a second layer they will be stuck in the middle of the soap.

6. Let the soap solidify, then remove from the molds. To give as a gift, wrap each soap in wax paper and secure with twine or pretty ribbon.

Sewing a Washcloth

ADRIANA ORTIZ-ERICKSON

Adriana Ortiz-Erickson is a true Renaissance woman, with more hobbies, interests, and jobs than anyone we know. Her artistic talent and genuine appreciation of ethically made, interesting things influence her as the buyer and manager of Heritage Goods & Supply. She has cultivated a love for art, textiles, and gifts. Drawing inspiration from the handmade clothes and gifts of her Mexican roots, Adriana's passion is also passed through her crafts. These days, sharing joy and wonder is a cornerstone of Adriana's new life as a mother and can be seen and felt in her simple, sustainable, and fun-to-make projects. This easy handmade washcloth is perfect to use in your skincare routine. You can use new material, or, if you have an old towel and some cotton or flannel cloth (and permission to cut them up), you can use those.

Terry cloth material, old or new

Ruler

Washable fabric pen

Sharp scissors

Cotton or flannel fabric

Cotton thread and a universal sewing needle, or a sewing machine

1. For this project, you will make a washcloth that is 7 inches square. Lay out the terry cloth on a flat work surface. Take the ruler and washable fabric pen and measure and mark a square with 7-inch sides.
2. Use the scissors to cut the square out of the terry cloth fabric. Repeat these same steps with the cotton or flannel fabric.
3. Once you have both pieces of fabric cut out, you can match them up so all four sides line up.

Then it's time to decide on your preferred method of sewing the washcloth together.

To hand-sew the washcloth:

1. Get the thread and sewing needle. Unspool an arm's length of the thread. Make a clean cut on the thread end and thread it through the sewing needle until you have a 2-inch tail (longer if you would like). Having this tail helps ensure that the thread will stay on the needle as you work the stitch through the fabric. On the longer end of the thread, tie a knot 1 inch from the end. This helps hold the thread in place so you can start the row of stitches as you work your way around the project.

2. Get the terry cloth and cotton fabric that you have cut into squares and lay them against one another so all four corners are paired. Pick the corner where you would like to start. Two beginning stitches Adriana recommends for this project are a running stitch or a whip stitch. You could also use a blanket stitch. (A running stitch will leave the fabric edges loose, while a whip stitch or blanket stitch will hug the edges.)

3. Using your preferred stitch and starting from your chosen corner, sew around the perimeter of the washcloth until you come back to where you started. On the last stitch, finish with a double knot.

To machine-sew the washcloth:

1. Get the terry cloth and cotton fabric that you have cut into squares. Lay them against one another so all four corners are paired. Using the edge of the presser foot as a guide, start on the corner of your choice.

2. After anchoring in a few backstitches, sew around the edge of the washcloth, ¼ inch in from the edge. Once you are back to where you started, you can end with a few more backstitches to lock in the work.

3. As an extra finishing touch, you can brace and add structure to the washcloth by sewing a diagonal line from corner to corner. Sewing an X across the washcloth will prevent the fabric from bagging and help it hold up while it is being used and washed.

Types of Stitches

If this is your first time hand sewing, here's a brief overview of how to do three basic stitches. For detailed explanations of different stitch techniques and more fun projects, we recommend checking out *Stitch Camp* by Nicole Blum and Catherine Newman.

RUNNING STITCH: To sew a running stitch, put the threaded needle through the cloth from underneath. The knot you made will hold the thread in place, so pull the thread through until the knot is up against the cloth. Now, find a spot about ¼ inch in front of where the thread is coming out, and put the needle down through the cloth from top to bottom. Next, find a spot about ¼ inch in front of where the thread is coming out of the underside of the cloth, and push it back up to the top of the cloth. Repeat this up-down, up-down stitching until you come back to the spot where you started. Tie a knot close to the cloth to secure your sewing.

WHIPSTITCH: To sew a whipstitch, put the threaded needle through the cloth from underneath. Pull the thread through until it stops when your knot reaches the cloth. Now, instead of putting the needle down through the top of the cloth, bring it around and push it up through the bottom of the cloth again. Space the stitches about ¼ inch apart. You will continue to put the needle through from underneath and bring it up to the top until you get to the place where you started. Tie a knot close to the cloth to secure your sewing.

BLANKET STITCH: To sew a blanket stitch, put the threaded needle through the cloth from underneath. Pull the thread through until it stops when your knot reaches the cloth. Now, bring the needle back to the underside of the cloth, in the same spot or very close to the same spot where you first put the needle through, and push it through to the top again. Before you pull the thread all the way, put the needle down through the loop made from the thread. Next, bring the needle around to the underside of the cloth again, this time ¼ inch past the last stitch. Push the needle through to the top, and put it down through the loop again before pulling the thread taut. Bring the needle around to the underside of the cloth again, to a spot ¼ inch past the last stitch. Push the needle through to the top, and down through the loop again. Continue in this way until you get to the place where you started. Tie a knot close to the cloth to secure your sewing.

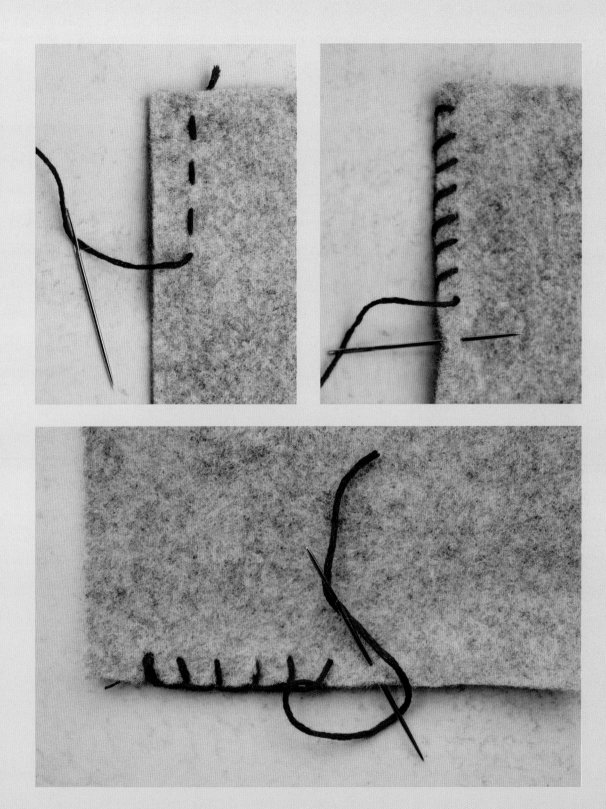

French Braids

Everyone's hair is different and beautiful, and of course not everyone has hair—that is beautiful too! While French braids work better on some hair types than others, we've included some great books on different hairstyles for many hair types in the Resources section in the back of this book.

Long, straight hair is the easiest to French braid or fishtail braid, although curlier and shorter hair can be braided both ways with enough patience and practice. For those of you ready to start braiding, you may want to grab a sibling or a friend. It's tricky to French braid your own hair, so it works best if you and a friend braid each other's hair.

To prepare the hair for braiding, carefully brush out all of the tangles, using a brush for straight hair or a pick or your fingers for curly hair. Isla's hair is very straight, so she uses a brush to comb out the tangles. Her friend Ellie has curly hair, so she likes to pick out tangles with her fingers to keep her curls smooth.

Gather the top one-third of the hair on your friend's head, as though you were doing a half-up, half-down style. Separate this hair into three sections. Begin to braid by taking the outside section of hair from the right-hand side of the head and bringing it over the middle section to the center. Now you have a new section in the center. (The section that was originally in the center is now on the right side.) Take the outside section of hair from the left-hand side and bring it over the new middle section all the way to the center.

Now comes the tricky part. Gather a new section of hair from the right side of the head about the size of the other sections you have, and add it to that section you are holding at the right side. (This is the section that used to be the middle section.) Take that combined section and bring it over the middle section to become the new middle section. Now, gather a new section of hair from the left side of the head, making it about the size of the other sections you have, and add it to the section you are holding at the left side. Bring that combined section over the middle section, making it the new middle section.

Repeat this process all the way down the head until you have put all of your friend's hair into the braid. If her hair is long, you will have a long tail of hair left over. Continue to braid this hair, although you won't be adding anything to the sections anymore, just repeating taking the hair from the outside section and moving it over to the center, then switching sides. When finished, secure the hair 1 to 2 inches from the bottom with a hair tie.

Fishtail Braids

Fishtail braids are similar to French braids and just as easy to accomplish, but they have a different twist to them.

Begin by brushing out or picking out any tangles. (Ellie's hair is curly, so she uses her fingers rather than a brush to keep her hair smooth and her curls bouncy.)

To braid, gather the hair into two sections at the base of the head. Take a small section from the right side of the section on the right, and bring it over the top, adding it to the right side of the section on the left side. This might sound confusing, but just think of it as taking that

section over to the section on the left, but at the right side of that left section. Next, take a small section of hair from the left side of the section on the left, and bring it over the top, adding it to the left side of the section of hair on the right side.

Keep going this way, trading off sides, until you are about 2 inches before the end of the hair. Secure with a hair tie. Now, gently tug along both sides of the braid from top to bottom. This will make the braid thicker. For more braiding inspiration, check out the books in the Resources section in the back of this book.

Lice Treatment

One of the most dreaded hair problems we can think of is head lice—those tiny parasites that crawl from head to head, laying eggs on our hair and biting our scalps! Getting lice can be embarrassing, itchy, and uncomfortable, and if you have it, it's important to treat it right away.

Louse is the word for a single parasite; *lice* is the word for more than one. A head lice infestation happens when a single louse crawls off of one person's head and onto another's. That louse then lays eggs on the hair, close to the scalp. When those eggs hatch into more lice, they lay more eggs, and by this time the poor person unknowingly hosting the lice begins to notice they have an itchy scalp, especially behind the ears. Lice multiply very quickly, and they can be passed to other people by direct head-to-head contact as well as by sharing hairbrushes.

Drugstores sell lice shampoo and lice combs, but over the years lice have become resistant to the treatment. This shampoo is also known to irritate the skin on the scalp and is filled with harsh chemicals. The natural, very effective way to treat lice is with olive oil. The oil is used in combination with a metal lice comb and lots of patience.

At the very first sign of lice, check everyone else in the household. Look on the hair about ¼ inch away from the scalp, especially behind the ears, at the nape of the neck, and along the part. If even only one egg is spotted, or one little bug running around on the scalp, that person also has lice, and there's probably a lot more lice and eggs hiding on their head.

The first step is to kill all of the live lice on the head, and the best way to do so is with olive oil. Go outside and use a hairbrush to brush out all the hair so there are no tangles. (Now, either throw the hairbrush away or put it in a ziplock bag and keep it in the freezer for a week to kill the lice so you don't end up with another infestation.)

Next, cover the whole head with olive oil. Gather the strands of hair and pile all the hair on top of the head. Make sure the whole pile of hair is completely saturated with oil. This is best done outside because it can be drippy and messy. Drape an old towel over the shoulders of the person with lice to keep the oil from getting on their clothes. Once the whole head and hair are covered, you can put a shower cap on to keep everything contained. Leave the towel around the shoulders for a while because the oil will drip.

The oil needs to be left on for about 8 hours to suffocate the lice. During this time, you can start combing out the lice and their eggs with a metal lice comb. (The plastic combs do not work nearly as well.) As you go along, wipe the comb with toilet paper and put it in the toilet or a lit fireplace. You can also wait until the oil has been on for 8 hours before you start to comb.

When combing the hair, separate it into sections to make sure you comb every last part. Then, when you are sure you've combed the whole head and every hair, do it again. You'll almost always find there are still either lice or eggs, or both, on the head. After you comb the whole head through twice without finding one louse or egg, you can let the person wash their hair. Wash the hair twice with shampoo to get the oil out.

After the hair is washed, comb with a wide-toothed comb (preferably metal or another material that can be boiled or washed well to remove any lice or eggs) to remove any tangles. Then, separate the hair into four to six sections and go through every hair again to check for eggs.

This process of searching every hair can be done as many times as you can stand. I recommend repeating this process of sectioning the hair and searching thoroughly every day for a week.

The last step is to repeat the olive oil treatment and combing 10 to 12 days after the first treatment. This is to make sure you kill any lice that may have hatched from an egg you did not see during the first round. This happens often! After this second treatment, you are all set.

Sometimes sand or dandruff on the scalp can look like lice eggs. The best way to tell the difference is that sand or dandruff can be easily removed by blowing it off the scalp or wiping it away. Eggs are different because they are attached to the hair with a sort of glue, so they are hard to remove. To get an egg off of a strand of hair, slide it off down the length of the hair with your fingernails. Then make sure to carefully toss the egg in the toilet.

CREATIVITY

Creativity means using your imagination—something you do when you play imaginary games, act on a stage, and make artistic projects. When we knit, sew, mend, carve, weave, and felt, we are using our imagination and being creative. The best thing about creativity is that there are no limits. We can draw, paint, write, and build whatever we can dream up! We often use our creative impulse to make beautiful and useful things we need or gifts for our friends and family. We make things to decorate our home, keep us warm, or bring a smile to someone's face. We use our creativity to express ourselves, have fun, connect with others, pass the time, and solve problems. It's such a great feeling to learn something new or make something with your own two hands. To spark your imagination, this chapter offers some ideas and things to try, but it's just the beginning. We hope you will find many more opportunities to be creative in your daily life.

Strohsterne (Straw Ornaments)

Beautiful straw Christmas ornaments have been made in Scandinavia and Germany for many generations. In Germany, they are called *strohsterne*, which means "straw star." We decorate our house with these delicate stars all year long. You can buy different colors of straw at craft stores, or try coloring your own with watercolors or markers, to make stars in all sorts of colors.

Disposable paper cup

Scissors or sharp knife

Hole punch

Handful of dry straw, at least 5 inches long

Butter knife

Thread

1. Carefully cut a disposable paper cup in half at the middle with scissors. Or, if you draw a line around the middle of the cup, an adult can help you cut all the way around it with a sharp knife. Use the hole punch to make eight evenly spaced holes around the new rim of the cup. They should be all the way at the top of the rim so that straw can be placed in each of the holes.

2. Next, take one length of straw and split it down the middle with a butter knife. Take the halved lengths of straw and split each of those down the middle. It's OK if your splits are not exact.

3. Continue splitting the other lengths of straw into quarters until you have 12 pieces. (This takes three lengths of straw, if all four pieces per length turn out pretty even. Sometimes when you split the straw it ends up much too thin on one end. If this happens, you might need an extra piece of straw or two until you get 12 even pieces.)

4. Trim the 12 pieces to be the same length, at least 4 inches long.

5. Next, set the cup on a flat surface like a table and arrange the straw around the cup. Each piece of straw sits flat across the cup, with either end nestled in the holes made by the hole punch. There are 8 holes. You will skip two spaces in between the spots where each straw end sticks out. The first straw sits in the first and fourth holes, with nothing in the second and third holes. The second straw sits in the second and fifth holes, skipping the third and fourth holes. The third straw sits in the third and sixth holes, and so on.

6. Continue around the cup in this way until you place the eighth piece of straw in the eighth and third holes. You will have two ends of straw sticking out at each hole-punched spot. Already it makes a nice star shape.

7. You have four pieces of straw remaining. Intersect the star with an X through the center. You don't have to use different colors of straw, but if you would like to, you can change colors for this part.

8. Intersect the X you just made with another X. Now you will have three ends of straw coming out of each hole-punched spot.

9. The last step is to secure the star. Ask someone to put a finger gently on the center. Take the thread and tie a knot around the first group of straw ends, at the first hole-punched spot, leaving a tail of thread at least 4 inches long. Wrap the thread around three times.

10. Don't cut the thread, but go on to the next group of straw ends at the next hole-punched spot. Wrap the thread around this group three times, but don't tie a knot. You don't need to tie any more knots until the end.

11. Continue on to the next group, and the next, wrapping three times at each. When you get back to the first group, wrap around one more time, then secure with a knot. Cut the thread, leaving a 4-inch tail. You will have two ends of thread, both 4 inches long, attached to that first group of straw you tied. Tie a knot at the end of those threads, making a loop, so you can hang the star. When you've finished tying, you can trim the ends to make them more even.

Whittling Safety with Liam

Whittling is the art of carving a stick of wood into something. I tend to whittle when I have extra time either at home or in nature. I like to whittle knives and spears the most because it's fun and a good way to spend time. But carve what you would like!

My favorite first knife for whittling is an Opinel knife. It's easy to use and the kid's version has a sharp blade but a blunt outer edge. I find it easy to work with, and I like that I can fold it into a closed position for safety. The knife must always be closed and locked when not in immediate use. This means if you are stopping to talk, putting it down to adjust your position, or passing it to a friend, it should be closed.

A sharp knife is a safe knife. Simply put, you have to use a lot more force with a dull knife so it can actually be more dangerous for that reason.

Keep your eye on the blade. You're less likely to cut yourself if you are watching the blade and the tip. So stay focused. It is also important to always cut away from your body, never toward it, to help control the cut and keep yourself safe from potential injury.

Make small cuts. Smaller cuts take less force, making slips less likely and less harmful. Plus, whittling requires you to slow down and work a little at a time, which means stopping, checking, and realigning every few cuts.

Never hold the wood in your lap. One slip of the knife can cut into the large blood vessels in your thighs. Instead, hold it past your knees or to the side, or sit at a table.

You are responsible for keeping your blood circle clear. Your blood circle is the area you cover if you hold the knife in your hand, extend your arm outward, and turn around. The rule in our family is that if someone enters your blood circle, you have to close your knife and then negotiate how to clear the space around you. It is the knife user's responsibility to notice when someone enters their blood circle. Have a first-aid kit handy just in case. It's important to be prepared if you do cut yourself or someone else.

Window Stars

Window stars add beauty and fun to a room, and they also serve the purpose of helping remind birds that there is glass there so they don't fly into them as often.

Kite paper squares or tissue paper

Scissors (if using tissue paper)

Glue stick

1. If you are using kite paper already cut into squares, which can be found at craft stores, you can skip to step 2 and begin folding. If you don't have kite paper, you can use tissue paper instead. Before making the stars, you will need to cut the tissue paper into squares. You will need eight squares of the same size, and they should be as even and precise as possible. A good size for the squares would be anywhere from 6 by 6 inches to 10 by 10 inches. We've found that making a template in the size you'd like and then tracing it onto the tissue paper works well. If you already have something that is square, such as a thin book, you could also use that as a template.

2. Once you have eight pieces of kite paper or tissue paper, you're ready to begin folding. Fold a square in half diagonally, then unfold.

3. Take one corner and fold it in so that one side of the square now lines up with the middle crease. Fold the other side of the square in the same way.

4. Fold in the long outside edge of one side to meet the center crease again. Fold the other side in the same way.

5. Repeat this process with all eight pieces of paper, applying the tiniest dot of glue with the glue stick here and there so the pieces do not come undone.

6. You will see that one end comes to a very sharp point, and the other end is a bigger point, with a 90-degree angle. That larger point will form the center of the star.

7. Put a little glue on half of the area at the large point, before any folds.

8. Layer a second piece on top of the first piece so that the outside of the large point of the second piece lines up with the center crease of the first piece.

9. Repeat this process, layering the new piece over the previous piece, until you have gone all the way around and have one piece left. For this piece, you will need to tuck one half of it under the first piece. Secure it with a little glue.

10. The last step is to stick it to the window, using a tiny little dab of glue from the glue stick.

Fabric-Wrapped Presents

When you use fabric to wrap gifts instead of paper, you can reuse the wrapping over and over. All you need is a square of fabric, like a handkerchief, scarf, or even a kitchen towel, that is big enough to cover the present.

1. Put the gift in the center of the square of fabric, and turn it so that each of the corners point to a flat side of the fabric.
2. Gather two corners of the fabric, opposite from each other, and tie one knot.
3. Gather the other two corners of the fabric and tie another knot directly over the first one, so you can still see the ends of the first knot.
4. Take the ends of the first knot and tie a third knot right on top of the second knot. Now the gift is secure. Tuck a flower under the knot and you're all set.

Square piece of fabric large enough to wrap the gift

Flower

Homemade Knitting Needles

If you knit, you can make yourself a pair of wooden needles for your next project. If you don't knit, you can make a pair for someone in your life who does. If you'd like to learn how to knit, there are some great knitting books suggested in the Resources section in the back of this book.

Pencil sharpener

2 wooden dowels, 12 inches long and ¼ inch thick

Fine and extra-fine sandpaper

Wood glue or craft glue

2 wooden beads with ¼-inch holes

Herbal salve or beeswax furniture polish

1. Using the pencil sharpener, sharpen one end of each of the wooden dowels as you would a pencil.
2. Next, use the fine sandpaper to sand each dowel well. Then use the extra-fine sandpaper to sand each dowel very well.
3. When the dowels feel silky smooth, put a drop or two of glue in each wooden bead and attach the beads to the flat ends of the dowels. Wait a couple of hours so the glue has a chance to dry.
4. Use a paper towel or cloth to rub the dowels with a dab of herbal salve or beeswax furniture polish. Make sure all of the wood gets a little salve on it.
5. Set the knitting needles aside so the salve or polish can soak in.
6. After a couple of hours, wipe any excess salve off the needles, and then they are ready to use or give as a gift.

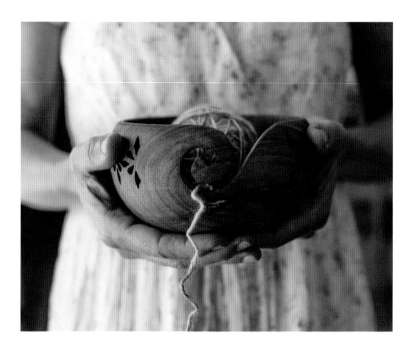

Finger Knitting with Jupiter

Finger knitting is really just crocheting a chain stitch with your hands. There are plenty of uses for a finger knitting chain. You can use it instead of ribbon to wrap a present, use it as a belt, make a spiral and stitch it together to make a potholder, tie it at the ends for a headband, or use it as a base for a flower crown (see page 317). You'll probably come up with your own ideas for using one too.

1. Make a slipknot with the bulky weight yarn.
2. Once you have a slipknot, put your finger through the loop and pull another loop through the first loop by hooking it around your finger.
3. Now, reach through the new loop you just made to grab the yarn again, and bring it through to make another loop.
4. Continue until you have a long line of finger knitting.
5. You may find that the loop keeps getting bigger and bigger as you go. To keep this from happening, tug gently on the long line of yarn. This will make the end loop smaller.
6. When you have made the finger knitting chain as long as you like, cut the yarn, then stick the tail (the end of the yarn) through the loop on the end of the chain. Pull it tight, and that will lock in all your work so it doesn't come undone.

Bulky weight yarn

Using a Drop Spindle with Lyra

Drop spindles have been used to spin wool into yarn for thousands of years. Making yarn with a drop spindle is challenging, especially at first, but they work really well if you take the time to learn how to use them. The parts to the drop spindle are the shaft, hook, notch, and whorl. The shaft is the stick. The whorl is the big wooden disk toward the bottom of the spindle. The hook is just what it sounds like—the little hook—and the notch is the little cutout in the wood where you can secure the yarn.

Wool roving

Drop spindle

1. The first thing to do is pull a bit out from the wool roving. You want it to be thin, but not too thin, because you don't want it to break. Twist the bottom of the roving with your fingers, and then tie it around the notch at the top of the spindle.
2. Once you have tied the roving on the spindle, you can start spinning it. Make sure you always spin it the same way so the yarn won't unravel. Keep pulling the wool thin and twisting as you go.
3. If the yarn does break, take both ends of the yarn together and start twisting until the ends are twisted together. They will kind of grab onto each other. Then you can continue spinning.
4. Once the yarn is too long for your arm to hold it (it always has to be held straight), take the bottom of the yarn off the notch and tie it onto the hook at the bottom of the spindle. Some drop spindles have a hook or notch at both the top and the bottom of the spindle. Some spindles don't have a hook at the bottom. That's OK. If yours doesn't have a hook at the bottom, you can tie the yarn to the bottom of the shaft, right where the whorl begins.
5. Keep spinning and wrapping the yarn around every time it gets too long to keep straight. After you have a lot of yarn, you can take it off the drop spindle and wind it into a ball.

Rolled Beeswax Candles

Rolled beeswax candles are a great introduction to candle making. They burn quickly compared to dipped candles, but if you roll them tightly it will help them burn more slowly.

1. Cut each of the beeswax sheets in half with scissors. (If you'd like to make taller candles, you can leave them whole. Just be sure to use a longer piece of wick.)

2. Cut a length of wick to be an inch or so taller than the beeswax sheet. This will be the part of the wick that sticks out at the top of the candle.

3. Take one piece of the now rectangle-shaped beeswax sheets and put it in front of you, landscape-style, so it is short and wide rather than tall and skinny.

4. Lay the wick vertically about ¼ inch away from one side, with the end sticking out past the top of the sheet. Carefully fold the edge of the sheet over the length of the wick that will be inside the candle. Now you have all but the very top of the wick covered up with wax.

5. After this first bit of wick is covered in wax, it should be easy to roll the rest. Continue rolling the candle from the wick side until all of the beeswax sheet is rolled around the wick. Now you have the first candle.

6. Keep going until you've made all of the candles. Trim the wick a little if it is longer than ½ inch, and be sure to have adult supervision and permission before lighting the candle.

6 beeswax sheets
(8 by 8 inches)

Scissors

6 feet cotton candlewick

Theater and Creative Play

PESHA RUDNICK

Pesha Rudnick is the cofounder and artistic director of Local, a theater company based in Boulder, Colorado. From a very young age she knew she wanted to be an actor or director. Losing herself in a story and inventing new worlds has always been her happy place, and she has always loved being around creative and emotionally curious people. This passion has helped her develop, direct, and produce more than 50 plays nationally. Pesha graciously agreed to share some of her thoughts on creative play with us and offer tips about how we can all bring more of it into our own lives. To learn more about Pesha and Local, please visit localtheaterco.org.

According to Pesha, creative play helps us make sense of a complicated world. For children and adults, tapping into our imaginations allows us to tackle absurd and challenging situations, understand other peoples' experiences, and ultimately enhance our empathy for one another. A few years ago, Pesha read an article that rocked her world. Apparently, live theater and creative play activate the mirror neuron system in our brains. A pair of scientists discovered these neurons and found that we have brain cells that respond equally when we perform an action or when we witness someone else perform that same action or experience. It's why we cringe when someone stubs their toe or laugh when someone near us has the giggles. As humans, we are genetically disposed toward empathy; however, as with any skill, it can grow with training or wither with lack of practice. We humans often need practice or our worldview can become pretty narrow.

Pesha suspects that most of us don't think of ourselves as "creative" in daily life, but many of us do talk to ourselves and imagine creative solutions to our daily life problems. Creative expression helps us manage big, important feelings. Journaling with a purpose—for example, writing a problem and coming up with three possible creative solutions—is a great way to bring creative expression into our lives. (Or you can dictate into a phone if you're someone who avoids writing.) She also recommends seeing live theater or music. Often the performing arts enable us to get out of our own head and experience how other people react and respond to conflict, love, or friendship. Finally, playing make-believe means you

can experience big feelings like joy, rage, revenge, or uncontrollable laughter in a safe environment.

If you are interested in learning more about theater, there are many ways to begin. If your school or community has a theater or improvisation group, sign up to participate. If not, make your own backyard or living room theater. Often if you create a stage, people will figure out how to fill it and what stories to tell. Start with an imagination game like, "This is not a stick." Simply find a stick or branch and show—don't tell—the many ways it can be used on stage. For example, you might say, "This is not a stick, it's a . . ." and then you would *show* (silently, by acting it out) that it's a hairbrush or an umbrella or a skateboard or a baseball bat. Get four or five friends together and go around in a circle at least four or five

times. The game gets more challenging each time, and this is where the imagination really lights up.

You could also host a talent show, lip sync, or poetry night at home. Have everyone write or prepare something they are willing to share and perform it from the stage. Encourage costumes and be sure to applaud. You'll be surprised how much you learn about your friends and family.

Create a play. Ask your neighbors or friends to join. Choose a story you all know, or make up an original play. Gather costumes and build a set if you'd like. Remember that most plays contain four things: characters (human or nonhuman), a conflict (or a "problem" the characters need to solve), words (written ahead of time, or improvised on the spot), and music or a song. Above all, have fun!

Resources

EAT

LACTO-FERMENTATION

Sally Fallon and Mary G. Enig, *Nourishing Traditions: The Cookbook That Challenges Politically Correct Nutrition and the Diet Dictocrats*

Sandor Ellix Katz, *The Art of Fermentation: An In-Depth Exploration of Essential Concepts and Processes from around the World*

Emillie Parrish, *Fermenting Made Simple: Delicious Recipes to Improve Your Gut Health*

SOURDOUGH

Vanessa Kimbell, *The Sourdough School: The Ground-Breaking Guide to Making Gut-Friendly Bread*

Emilie Raffa, "Sourdough Bread: A Beginner's Guide," theclevercarrot.com/2014/01/sourdough-bread-a-beginners-guide

DAIRY AND NONDAIRY

David Asher, *The Art of Natural Cheesemaking: Using Traditional, Non-Industrial Methods and Raw Ingredients to Make the World's Best Cheeses*

Gianaclis Caldwell, *Homemade Yogurt & Kefir: 71 Recipes for Making & Using Probiotic-Rich Ferments*

Karen McAthy, *The Art of Plant-Based Cheesemaking: How to Craft Real, Cultured, Non-Dairy Cheese* (Second Edition)

SEASONAL EATING

Andrea Bemis, *Local Dirt: Seasonal Recipes for Eating Close to Home*

Jeff Crump and Bettina Schormann, *Earth to Table: Seasonal Recipes from an Organic Farm*

Tom Hunt, *The Natural Cook: Eating the Seasons from Root to Fruit*

Alice Waters, *We Are What We Eat: A Slow Food Manifesto*

Andrew Weil, *True Food: Seasonal, Sustainable, Simple, Pure*

HEALTHY SNACKS

Erin Gleeson, *The Forest Feast for Kids: Colorful Vegetarian Recipes That Are Simple to Make*

Julie Morris, *Superfood Snacks: 100 Delicious, Energizing & Nutrient-Dense Recipes*

My New Roots, mynewroots.org

DRINKS AND TONICS

Kathryn Lukas and Shane Peterson, *The Farmhouse Culture Guide to Fermenting: Crafting Live-Cultured Foods and Drinks with 100 Recipes from Kimchi to Kombucha*

Andrew Weil, *True Food: Seasonal, Sustainable, Simple, Pure*

FORAGED FOODS

Sonya Patel Ellis, *The Botanical Bible: Plants, Flowers, Art, Recipes & Other Home Remedies*

Emma Rollin Moore, Lauren Malloy, and Ashley Moore, *The Women's Heritage Sourcebook: Bringing Homesteading to Everyday Life*

Jerry Traunfeld, *The Herbfarm Cookbook*

RAISE

CHICKENS

Melissa Caughey, *How to Speak Chicken: Why Your Chickens Do What They Do and Say What They Say*

HORSES

Debbie Busby and Catrin Rutland, *The Horse: A Natural History*

Kelly Milner Halls, *All About Horses: A Kid's Guide to Breeds, Care, Riding, and More!*

H. A. Levin, *A History of Horses Told by Horses: Horse Sense for Humans*

Robyn Smith, *Horse Life: The Ultimate Guide to Caring for and Riding Horses for Kids*

Heather Smith Thomas, *Storey's Guide to Training Horses: Ground Work, Driving, Riding* (Third Edition)

MULES

Cynthia Attar, *The Mule Companion: A Guide to Understanding the Mule*

John Hauer, *The Natural Superiority of Mules: A Celebration of One of the Most Intelligent, Sure-Footed, and Misunderstood Animals in the World* (Third Edition)

Donna Campbell Smith, *The Book of Mules: An Introduction to the Original Hybrid*

PIGS

Kelly Klober, *Storey's Guide to Raising Pigs* (Fourth Edition)

Robin Nelson, *Pigs*

DOGS

Tammy Gagne, *The Dog Encyclopedia for Kids*

Vanessa Estrada Marin, *Dog Training for Kids: Fun and Easy Ways to Care for Your Furry Friend*

Ádám Miklósi, *The Dog: A Natural History*

Myrna M. Milani, *The Body Language and Emotion of Dogs: A Practical Guide to the Physical and Behavioral Displays Owners and Dogs Exchange and How to Use Them to Create a Lasting Bond*

Clive D. L. Wynne, *Dog Is Love: Why and How Your Dog Loves You*

CATS

Thomas McNamee, *The Inner Life of Cats: The Science and Secrets of Our Mysterious Feline Companions*

Arden Moore, *The Cat Behavior Answer Book: Solutions to Every Problem You'll Ever Face, Answers to Every Question You'll Ever Ask*

MAKE

GARDEN AND HERBS

Michael J. Caduto and Joseph Bruchac, *Native American Gardening: Stories, Projects, and Recipes for Families*

Julie A. Cerny, *The Little Gardener: Helping Children Connect with the Natural World*

Herb Fairies, learningherbs.com/herb-fairies

Herbal Roots Zine, herbalrootszine.org

Patricia Kaminski and Richard Katz, *Flower Essence Repertory: A Comprehensive Guide to the Flower Essences Researched by Dr. Edward Bach and by the Flower Essence Society*

Lesley Tierra, *A Kid's Herb Book for Children of All Ages*

HAIRCARE

Moniruzzaman Publishing, *Curly Hair Book for Girls, Age 9–12*

Kaye Nutman, *Headscarves, Head Wraps & More: How to Look Fabulous in 60 Seconds with Easy Head Wrap Tying Techniques*

Fiona Watt and Lisa Miles, *The Usborne Book of Hair Braiding*

CREATIVITY

Nicole Blum and Catherine Newman, *Stitch Camp: 18 Crafty Projects for Kids & Tweens*

Bonnie Gosse and Jill Allerton, *A First Book of Knitting for Children*

Bonnie Gosse and Jill Allerton, *Knitting for Children: A Second Book*

Deborah Jarchow and Gwen W. Steege, *The Weaving Explorer: Ingenious Techniques, Accessible Tools & Creative Projects with Yarn, Paper, Wire & More*

Cecily Keim and Kim P. Werker, *Crochet: Teach Yourself Visually*

Irmgard Kutch and Brigitte Walden, *Autumn Nature Activities for Children*

Irmgard Kutch and Brigitte Walden, *Spring Nature Activities for Children*

Irmgard Kutch and Brigitte Walden, *Summer Nature Activities for Children*

Irmgard Kutch and Brigitte Walden, *Winter Nature Activities for Children*

Nina and Sonya Montenegro, *Mending Life: A Handbook for Repairing Clothes and Hearts*

Carol Petrash, *Earthways: Simple Environmental Activities for Young Children*

Reader's Digest, *Complete Guide to Needlework*

Kelli Ronci, *Kids Crochet: Projects for Kids of All Ages*

OTHER

FOR TEACHERS, PARENTS, AND CAREGIVERS

Dawn Casey, Anna Richardson, and Helen d'Ascoli, *The Children's Forest: Stories and Songs, Wild Food, Crafts and Celebrations All Year Round*

Emma Rollin Moore, Lauren Malloy, and Ashley Moore, *The Women's Heritage Sourcebook: Bringing Homesteading to Everyday Life*

Naomi Walmsley and Dan Westall, *Forest School Adventure: Outdoor Skills and Play for Children*

Acknowledgments

This book was a labor of love, made possible through many helping hands and the encouragement and support of so many people. We want to thank Jim Muschett, Susi Oberhelman, Candice Fehrman, and the whole Rizzoli team for believing in us and taking on another Women's Heritage book project. What an honor it has been!

Thank you to Sara Prince for her exquisite photography and fabulous friendship, and for the time and work that went into countless photo shoots and many hours of editing.

Thank you to all of the wonderful and inspiring families who contributed features to this book, shared their experiences, and inspired us with their hobbies and crafts.

Thank you to our partners and children for your participation in the photo shoots and for your patience at home while we worked on this book.

Big thanks also to the whole Women's Heritage team, the incredible people who run our retail stores with savvy, grace, diligence, and insight. We are so grateful to all of you.

And last, thank you to all of the children, teens, caregivers, teachers, and parents who read this book. Thank you for opening up your hearts and hands. We hope this book brings you joy and inspiration that you can share with others.

TO ADVENTUROUS
CHILDREN
EVERYWHERE

First published in the United States of America in 2023 by
Rizzoli International Publications, Inc.
300 Park Avenue South
New York, NY 10010
www.rizzoliusa.com

The goal of **Women's Heritage** is to bring elements of the homestead into everyday life. We understand today's world can feel very busy, and making things from scratch or even learning a new skill can seem daunting. We hope to inspire children and teens to explore, discover, and learn new passions and skills. For more information, please visit heritagegoodsandsupply.com.

Publisher: Charles Miers
Associate Publisher: James Muschett
Managing Editor: Lynn Scrabis
Editor: Candice Fehrman
Design: Susi Oberhelman

Printed in China

2023 2024 2025 2026 / 10 9 8 7 6 5 4 3 2 1

ISBN: 978-1-59962-167-8

Library of Congress Control Number: 2022946516

Visit us online:
Facebook.com/RizzoliNewYork
Twitter: @Rizzoli_Books
Instagram.com/RizzoliBooks
Pinterest.com/RizzoliBooks
Youtube.com/user/RizzoliNY
Issuu.com/Rizzoli